Your Library

A REFERENCE GUIDE

Your Library

A REFERENCE GUIDE

William Katz

State University of New York
at Albany

HOLT, RINEHART AND WINSTON
New York   Chicago   San Francisco
Atlanta   Dallas   Montreal   Toronto

Library of Congress Cataloging in Publication Data
Katz, William A.
   Your Library.

   Includes Index.
    1. Libraries—Handbooks, Manuals, etc. 2. Reference
books I . Title.
Z710. K38   021   78–21993

ISBN 0-03-043801-2
Copyright © 1979 by Holt, Rinehart and Winston
Printed in the United States of America
9 0 1 2 090 9 8 7 6 5 4 3 2

For Janet and Jeffrey

Preface

The purpose of this manual is to make you feel at ease in your library. It is directed to you, not to a librarian. If you are an intelligent person who is baffled by the library system, you have a lot of company.

The manual is in two sections. The first tells how to make good use of the library, librarians, and various types of reference works. You should read straight through the first section.

The second section tells where to find sources on any subject. Whenever you have a specific question—say, where to find reviews of a new novel—just skip to the chapter on your subject. Here there is a chart to give you an answer, and other advice on sources.

There is usually too much, not too little, in a library. You are a beginner or a baffled amateur, not a professional researcher. Your problem is how to find an answer to your question somewhere in all those books and magazines. You don't want everything in the library on your subject; you only want a quick, direct answer.

With that purpose, the first section of this manual makes you familiar with the general kinds of reference works. It tells you *how* to find information.

The second section covers many more reference works. When you need specific help, this section will tell you *where* to turn, quickly and easily. It is important to realize that the books listed in the second section are only representative of what you may find in your library. Scores, even hundreds, of other titles may help, too. But if you learn to find the books considered here, you can find anything.

In both sections, after each reference book discussed, you will find two sets of numbers and letters. (These "call numbers" are explained in Chapter 3.) You can think of them as the key to finding the books on the library shelves. The number of the book you need is located on the spine of the book.

In your quest for answers, never forget the librarian, your first and best source of information. You should depend as much upon the librarian as you would upon your family doctor or mechanic. The librarian is your best defense against frustration.

A Word to Librarians and Teachers

This manual is not for the professional librarian. It is for anybody beginning to use the library. A sincere effort has been made to eliminate library jargon. When jargon could not be avoided, it is always explained.

The focus is on finding the reference work that will produce answers. Nothing is said about reference services, evaluation of reference books, the history of libraries, and so on. These topics are of major importance—but only to librarians. Manuals that cover them only confuse beginners.

On the other hand, I dwell upon procedures in using the library that trained reference librarians may not think important. Always I have taken the point of view of the struggling beginner.

The reader is told over and over again that the best single resource is the librarian. This idea can never be stressed enough.

My particular thanks to Anne Roberts of the State University of New York at Albany library. She gave me many useful suggestions, which helps to explain why she is a favorite reference librarian among students and, incidentally, an expert on methods of teaching the use of the library.

For their helpful criticisms and suggestions about the manuscript, I wish to thank Matyne Easton, Iowa State University; Teresa G. Poston, George Peabody College for Teachers; and Penny Pypcznski, Trenton State College.

I also am grateful to Amy Dykeman, who read the manuscript several times and offered useful suggestions. Mary Wilken took many of the photographs. Elizabeth M. Horvath read the manuscript and ran down elusive titles, and Nancy Kane typed the finished work. My thanks, too, to my editor Susan Katz—unfortunately not a relative.

January 1979   *William Katz*
Albany, N.Y.

Contents

Your Library

A REFERENCE GUIDE

section one
How to Use the Library

Chapter **1**

Get Your Bearings

How can you do your best with a paper, speech, or project?

At least part of the answer is how well you use your library.

The library is a workshop where you may find the information you need for almost any purpose. You may begin a paper or a revolution in the library. Here is useful information on just about any subject or person you can name.

The problem is learning how to get what you need, and that's what this manual is all about.

If you are a typical beginner you have certain difficulties. You wander into an academic or public library. Other people are confidently walking about, but you stagger around, lost. With luck, you find the door again.

Take heart. More precisely, look for a librarian before you give up and leave.

LOOK FOR THE LIBRARIAN

The average librarian is eager to assist. An expert with an advanced degree and a ready sympathy, the librarian has been talking to people like you for years. The librarian not only has heard versions of your question a hundred times, but also knows just where to find the answer.

Once you've found the librarian, don't hesitate to ask questions. Beyond that, if you don't understand the answers, or if you need additional help, trot right back to the librarian.

LOOK AROUND THE LIBRARY

Almost all libraries have printed materials, floor plans, and signs to direct you. Gather up the printed material to study at home. Pay particular attention to floor plans and aids that direct you to works in your fields of interest.

Most medium to large public libraries and almost all school libraries have formal tours and orientation sessions. They may be simple or elaborate, often augmented by lectures, slides, television presentations, films, and even cassette tape players you can carry around the library much as you would in a museum tour. Ask the librarian about tours, courses, and other ways to familiarize yourself with the library.

Either before or after the directed tour, take your own personal trip around the library. The advantage is that you can *browse*—a magic word for pulling down this or that book, looking at a magazine, tinkering with a microform machine, or just sitting in a study space and considering the world.

Let's say you are going on a personal tour. What should you look for?

Before you begin, think of something that interests you. Try to keep it simple. Take a broad subject such as art, baseball, or business. As you are walking, casually see where you might find information on your topic.

Three Key Points

Begin your tour by locating three key points. First, look for the *card catalog,* the primary device for finding books. The card catalog is described in Chapter 3.

Second, on the way to the card catalog you will probably pass a large desk called *circulation,* or the *loan desk.* Here you will check out books, renew books, or ask where missing books and magazines are. If there are mimeographed rules and regulations, take one. Find out what you need to check out material—a card, an identification number, or what?

Ask at the circulation desk whether there are branch libraries. Branches are likely in a large university or college library. Sometimes a reference in the card catalog may be to a branch library, so it is important to know where the branches are located.

Near the catalog is likely to be the third key point, the *reference books and the reference desk.* Behind the desk will be those friendly librarians who will help you.

Close to the reference desk will be shelves of much-used reference books. They are the ones the librarians tend to use over and over again to answer questions. When you have time, and if it's permitted, look at some of these books.

Beyond this small collection will be shelves of other reference books. Again, when you have time it will pay you to cruise up and down looking over whatever interests you (see Chapter 4).

Library Materials

Now that you have found the three key points, walk around to discover where the various kinds of materials—books, magazines, and so on—are kept.

Most libraries have the books and magazines out where you may look at them, but other libraries (particularly large ones) sometimes close off the books from the public. In order to get what you want, you first have to write down the name of the book on a certain form.

A fast way to see how the books are organized is to look for descriptive signs on the ends of book stacks, which may tell you whether the section has fiction, biography, history, or something else. Here and there look at a few of the book titles, which are often descriptive of content. You will notice numbers on the spines (backs) of books. They allow you to find what you want when you use the card catalog.

Find out also where the *magazines* are located. Most librarians refer to magazines as "periodicals"—a good umbrella word that includes both popular magazines and scholarly journals. The periodicals may be in bound volumes or in single issues. Sometimes single current issues and bound volumes of back issues are together; sometimes they are separate. Look, too, for the newspapers.

There may be a special section for *microform*—materials in reduced size on film somewhat like the film in cameras. You can read it through a microform reader (Figure 1-1). Often back issues of magazines, newspapers, and hard-to-find copies of older books are on microform.

If you are in a school or academic library, find out where the *reserve books* are kept. Materials on reserve are temporarily taken out of circulation by a teacher. You will be using them for assigned readings. In other words, they are reserved for class members. Ask how long you can keep reserve books out.

Depending on your needs and the size of the library, you will want to know where to find other materials. *Pamphlets* are usually in filing cases near the reference books. *Government documents* may be in a separate section of the library. *Films and slides* are likely kept with other *audiovisual materials* such as *records, tapes, pictures,* and *photographs.*

There may be a part of the library given over to *rare books* or other special subject collections, such as *maps.* If you are likely to be using these facilities, see whether they have separate card catalogs.

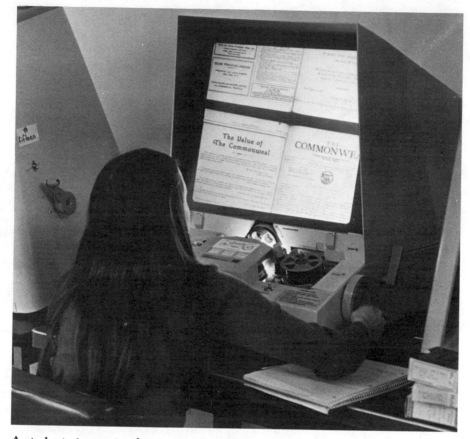

A student views microform on a microform reader.

Library Facilities

Finally, explore your library's facilities. With any luck the library will have one or several *Xerox or copying machines.* Check to see how much is charged to make a copy, and whether the machines really work. Look, too, for microform reader-printers. From them you can get material on microform.

Look also for such facilities as rest rooms, drinking fountains, telephones and places to study. Some libraries have typing rooms or spaces for typewriters.

Information Retrieval by Computer

More and more libraries now offer to do searches for you by means of computer. The computer searches through indexes and *abstracts* (summaries) to help you locate articles and books on any topic you request.

You should inquire whether such computer searches are available in your library. Find out what you have to do to have such a search made. The librarian will tell you whether or not your request requires computer assistance. The librarian also will tell you whether there is a charge for such a service. Charges are common for computer searches.

Special Events

Your library's resources are not restricted to print. Libraries often offer special programs that you may enjoy. Some have concerts, poetry readings, talks by authors, or book discussion groups. Some display art or literary memorabilia in special areas. Keep your eyes open. Maybe your library can enrich you in these extra ways.

Chapter **2**

Ask the Librarian

Never preface an inquiry to a librarian with "I know this is a stupid question, but. . . ."

There are no stupid questions.

The fact that you are interested in something gives your query importance. The quest may be for no more than the nearest phone or for information on how to send a rocket to Mars. In either case you are following the traditional way of learning—asking a question.

One Greek philosopher summed it up nicely: "Questions are the creative act of intelligence."

No one wants to seem foolish. Consider, though, how much more foolish it is to spend hours looking for something that a librarian might find in seconds. For instance, the librarian will answer short, quick questions—such as who won a certain prize, the address of a company, the name of a prominent author, or the exact title of a book—in a matter of seconds or minutes. Remember that the librarian can find this material much faster and much more easily than you can.

Librarians are eager to help. At the same time you must realize that when a library is understaffed, you may only get limited assistance. Chances are there will be someone else, or a whole group of people behind you with other queries.

No matter how many people are about the reference desk, you are as important as any of them. This fact is worth stressing because study after study finds that you don't think you have the right to ask the librarian for help. Most librarians are amazed by these results. If you learn nothing else from reading this manual, remember you can talk over problems with your librarian. It's your right. Use it.

TYPES OF QUESTIONS

Everyone has a different way of asking questions. However, we can fit questions in the library into three large categories: directional, ready reference, and research.

The directional question is familiar. In a supermarket you ask directions to the cheese section. In a library you ask where the card catalog is located. Room for misunderstanding is limited.

The ready reference question is equally familiar. You want a single piece of information. In the supermarket you might ask which cheese is mildest. In the library you might ask which country exports the most cheese, or which cheese is most popular in the United States. There is usually only one answer to ready reference questions—an answer often found in reference books.

The *research question* requires a more detailed answer. You might ask, for example, the methods by which cheese is manufactured. The answer is built up by borrowing a fact here, a paragraph there, until you know enough. At that point you would decide how to use the material. If you were planning a paper, you might decide that your paper should recommend making cheese at home. If you were planning a project, you might choose the easiest way to make some cheese yourself.

It is with the research or search question that most of this manual is concerned. This type of query causes the most difficulty.

THINKING OUT YOUR QUESTION

What do you really want?

That's the basic question about any question.

Before you approach the librarian, try to think out your question. Figure out its scope and purpose.

The Scope of Your Question

The *scope* of the question is how general or specific an answer you need. You would not go to the supermarket and ask the clerk for food; you would ask for bread or for milk. In the library you have to be equally precise.

If you want to know the best modern compact car, say so. Do not ask: "What do you have on cars?" When you need material on the causes of the French Revolution, say so. Do not ask: "What do you have on France?" Limit your question to the smallest possible unit.

Try to use key words for that small unit. For example, the key descriptors above are "best," "modern," and "compact" for the car, and "causes" and "Revolution" for France. You would not simply ask about "cars" or "France."

The Purpose of Your Question

You know the purpose of your question. Maybe you need material for a long paper, a ten-minute oral report, or your own reading pleasure. Whatever your reasons, try to make them clear to the librarian.

To clarify your purpose, ask yourself these related questions:

How much do you want on the subject?   Tell the librarian approximately how long a report or talk you are planning. Without knowing how much material you need, the librarian may give you too much or too little. Say, for example, "I need three articles and two books." Or "I need a short encyclopedia article." Or "I need a short book, no more than 100 pages."

Do you want difficult or elementary material?   Tell the librarian the level of the course for which you are doing an assignment—Introduction to Geometry or Advanced Calculus. Specify whether you want something "elementary," "average in difficulty," or "fairly technical."

Do you need only current materials?   The librarian can't always tell from your question whether you can use old materials or only current materials. Tell the librarian, for example, "I need an article that is relatively current, not more than one year old." Or explain that it does not matter how recent the material is.

Do you have time?   Let the librarian know when you are pressed for time. If you are in a rush, tell the librarian you only have five minutes. If you have just one day in which to gather information, say "I need something from the library today. I can't wait for a book to come back."

On the other hand, you may have time to wait for material ordered from outside the library. If the librarian orders something for you from another library it may take a few hours or weeks to arrive. Be sure you understand the approximate time, and let the librarian know whether you can wait so long.

Do you need material in a particular form?   Perceptive librarians may know when a government document, a pamphlet, or a film is in order. However, sometimes it is not obvious that you want information in a specific form. Say so.

Write Out the Question

You should give yourself time to think about your question. One good method is to write out the query. Have you included everything you really want to know? Will it be clear to the librarian?

Next, say the question aloud to yourself or to someone else. Is it still clear? If not, back to pencil and paper.

Still No Question

There are times when you can't make the question clear.

The usual reason is that you don't know the special language of the area about which you are asking. Let's say you do not know the name of the war that liberated the United States from England. Now how do you ask for material on the "Revolutionary War"? You have to explain in a roundabout fashion until the librarian comes up with the key words.

When you don't know the language of the subject, that is precisely the time to ask for help. At least you can state clearly that you don't have a clear question. You can state your purpose, too. Now the librarian will enter into a dialog with you. With skill, and a dash of luck, the two of you will shortly come to some agreement on the subject and its scope.

The important rule is: *If you can't ask clearly, say so!* Any other effort will only lead to misunderstanding and a vast waste of time.

TALK OVER THE QUESTION

For a directional or a ready reference question, the dialog with the librarian is likely to be limited to a direct question and a direct answer. The real dialog takes place over the research query.

There are four rules to help you in this exchange.

First, try to make your question open-ended. To some questions the librarian can simply answer "yes" or "no." For example: "Do you have books on the French Revolution?" Answer: "Yes, check the card catalog." An open-ended query requires a dialog: "I'm looking for an article on the causes of the French Revolution. Would you help me?" Notice too, that this wording is more precise. Precision tends to follow the open-ended query.

Second, try to be brief and avoid pointless rambling. You can be brief when you've thought out the question.

Third, learn to listen. You may be so anxious to be understood, or so nervous, that you don't hear what the librarian is saying.

Finally, observe how the librarian is handling your question. When you are not getting the right kind of help, say so. Say "I'm sorry, that's not what I mean" and begin again.

The reference interview normally ends with the librarian giving you the material you asked for or telling you where to find it. In either case, if you don't find what you want, go right back to the librarian for assistance.

The Final Word

Be prepared to help yourself as much as to ask for help. The librarian can find you what you ask for, but only you can determine whether what is found is what you really need.

Don't expect the librarian to do all of your work. The librarian is there to help you find what you need, not to write your paper or prepare your talk.

Chapter **3**

The Card Catalog

The giant information source in the library is the card catalog. The catalog is often your best guide to information.

The typical card catalog consists of cabinets with many trays or drawers arranged in alphabetical order. Within each drawer 3 × 5 cards are arranged alphabetically. Catalogs can take other forms,[1] but this type of catalog is the most popular.

HOW TO USE THE CATALOG

The card catalog helps you find information by means of three types of cards. The first type tells you what books the library has by a certain writer. These cards are the *author cards*.[2] Second, the *subject cards* tell you what books the library has on a certain subject. The "See also" cards tell you the related subjects. Third, the *title cards* list the books by title.

---

[1] Some catalogs are computer printouts in a book or a binder. Others are recorded on microform or displayed on a cathode ray tube (CRT), similar to a television screen.

[2] Sometimes an author card does not name a person. If, for example, you are looking for a book from a government agency, such as the U.S. Office of Education, you must look under the agency name. The same is true of a book prepared by a committee such as the Committee on Flying Saucers or by an organization such as the American Science Foundation. Oddly, none of these organizations are writers. Someone who did the actual writing gave way to the name of the group.

Every card tells you where the book is in the library. Remember, your library may have several departments or branches. The card will show you in what branch to look.

Find out before you use the catalog whether it is a divided catalog (with two separate files for subjects and authors) or a single, dictionary catalog with all the cards in one file.

Locating a Card

You may locate a book if you have an author, a title, or a subject. For example, if the library has Walter Terry's book *The Dance in America* on the shelves, you will be able to locate it in the card catalog three ways: by the author (Terry, Walter), by the title (*The Dance in America*), and by the subject of the book (Dancing—History, or Dancers). All and all, then, there are four cards that will lead you to the book.

How do you find the cards in the catalog?

The same way you look up a name in a phone book. To find an author, you look for the last name first. To find a title, you look for the first word in the title, *not counting* "the," "a," "an," and other minor introductory words.

Librarians make it easy for you: the top line on the card is always the key to what you are seeking. On an author card, the author's name is always first; on a title card, the title is always first; and on a subject card, the subject is always first.[3]

Finding the Call Number

Just as a phone book without a number after the name would be useless, so would a catalog card without its number. This *call number* is found in the upper left-hand corner of the card.

The call number identifies the book. The same number is on the spine (back) of the book. Each book has its unique call number.

Look at the cards for Dan Morris' *Fisherman's Almanac* (Figure 3-1). No matter if you find the book under the author (Morris, Dan), under the title (*The Fisherman's Almanac*), or under the subject (Fishes, Fishing), the call number (SH441. M59) in the upper left-hand corner of each of the cards is always the same.

---

[3] Librarians call the author card the *main entry* or *unit card*. The subject and title cards are *added entries*.

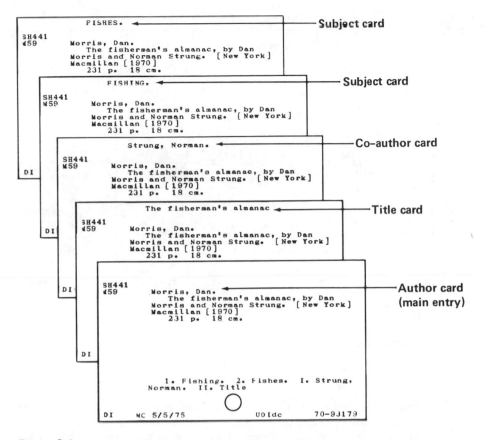

Figure 3-1

You can find the same book with these five different catalog cards. Notice that they all carry the same call number.

The Rest of the Catalog Card

Most of the other information on the catalog card you can skip. (*Go to the following section, if you like, and ignore this section.*)

In case you do need to decipher the data, you will find an author, a title, and then, pretty much in this order as you read down the card (see Figure 3-2):

1. A subtitle, if there is one.
2. The number of the edition.
3. The illustrator, translator, coauthor, and so on.

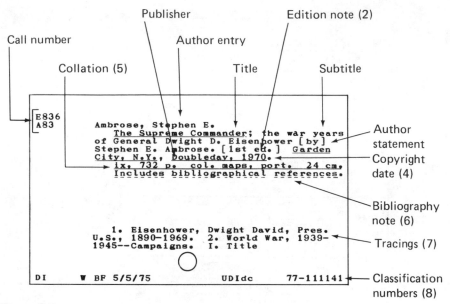

Figure 3-2

The information on a catalog card.

4. The place of publication (New York), the publisher (Doubleday), and the date the book was published (1970). These facts are called the "imprint."
5. The descriptive notes or "collation": the number of pages in the book, whether it is illustrated, its height, whether it is a series, and so on.
6. The "bibliographical notes": the page on which the bibliography begins and similar information.
7. The "tracings": the subject headings under which the book is listed in the catalog, followed by the full names of any people besides the author who also rate separate catalog cards.
8. A series of numbers at the bottom of the card, which includes the Library of Congress classification, Dewey Decimal classification, and the catalog card number.

Of all this extra information, two items are most likely to help you. If you wanted current material, you would check the *date* the book was published. And if you wondered how much or how little you would have to read, you would check the number of pages.

Remember, catalog cards do not tell you what is in the book. You can sometimes guess content by the subject headings (at the bottom of the card) by the title, or even by the author. Comedian Woody Allen is going to write quite a different book than Walter Allen, who is an authority on the novel. And while the title *Looking Outward* may not tell you much about the book (it concerns the United Nations), you won't have difficulty recognizing the topic of such books as *Wines of Portugal* or *Field Book of Freshwater Life.*

Using the Card

Once you know the library has the book you need, what do you have to copy from the catalog card? As you can see from Figure 3-3, not much. First, copy the call number in the upper left-hand corner of the catalog card. It tells you where the book is located. If you want to be safe, copy the author's name and the first few words of the title, but that's enough.[4]

Now look for the chart, floor plan, or directional signal that points you in the direction of the book with the call number you've copied down.

Go to the shelf and look at the numbers on the backs of the books. When one matches the call number, there is your book.

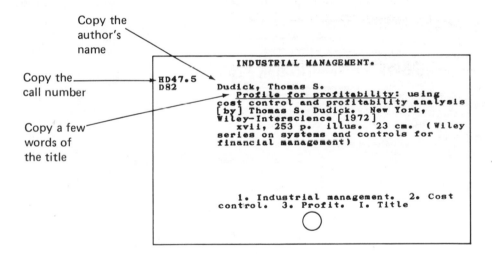

Figure 3-3

The three elements you need to copy from a catalog card in order to find a book.

---

[4] *Exception:* In some libraries there are no open book shelves. The books are closed off from the public. To get a book you must fill out a *call slip* with certain information from the catalog card, and give it to a clerk. Before you begin to use the catalog, ask for the call slip and see whether you understand it clearly. It probably will require more than just the call number. If you don't understand what is needed, ask a librarian. Ask before you fill out more than one slip—or you may have to go back and do them all again.

HOW BOOKS ARE ARRANGED

Even with a personal library of a few books, you've probably wondered how to arrange them on the shelves. When the number grows to 100 or more, you may take action. Perhaps you put the paperbacks in one place, the hardbound volumes in another. Some you arrange by subject, others by author or even by size.

Multiply this challenge by 30,000 volumes and you are in the same position as Melvil Dewey, approximately 100 years ago. He came up with a logical way of arranging those 30,000 books that has been followed by libraries throughout the world. The arrangement is called the *Dewey Decimal classification system.*

Can you use the same plan for 3 million books that you used for 30,000? Many librarians say no, and turn to another classification—one usually favored in larger academic and public libraries. The second major arrangement plan is called the *Library of Congress classification system.*

You can tell instantly which system your library uses from any call number. If the call number begins with one or two letters, it is a Library of Congress arrangement. If there are no beginning letters, your library uses the Dewey arrangement.

Dewey Decimal Classification System

Dewey began by dividing all knowledge into ten major classes. He assigned a fixed number in the hundreds to each class:

000	General works
100	Philosophy and related disciplines
200	Religion
300	Social sciences
400	Language
500	Pure science
600	Technology (Applied science)
700	The arts
800	Literature
900	General geography and history

Within each of these broad areas finer subdivisions are numbered by tens. For example, consider the 700s:

710	Civil and landscape art
720	Architecture
730	Plastic arts (Sculpture)
740	Drawing, decorative & minor arts
750	Painting and paintings
760	Graphic arts (Prints)
770	Photography and photographs

780   Music
790   Recreational and performing arts

With beautiful logic, this system allows further and further subdivisions. For example, 320 is political science, which falls under 300, the more general category of the social sciences. Now within political science, subtopics are numbered by ones. Books numbered 323 concern the relations between states and their residents. Even this topic is subdivided, by placing numbers after a decimal point. For example:

323.4   Civil rights
323.44   Freedom of action
323.6   Citizenship

You need not memorize these numbers; only remember they follow a logical pattern. Once you know, for example, that the pure sciences are 500, it is easier to recall that 510 is mathematics and 530 is physics.

With the development of new fields of knowledge and more specialization within each, the Dewey Decimal classification system is running out of room. It could not, for example, provide a satisfactory range of numbers for new subdivisions under physics. Consequently, larger libraries, with more specialized collections, prefer the Library of Congress method.

Library of Congress Classification System

The Library of Congress system is as logical as the Dewey system, but more capable of expansion.

You know you are in a library with a Library of Congress system when you see a letter before the number. Here knowledge is divided not into 10, but into 21 major sections, each designated by a letter of the alphabet:

A   General works
B   Philosophy, psychology, religion
C   Auxiliary sciences of history
D   History and topography (except American)
E   American history
F   United States local history
G   Geography, anthropology
H   Social sciences
J   Political science
K   Law
L   Education
M   Music
N   Fine arts
P   Language and literature
Q   Science

R Medicine
S Agriculture
T Technology
U Military science
V Naval science
Z Bibliography and library science

The basic subject area is modified by another letter. Thus M for music becomes ML for the literature of music and MT for musical instruction and study. You soon learn the letters for categories you need, such as PS for American literature.

Beyond the broad categories, further subdivision is achieved by adding numbers between 1 and 9999. For example PN stands for literary history and collections (P is language and literature). Add a few numbers and you have PN 6413, the call number for collections of Greek proverbs.

You need not memorize the designations; only realize the logic behind the classification—a logic that makes it easy for you to locate what you need in the library.

Two Major Differences

There are two differences to learn about the Dewey and the Library of Congress systems, particularly if you grow used to one and then are in a library that uses the other. These differences concern the handling of fiction and biography.

Fiction. Fiction is arranged in the Dewey system by the last name of the author. It is in a separate section, and it does not have a classification number other than possibly "F," with a letter and number below to help the librarian shelve the title.

In the Library of Congress system, fiction is not separate; books by and about the author are grouped together. For example, on the same shelf with novels by Henry James will be critical works about Henry James.

Biography. Like fiction, biography is in a separate section in the Dewey system. Biographies are arranged alphabetically by the subject (not the author), or the biography. They are classified simply as "B" or 920, with a letter and number below to help the librarian shelve the book.

In the Library of Congress system, biography is not separate. It is arranged under the area in which the subject of the biography took part. For example, a biography of the painter Frederick Remington would be with the books on American art.

WHEN YOU CAN'T FIND A BOOK

Now that you know how to use the card catalog and how books are arranged in the library, you will usually have an easy time finding a book. Let's consider the times when you *can't* find your book on the shelf or in the catalog. Don't despair!

Not on the Shelf

Let's say you have written down a call number, and you find the place the book should be on the shelves. It's not there. What do you do?

First of all, double back and be sure you have copied the call number properly from the catalog card. Often a simple mistake in numbers explains why the books on the shelf were about drugs and not dance.

If you have the number right, look around the shelf again. Perhaps the book is not shelved properly.

Still no luck? Look at other titles with approximately the same call number. Often one or more of them may be as good as or even better than the title you are pursuing. Or if you can't find a book, how about two or more periodical articles (see Chapter 6)? They are generally easy to find, and you can read them quickly. The magic word is: *compromise.* Rare is the time when you need a book and nothing else will do.

Still want the exact book? Then go to the circulation desk and ask the clerk where it is. Be sure you have not only the call number, but the author's name and the title, spelled properly. You may discover that the book is on reserve, or that someone else has checked it out. Often the librarian will arrange to have the book recalled for your use.

The clerk may tell you the book is unshelved, lost, or stolen. If you still need it desperately, try to find it in another local library, or go to the interlibrary loan office for help.

Not in the Catalog

Just because you cannot find what you are looking for in the card catalog does not mean it is not in the library. There are certain types of materials that you will not find in the card catalog. You can find some of them by consulting the proper index. Such materials include articles from magazines (see pp. 38–40); short stories, essays, and collected materials (see chapter 11); biographical material about a person in a collection of biographical sketches (see pp. 61–67); newspaper articles and clippings (see p. 43); fiction by subject (see the *Fiction catalog,* (p. 134); and first lines of poetry or poetry by subject (see *Granger's Index to poetry,* p. 135).

Look for file drawers or cabinets where the library may have articles, clippings, illustrations, pamphlets, and so on filed by subject. Librarians call this collection the *vertical file,* and if you don't see it: ask.

Some libraries also may not list the following materials in the catalog:

government documents (which may be separate or part of the overall collection), periodicals, films, recordings, microforms, and audiovisual aids.

Not in the Library

The card catalog is a list of materials in your library. The card catalog has a severe limitation. It does not tell you what materials are available *beyond* your library.

Bibliographies often tell you which library has which books. They tell you, too, the key materials in a given subject area, and they tell you what is available from publishers.

When you want to find out whether or not you can buy a book, you have to discover whether it is still available. Two bibliographies will help you do so.

Books in Print. N.Y.: Bowker, 1948 to date, annual. 4 vols. Z1215. P97   015

This work includes more than 500,000 books you or the library can buy from American publishers. As the title indicates, these books are "in print." (When you no longer can purchase the book, it is "o.p." or "out of print.") Figure 3-4 shows a typical page.

You can look up either the author or the title in *Books in Print*. The entry for each gives you the full name of the author and the full title of the book, plus the name of the publisher, the year of publication, and the price. You can look up the address of any of the 7000 publishers represented in the four volumes.

You may find the second title in this series more helpful:

Subject Guide to Books in Print. N.Y.: Bowker, 1957 to date, annual. Z1215.P973   015.

Here the books from *Books in Print* are rearranged under subject headings—the same headings you are likely to find in the card catalog or in a periodical index. There are also numerous cross-references.

This guide is particularly useful when you want to find any current books on a given subject. A quick look at *Subject Guide to Books in Print* will tell you, for example, what books are available on dance, automobiles, or energy.

Just about any subject of interest to you will be in *Subject Guide to Books in Print,* with two restrictions. First, novels are not listed under subjects. For that, you have to turn to *Fiction Catalog* (p. 134). Second, only books currently in print are listed, not everything ever published on a given subject. For that you would need a special bibliography.

For example, you might look up books about the composer Maurice Ravel in *Subject Guide to Books in Print.* You would find all the books now available.

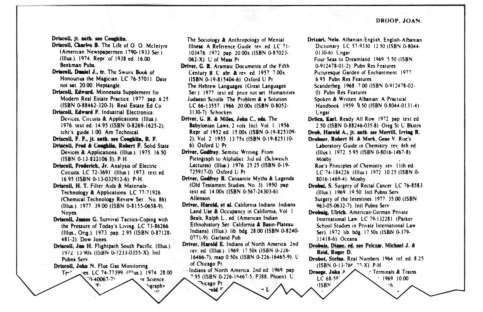

Figure 3-4

Part of a typical page from the author section of *Books in Print*. Reprinted from *Books in Print 1977* with permission of R.R. Bowker Company, 1180 Avenue of the Americas, New York, New York 10036. Copyright © 1977 by Xerox Corporation.

You would not find a definitive biography of the composer published in the 1940s. It is out of print. To find the name of that biography (unless you are lucky and it is in your library card catalog), you would have to refer to a later book or possibly to a good encyclopedia.

Never Give Up!

If you find a title in either of these bibliographies or in your readings and you want to borrow the book, the first place to look is your library card catalog. If it's not in the catalog (and you've looked it up properly), make sure you are looking for something that ought to be in the catalog (not a magazine article, for instance).

If you still can't find it, ask the librarian. The librarian has many ways of telling whether or not the material you want is available in a nearby library, and the interlibrary loan office may arrange to borrow the material for you.

Never, but never give up! There is something in the library to help you—and if you can't find it, the librarian will.

Chapter **4**

Reference Works

Just about anything or anyone—a government document, a pamphlet, a film, an expert—can be considered a reference source. However, one section of the library contains special reference books, usually marked with an "R." You have to use these books in the library.

You are familiar with some reference books. One of the world's all-time best sellers is a reference book: *Guinness Book of World Records.* So are equally well-known titles like the *People's Almanac* and the *Encyclopaedia Britannica.* So are the dictionary and the phone book.

Generally a reference book is arranged so that you can extract information quickly and painlessly. It rarely is meant to be read cover to cover, and the arrangement is usually alphabetical or even chronological.

In addition, all good reference books share two features. All of them have an index. With the exception of the white pages of the phone book and other books arranged in alphabetical order, an index is imperative for a good reference book. Second, they are timely. Unless the information is fairly current, it is likely to be of little value for most of your projects.

TYPES OF REFERENCE WORKS

There are two basic forms of reference works.

The "where to find" form includes the card catalog, periodical indexes, and bibliographies. Here you must take two steps: first you go to the reference work; then you find the book. The catalog tells you where to find the book.

By contrast, the self-contained form, such as an encyclopedia or almanac, has the answer, either in part or complete. You do not have to go any further— unless, of course, you want more information.

The Big Three

To begin almost any quest for information you can use one of three basic types of reference works. These are the "big three".

An *encyclopedia* supplies background information, an overview, definitions, dates, history, and so on. (Chapter 5 tells you more about encyclopedias.)

A *periodical index* (Figure 4-1) offers more current, specialized information than you are likely to find in an encyclopedia. (Chapter 6 describes the periodical index.)

The *card catalog* helps you locate materials to expand your topic.

You will not always use these sources in that order, or even all of them for one question. Still, it is amazing how much information you can find with them.

Beyond the three you may need other types of reference works.

"Where to Find" Works

Bibliographies list books or other materials by subject or by author. They tell you what is available on a given subject or by a given writer. The card catalog (which tells you the holdings of your library) is a type of bibliography. Another example is *Subject Guide to Books in Print* (see p. 22). Specialized bibliographies are available on almost any subject.

Indexes list sources of other materials. Besides the indexes that tell you where to find an article in a magazine, there are indexes to newspapers (*The New York Times Index,* p. 181) and indexes to collections of short stories, plays, and so on (such as the *Short Story Index* p. 139.)

Self-Contained Works

Dictionaries give you the meanings of words. In addition they give spelling, pronunciation, word origins, word division, abbreviations, and personal names, and answer numerous other questions about language.

Biographical sources give you brief data or long essays on people, both living and dead. A cursory look at the preface will tell you quickly which type of biographical aid you are using. An example of a biographical aid is *Who's Who in America.*

18 READERS' GUIDE TO PERIODICAL LITERATURE

DINOSAURS
Dinosaurs. J. Bosveld. il Sci Digest 82:31-2+
S '77
DIPHENYL compounds
Widespread PBB contamination can affect im-
mune system. B. J. Culliton. Science 197:849
Ag 26 '77
DIRECTORIES
Born again businessmen; Christian business di-
rectories. America 137:140 S 17 '77
Buying Christian; Christian business directories.
A. B. Haines. Chr Cent 94:804-5 S 21 '77
DIRECTORS, Bank. See Banks and bank;•g—Di-
rectors
DISADVANTAGED children. See Socially handi-
capped children
DISASTER relief
Climatic change; coping with nature's forces.
R. C. Cowen. Current 195:53-6 S '77
We've been asked: about the big surge in
disaster aid. il U.S. News 83:55 S 19 '77
DISASTERS
See also
Disaster relief
DISCRIMINATION
Aspects of institutional discrimination. J. J.
Harris, 3d and W. R. Bentzen. bibl il Clearing
H 51:7-10 S '77
Quota conflict; reverse discrimination vs affirma-
tive action. Time 110:25 S 26 '77
Some are more equal; Supreme Court decisions
affecting discrimination in education and politi-
cal representation. B. Odom. Nat R 29:1114-15
S 30 '77
DISCRIMINATION in employment
Bona fide seniority and racial bias; Supreme
Court decision. bibl M Labor R 100:48-9 Ag '77
Furor over reverse discrimination. J. K. Footlick
and others. il Newsweek 90:52-5+ S 26 '77
Immigrants, employers, and exclusion. B. W.
Parlin. Society 14:23-6 S '77
DISCRIMINATION in sports. See Segregation in
sports
DISEASES
Leads on the causes of Legionnaires' disease.
il Sci N 112:180 S 17 '77
War on germs. M. Clark. il Newsweek 90:98
S 19 '77
DISEASES, Industrial
Unhealthy jobs; excerpt from The picture of
health: environmental sources of disease. E.
Eckholm. bibl il Environment 19:29-38 Ag '77
DISSENTERS
No to Maoism; Chinese. il Time 110:54 S 19 '77
Ten days that shook me up in Russia. B. Gelb
N Y Times Mag p21+ S 18 '77
DODOS
Plant-animal mutualism; coevolution with dodo
leads to near extinction of plant. S. A. Temple.
bibl Science 197:885-6 Ag 26 '77
DOGS
Diseases and pests
Guarding a new puppy's health. D. L. Hunter.
il Parents Mag 52:40 S '77
DOLPHINS (mammals)
Hawaiian spinner; thermoregulatory behavior of
the spinner dolphin. G. C. Whittow. il Sea
Front 23:304-7 S '77
DOMINICAN REPUBLIC
See also
Medical care—Dominican Republic
DONELSON, Kenneth L.
Some responsibilities for English teachers who
already face an impossible job. Engl J 66:27-32
S '77
DONER, Landis W. and White, J. W. Jr
Carbon-13/carbon-12 ratio is relatively uniform
among honeys. bibl il Science 197:891-2 Ag 26
'77
DORSETT, Tony Drew
Tony D comes to big D. J. Marshall. il pors
Tony D illus 47:38-43+ S 19 '77 •
DOUGLAS, William Orville
C & O Canal dedicated to Justice Douglas. il
por Nat Parks & Con Mag 51:20 Ag '77
DOUTY, Harry Mortimer
Slowdown in real wages: a postwar perspective.
bibl il M Labor R 100:7-12 Ag '77
DOWLING, Elizabeth
(ed) See Ashe, A. Arthur Ashe: on politics
& sports
DRAIN tiles
Tiling still pays; drainage boosts efficiency,
yields. G. Vincent. il Suc Farm 75:41 S '77
DRAINAGE tiles. See Drain tiles
DRAMA festivals
Cervantes at Chamizal; Siglo de Oro Drama
Festival, El Paso, Tex. W. M. Reid. il Améri-
cas 29:19-24 S '77
Scotland
See also
International Festival of Music and Drama,
Edinburgh
DRAMA reviews
Single works
See name of author for full entry
All for love. J. Dryden
Miss Margarida's way. R. Athayde

DRESANG, Eliza T.
There are no other children; special children in
library media centers. il SLJ 24:19-23 S '77
DREXLER, Arthur
Pushing future directions in modern design. B.
Diamonstein. il por Art N 76:43-5 S '77 •
DREYER, June Teufel
Ethnic relations in China. bibl f Ann Am Acad
433:100-11 S '77
DRILLING and boring
Plastic cube with memory. il Mech Illus 73:153
O '77
DROUGHTS
Water; the next resource crisis? il Nations Bus
65:50-2+ S '77
DRUGS
Physiological effects
Aspirin. il Sci Digest 82:54-7 S '77·
DRUNKENNESS. See Liquor problem
DRYDEN, John
All for love. Reviews
New Repub 177:22-3 S 24 '77 •
DRYING apparatus
See also
Grain dryers
DUBUFFET, Jean
Right to raze. Vasari. il por Art N 76:19 S '77 •
DUE process of law
Due process in discipline. C. E. Alberti. bibl
Clearing H 51:12-14 S '77
DUNBAR, Bonnie S. See Shivers, C. A. jt. auth
DUNCAN, Charles William, 1926-
Collective security and confidence; excerpt from
address. Aviation W 107:7 S 12 '77
DUNCAN, Isadora
Isadora reexamined. N. Macdonald. il pors
Dance Mag 51:51-66 Jl; 42-6 Ag; 60-3 S '77 •
DUNCAN, John James
Excerpt from address on Comprehensive Health
Care Insurance Act, January 17, 1977. Cong
Digest 56:201+ Ag '77
DU PONT, Henry Francis, Winterthur Museum.
See Henry Francis du Pont Winterthur
Museum
DU VAL, Miles P. 1896-
Panama Canal question; address, July 29, 1977.
Vital Speeches 43:685-9 S 1 '77
DYES and dyeing
See also
Batik

EFLA. See Educational Film Library Association
EAGLE, Joanna Shaw-. See Shaw-Eagle, J.
EARTH
Photographs from space
Massive dust cloud tracked in GOES-1 satellite
image. il Aviation W 107:58-60 Jl 25 '77
Surface •
See also
Faults (geology)
EAST TIMOR. See Timor (island)
EASTERN Airlines
Eastern A-300B crew training started. L.
Dunkelberg. il Aviation W 107:27+ S 5 '77
EASTERN Test Range. See Proving grounds
ECKHOLM, Erik P.
Unhealthy jobs; excerpt from The picture of
health; environmental sources of disease. bibl
il Environment 19:29-38 Ag '77
ECKSTEIN, Otto
To the prophet for the profits. il por Time 110:
90+ S 26 '77 •
ECOLOGICAL communities. See Ecosystems
ECOLOGISTS in government. See Scientists in
government
ECONOMIC Adjustment, Office of
See also
United States—Defense, Department of—Eco-
nomic Adjustment, Office of
ECONOMIC assistance, Domestic
See also
Food relief—United States
ECONOMIC conditions
See also
Business depression
ECONOMIC conferences
Requiem for the North-South conference; Con-
ference on International Economic Cooperation.
J. Amuzegar. bibl f For Affairs 56:136-59 O '77
ECONOMIC development
Conferences
See Economic conferences
ECONOMIC forecasting
Declining interest rates forecast; study by the
Academy for Contemporary Problems. il Am
City & County 92:34 S '77
Economics. Sr Schol 110:30-1 S 22 '77
Storm warnings. Nat R 29:1039-40 S 16 '77 •
To the prophet go the profits; Data Resources,
Inc. il por Time 110:90+ S 26 '77

Directories literally direct you to phone numbers, addresses, and names of institutions, organizations, or individuals. Some directories give much more detailed information. The best-known example is the phone book.

Almanacs, handbooks, and manuals differ slightly from each other, but they serve the basic purpose of giving you current, usually outline, information on a topic. Almanacs tend to gather miscellaneous facts, such as the *World Almanac* (p. 69), while handbooks and manuals concentrate on a subject area.

Yearbooks are just that, and often supplement your encyclopedia.

Geographical sources include maps and atlases, gazeteers (a list of places and where to find those places), and travel information.

WHICH REFERENCE WORK?

Which type of reference work should you select? It depends on the kind of question you want to answer. Figure 4-2 shows the right kind of source for many kinds of questions. If you don't know where your question fits, ask the librarian.

Comparing Works

When there is only one book available of the type you need, your task is easy. But usually you have a choice of several encyclopedias, for example. Whenever you have a choice, select the book on five criteria.

First, which source is the *most up-to-date*? You can find the date of an index on its cover, and the date of a book on the title page or on the back of the title page. There may be several dates; look for the latest. The card catalog or a bibliography also tells the date or edition of a book.

Next, figure out which source is the *easiest to use*. Check how the material is arranged and whether there is an index. In addition, ask yourself whether there are too many abbreviations, and whether you understand the abbreviations. Skim the preface or introductory explanation. Usually the compiler explains the arrangement, the abbreviations, the scope (how much of a subject is considered), the audience, and the purpose of the work.

Figure 4-1

Part of a page from *Readers' Guide to Periodical Literature,* a magazine index found in most libraries. *Readers' Guide to Periodical Literature*: Copyright © 1975, 1976, 1977 by the H.W. Wilson Company. Material reproduced by permission of the publisher.

Types of Questions	Card Catalog	Yearbook	Manual	Index	Handbook	Encyclopedia	Directory	Dictionary	Biography (essay)	Biography (data)	Bibliography	Atlas/Gazetteer	Almanac
Abbreviations								X					
Addresses							X			X			X
Background/overview of subject						X							
Bibliographies and reading lists	X					X					X		
Biography: longer essays	X			X		X			X				
Biography: quick facts						X				X			X
Book prices and publishers											X		
Book reviews				X									
Books	X										X		
Countries—background, history, economics, government, and so on	X					X							X
Countries—current facts		X		X									
Countries—description	X					X						X	
Current news		X		X									X
Dates						X							X
Definitions						X		X					
Essays	X				X								
Ethnic history	X			X	X								
Geographical names—pronunciation/location								X				X	
Government		X	X			X							X
Historical documents	X					X							
"How many" questions	X			X	X	X							X
"How" questions			X		X								
Illustrations (see Pictures)													
Magazine articles				X									
Maps												X	

Figure 4-2

Use this chart to find out what type of reference source answers your question. If, for example, you are looking for book reviews, look in the "Types of Questions" column until you find book reviews. Then look to the right for columns marked x. (You will find reviews by means of an index.)

    Third, decide which source is the *easiest to read.* Is a work too technical or too simple for your need? An equally important, related question: Is the material too long, or too short?

    Fourth, which source is the *most complete*? Which work, no matter how long or how short the treatment of your subject, answers your question completely?

Types of Questions	Card Catalog	Yearbook	Manual	Index	Handbook	Encyclopedia	Directory	Dictionary	Biography (essay)	Biography (data)	Bibliography	Atlas/Gazetteer	Almanac
Name of communities, cities, rivers, physical features							X					X	
Name of institution, corporation, organization							X						
Notable persons									X	X			X
Occupations					X				X				
Outline for a talk or paper						X							
Periodicals (see Magazines)													
Periodicals in a subject field							X				X		
Pictures of people or places				X		X			X				
Political data		X		X		X							X
Presidents	X					X			X	X			
Quotations					X			X					
Record reviews				X									
Records		X											X
Statistics		X		X		X							X
Travel	X	X			X	X						X	
"What" questions	X		X		X	X							X
"When" questions		X			X	X							X
"Where" questions						X						X	
"Who was/Who is?"									X	X	X	X	
"Who wrote?"				X	X	X							
"Why" questions	X				X	X							
Words—definitions, pronunciations, and so on								X					

Finally, consider which source has the most useful *special features*, such as bibliographies, illustrations, and charts.

Works That List Reference Works

There is another approach to selecting the right reference work. You can go to a work that describes reference works! The best such guide is:

Guide to Reference Books (Eugene P. Sheehy, Ed.), 9th ed. Chicago: American Library Association, 1976. Z1035.1S43   011

This work lists most of the basic reference books in all subjects. It also *annotates* them—it describes them briefly. Easy to use, it is arranged under five broad subject headings, with a magnificent author, subject, and title index. Whenever you are doing lengthy research, it will pay you to begin here.

This guide gets rapidly out of date. Another work lets you keep up with new bibliographies:

Bibliographic Index. N.Y.: Wilson, 1937 to date, triannual.
Z1002.B59   016.016

This work lists bibliographies that are parts of books, separate books, or (most important) in articles in 2200 English and foreign language periodicals. It covers a wide area and it is fairly easy to use.

Remember, this source is two or three times removed from the information you really want. For example, you find a citation in the index. You then have to go to the magazine or book where the bibliography is printed. Next you scan the bibliography and pick out the name of the reference book you want—which means another trip to the periodical room or to your library card catalog.

You will not often have to be so persistent. For most purposes you will find a good source in *Subject Guide to Books in Print,* your own card catalog, or in the bibliography at the end of an encyclopedia article.

Chapter **5**

Encyclopedias

There are three basic forms of reference works that you can count on to answer most of your research questions: the card catalog, the periodical index, and the encyclopedia. You can begin searching for material in any one of them, but the encyclopedia is often the best. When you don't know much about the subject, the encyclopedia offers you a clear overview.

The encyclopedia has another advantage over the card catalog and periodical index. It is a one-stop information source. You don't have to go from there to the shelves to find a book or a magazine. All, or at least most, of the basic information you are likely to need for a start is in the encyclopedia.

Once you use the encyclopedia, it becomes easier to decide where to fill in with periodical articles and with books from the card catalog. Often the encyclopedia will even tell you books to look up.

In no case is it fair or honest simply to rewrite or condense an encyclopedia article for your paper. This temptation is one of the reasons some teachers suggest you avoid using an encyclopedia. Properly used, the encyclopedia is a basic place to start almost any research.

WHAT IS IN AN ENCYCLOPEDIA?

In an up-to-date, good encyclopedia, you will find the definition of a subject or the basic background of a person's life. You will read the history of a subject or event. Usually charts, diagrams, and other illustrations clarify difficult parts. At the end of most articles, a bibliography suggests additional readings.

Encyclopedia articles contain a built-in outline for your talk or paper. The order in which material is presented will suggest how to order your own work. When the article is divided into logical sections and subsections, you can borrow this structure, in whole or in part.

TYPES OF ENCYCLOPEDIAS

Most libraries have three types of encyclopedias—general sets, one-volume sets, and subject encyclopedias. This chapter concentrates on general sets.

Most of the encyclopedias, regardless of type, are in the reference section of the library.

General Sets

Three general sets are familiar sights in many homes—the *Encyclopedia Britannica* and the *Encyclopedia Americana* (called "adult sets"), and *Collier's Encyclopedia* (for students). These sets are described later in the chapter.

Two less familiar general sets may be in your library:

Encyclopedia International. N.Y.: Grolier. 20 vols. Adult and student.
AE5.E447   031

Compton's Encyclopedia. Chicago: Encyclopedia Britannica. 26 vols.
student AG5.C73   031

Non-American, English-language sets you are likely to find are:

Chamber's Encyclopedia. London: International Learning Systems. 15 vols.
A general adult British set, last published in 1973 and now much dated.
AE5.C44   032

Encyclopedia Canadiana. Ottawa: Canadiana Company. 10 vols. Dated
adult set. F1006.E625   971

One-Volume Sets

The one-volume encyclopedias are like the general sets, but they have less material. Most of them can be used with ease by high school students.

Three volumes are particularly useful when you are looking for a quick fact, such as a date or the spelling of a name. All are relatively up-to-date.

The New Columbia Encyclopedia, 4th ed. N.Y.: Columbia, 1975. AG5.C725   031

The Random House Encyclopedia. N.Y.: Random House, 1977. AG5.R25   031

The Lincoln Library of Essential Information. Columbus, Ohio: Frontier Press Co., frequently revised. AG105.L55   031

Subject Encyclopedias

The subject encyclopedias include *The Encyclopedia of Philosophy* and the *International Encyclopedia of the Social Sciences*. Their titles are self-explanatory. They are considerably more specialized and detailed than a general set or one-volume encyclopedia. Many of them are described in Section Two.

WHICH ENCYCLOPEDIA?

Which one of the general sets should you use? The one that has the easiest, usually the longest article on your subject.

How do you find that?

When you know absolutely nothing about the subject, and it appears to be difficult, begin with *Compton's* or an equivalent student set. Explanations are written clearly for younger people. For example, if you are a mathematical dunce and want something on the theory of relativity, the best place is the *Compton's,* not the *Encyclopaedia Britannica,* which will have a detailed, technical article.

On the other hand, when you feel relatively comfortable with the subject, you can begin with the *Britannica* or *Americana.* See which one is best for your needs. There are five tests:

1. Is the article too long or too short?
2. Is the language clear?
3. Are there helpful illustrations?

4. Can you use the outline form of the article?
5. Is the bibliography useful? Does it list up-to-date titles you are likely to find in your library?

Timeliness is not always important, but you should read a relatively current article. Check the last date on the opposite side of the title page. This date will give you the *approximate* year when the information you are reading was written. *Approximate* needs to be stressed, because while most sets are revised annually, not all of the material in the set is updated each time.

If you want to check the relative currency of the set quickly, look up your home town to see what population figure is given; check the article on a famous living person to see how much of the data is current; or look at a few illustrations to see whether the set is still featuring automobiles, airplanes, and fashions of one year ago, or twenty years ago.

As of this writing, the *Britannica* was more up-to-date than either *Americana* or *Collier's*—but the other sets do revise material each year.

HOW TO USE AN ENCYCLOPEDIA

Most encyclopedia are arranged in alphabetical order by subject. On the spine of each volume you will find the inclusive letters covered in that volume.

When you are in a hurry and looking for a large, common subject, the fastest way to find what you want is to pull down the volume with your subject. It is simple enough to find "Cannibals" or "Zebras" by consulting the inclusive letters.

AMERICAN INSTITUTE OF CHEMICAL ENGINEERS. See THE AMERICANA ANNUAL—*Societies and Organizations.*

AMERICAN INSTITUTE OF GRAPHIC ARTS. See THE AMERICANA ANNUAL—*Societies and Organizations.*

AMERICAN INSTITUTE OF MINING, METALLURGICAL, AND PETROLEUM ENGINEERS. See THE AMERICANA ANNUAL—*Societies and Organizations.*

Figure 5-1

Look for "see" references in the encyclopedia to send you to the right subject heading. Reprinted with permission of The Encyclopedia Americana, copyright 1978, The Americana Corporation.

Make use of the cross references.[1] Once you find the subject, look for the "see also" references at the end, which refer you to related articles. If the subject is not in the volume, there probably will be a "see" reference to the proper place (Figure 5-1).

The Index

When you still can't find something, or you are looking for a bit of detail, turn to the index (Figure 5-2). Don't assume what you need is not in the set. The odds are that it is, but you need an index.

Almost all sets now have indexes, including all discussed here, except for the new *Britannica.* There is no index to the *Britannica,* at least in the usual sense. When you are hunting for something, turn to the "Micropaedia" set and look up your subject. Here will be a reference to the longer articles in the "Macropaedia" set. (See p. 36 for details on the britannica).

If you do use an index, watch for letters after the page numbers. The letters usually refer to a section of the page. For example, 330a means what you want begins at the top of the left portion of the page. (The lettering is explained at the beginning of the index.)

Time-Saving Hints

Don't waste time looking for one general encyclopedia. Almost any set you find in the library will do nicely. If one is not sufficient, turn to another. Remember, though, that there are special subject encyclopedias.

---

[1] Cross-references, of major importance when using any reference work, are discussed in detail on page 55.

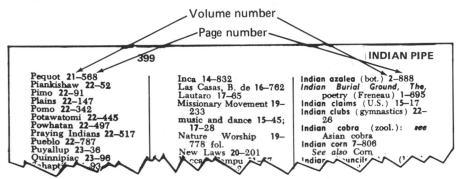

Figure 5-2

If you can't find your subject directly, turn to the encyclopedia index. Notice this detail from the *Americana* index. Reprinted with permission of The Encyclopedia Americana, copyright 1978, The Americana Corporation.

When you have trouble constructing an outline for a subject, try the outlines in the encyclopedias.

When you are looking for additional readings, you can save much time and energy by limiting yourself to two or three of the latest listed in the encyclopedia article bibliography.

If you have to take many notes, look around first for a photocopying (Xerox) machine. It is easier to xerox the pages and then to incorporate what you need into your notes by cutting and pasting.

Jot down the headings and subheadings. They are not likely to appear exactly in the card catalog or a periodical index, but they may suggest key words for searching.

THREE BASIC SETS

The New Encyclopaedia Britannica, 15th ed. Chicago: Encyclopedia Britannica, 1974. 30 vols. AE5.E363   031.

Totally revised in 1974, the *Britannica* is the most up-to-date of the general encyclopedias. It now consists of three parts: the "Micropaedia," 10 volumes of short facts for ready reference purposes; the "Macropaedia," 19 volumes of in-depth articles in the traditional fashion of encyclopedias; and the "Propaedia," a one-volume outline of knowledge, which is difficult to use, but may be of some help in outlining broad subject areas. There is no index, but you will find specific references to the "Macropaedia" in the "Micropaedia." The latter should be used for biography, because there are few full-length biographical articles in the fuller "Macropaedia." You can go directly to the "Macropaedia," but it may be faster in difficult cases to begin with the "Micropaedia."

Advantages.   Choose the *Britannica* when you want timeliness; it is the most up-to-date of the general sets. Choose it for depth; most articles in the Macropaedia are at least 1000 words. You will get good, but scholarly bibliographies and useful illustrations. Particularly strong in the arts, humanities, and technical aspects of science, the *Britannica* has a reputation as the most authoritative.

Drawbacks.   The new format is not easy to use. The style and language presuppose better than average education, and there is not an adequate index.

Encyclopedia Americana. N.Y.: Grolier. 30 vols. [1] AE5.E33   031

The *Encyclopedia Americana* has undergone numerous revisions. Articles are authoritative, generally short, and almost always easy to read. The index is superior. Next to the *Britannica,* the *Americana* is the most common set in American libraries.

Advantages.   The *Americana* should be your first choice when you want in-depth information on American cities and towns, understandable language and style, biographical information (particularly about Americans), and good illustrations. It is particularly strong for its detailed index, one of the best now available. Altogether, the *Americana* is one of the easiest sets to use.

Drawbacks.   The set is constantly revised, but it is uneven in timeliness. Also, while international in scope, it has much more materials on North America.

Collier's Encyclopedia. N.Y.: Macmillan. 24 vols. AE5.C683   031

Collier's Encyclopedia is a "bridge" set between the adult and the young people's encyclopedias. It is more advanced than the junior set, less detailed and scholarly than the senior works. It is much favored in high schools, and usually it is found in college libraries as well.

Advantages.   Go to *Collier's* first when you want a fast, not so detailed overview of a subject; easy short articles; bibliographies and reading lists (grouped in the last volume) that are graded for difficulty; and an easy-to-use, good index. Much of the material is based on current curriculum and therefore, if you are a student, you are likely to find what you need here.

Drawbacks.   While there are some long articles, most of the material is treated in much briefer form than in the *Britannica* or *Americana*. When you want depth, this brevity is a drawback.

Chapter **6**

Indexes

Once the encyclopedia has given you an overview of the subject, the next place to turn is the periodical index. *Periodical* is another word for magazine.

There are many reasons for using magazines. First, a magazine article is current. A periodical may come out once a week. The article often stands as the first statement by someone working on a new idea. By consulting the article you may find ideas and information still years away from appearing in a book.

Moreover, the subject may be too slight or unimportant ever to find its way into an encyclopedia or a book. In that case, the only place you can find information on the subject is in an article. For example, there may be a flurry of interest this week about a sighting of a two-ton shark that never will be included in a book.

Third, it is easier to find out about all sides of a controversial subject with magazine articles. Several articles may give different viewpoints about the same topic. Books, by contrast, are usually long explorations of one viewpoint.

Fourth, a magazine article often will zero in on your subject much faster than a book. Because the article is more specific about a narrow subject, topic, or individual than a book, it is easier for you to read, understand, and use.

Finally, articles are not only shorter than a book, but often easier to read. They are not all easy: some are quite technical. It depends on what kind of periodical you are reading—popular or scholarly.

TYPES OF PERIODICALS

When do you select a popular or semipopular magazine, and when do you select a scholarly journal?

It is common sense to select a popular magazine when you know little or nothing about a subject and want a quick overview. You would choose a scholarly journal when you want in-depth material about a subject you understand.

You will tend to select periodicals because you know them, or because their titles sound impressive, or because you come across a reference to them. Another reason you will choose one over another is availability.

When you have a choice, how can you tell the popular from the scholarly?

Popular Magazines

You know many popular magazines. Magazines such as *Reader's Digest, TV Guide, McCall's, Woman's Day, Better Homes & Gardens, Playboy, Rolling Stone, National Geographic, Ladies Home Journal, Time, Newsweek, Sports Illustrated, People,* and the *National Enquirer* are some of the most widely read.

Only experience will make it clear whether a magazine is popular, but there are several quick clues. It probably is popular if:

1. It is indexed in *Readers' Guide to Periodical Literature, Access,* or *Popular Periodical Index.*
2. It is published weekly, every two weeks, or monthly.
3. You find advertising, particularly for consumer goods like liquor and automobiles.
4. You recognize the magazine from home, the supermarket, or drugstore stands.

The articles are popular if:

1. The title is not too technical. For example, under tte heading "Wolves," "Showdown on the tundra" is more likely to be popular than "Wolf kill: Signals between predator and prey."
2. The author is a well-known popular writer.
3. The article is short—no more than one to three pages long.

There is a group of popular titles that are edited for well-educated readers. Among them are literary review magazines such as *The New Yorker, The New York Review of Books, Saturday Review, Harper's Magazine,* and *Atlantic.* Most of them are indexed in *Readers' Guide.* Some scientific and news magazines are of this type.

Another group of popular magazines is much more specialized. It includes trade magazines that tell you how to operate a steel industry or a hamburger joint and magazines directed to readers with special hobbies and interests.

Journals

Journals publish technical and scholarly articles. They are meant to be read only by a few people vitally interested in a field. By definition there are no "popular" (widely read) journals.

Journals are easy to identify, if only because many of them literally include the word "journal" in the title—*Journal of Agricultural Engineering Research, Journal of Dentistry,* and so on. Nine other clues will help you identify them. You probably have a scholarly journal if:

1. You find it in a subject index. For example, *Engineering Index, Business Periodicals Index,* or *Psychological Abstracts* direct you only to specialized journals.
2. It is published quarterly, twice a year, or even less often—and usually is late in getting published.
3. The title is longer and more descriptive than popular titles.
4. The authors are identified either at the beginning or end of the article. Most authors will clearly possess some expertise.
5. The articles tend to be long—from 8 to even 30 or 40 pages.
6. There is little or no advertising, except of a specialized nature.
7. There are no illustrations, or just a few charts and graphs.
8. There are footnotes and long bibliographies.
9. The title of the journal is unfamiliar.

Looking for a Periodical in a Field

When you are looking for the name of a periodical in a particular field, you can generally find it in these two reference sources:

Ulrich's International Periodical Directory, 17th ed. N.Y.: Bowker, 1977. Z6941.U5   016.05

This work lists by subject about 60,000 periodicals. Full information is given for each title, including where it is indexed.

Magazines for Libraries, 3rd ed. N.Y.: Bowker, 1978. Z6941.K2   016.05

This work is a selective list of magazines by subject. It lists about 7000 titles with descriptions.

WHICH INDEX?

Suppose you are looking for periodical articles on a particular subject. You do not have to look in all the periodicals in that general field. Your search is made easy by periodical indexes.

The library has many indexes. Which one should you use?

Articles in Popular Magazines

Three indexes are your best help when you need current articles that are not too technical or specialized. They are the *Readers' Guide to Periodical Literature, Access,* and *Popular Periodical Index.*

Readers' Guide to Periodical Literature. N.Y.: Wilson, 1900 to date, semimonthly. AI3.R48   016.05

Coverage.   This guide is the most general of the periodical indexes, covering 156 popular magazines.

Frequency.   *Readers' Guide* is published every two weeks in a green paper cover. The semimonthly issues are cumulated every three months, and there is an annual bound circulation. As this index comes out more often than almost any other, you should use it for material on current events and affairs.

How to Find an Article.   The index is arranged by author's name and by subject. For material *about* (not by) an author, you look under the name with the subheading "about." When you are looking for a subject, be sure to check three features: subheadings under that subject, "see" references (subject headings used by the index rather than the one you chose), and "see also" references (other subjects in the same area of interest). As an added feature, book reviews are listed separately in the back of the index, under the name of the author of the book.

Access. Syracuse, N.Y.: Gaylord Brothers, 1975 to date, 3/yr. AI3.A23   016.051

Popular Periodical Index. Camden, N.J.: Robert Bottorff, 1973 to date, semiannual. AI3.P76   016.05

Each of these sources has its own peculiar method of indexing. *Access* divides the author entries from the subject entries. They are both easy to use and a backup for the *Readers' Guide.* Warning: The catch to using these two indexes is that many libraries do not have all, or even a majority of the titles indexed—particularly those in *Access.* You are likely to have better luck with *Popular Periodical Index,* which indexes about 30 titles, than with *Access,* which indexes 200.

Specific Articles

For articles with more specific information, but still fairly broad, you will want to turn to one of three indexes: *Humanities Index, Social Sciences Index,* or the *General Science Index.* All are published by the publisher of the *Readers'*

Guide and follow much the same pattern. If you know one, you know them all.

As the titles indicate, the indexes sweep large areas, including both semi-popular and technical periodicals. You will use these indexes when you want more information than you can find in the *Readers' Guide.*

Humanities Index. N.Y.: Wilson, 1974 to date, quarterly. AI3.H85   016

Coverage.   Next to the *Readers' Guide,* the most heavily used of the Wilson indexes. It covers 259 titles in the humanities and related areas, and it is your first choice for articles about literature and literary criticism or history. It also considers area studies, folklore, performing arts, philosophy, religion, and so on. Book reviews are listed in the back of each issue.
Frequency.   The index is published every quarter, with an annual cumulation. If you want more up-to-date material, go back to *Readers' Guide.*
How to Find an Article.   Follow the same process as for the *Readers' Guide.* There is the same full dictionary arrangement by author and by subject. Be sure to check subjects subheadings and the many "see also" references.

There is at least one related index:

British Humanities Index. London: Library Association, 1963 to date, quarterly. AI3.B7   016

This index covers some 400 British periodicals. Most are in the humanities, but some are in the social sciences as well. Arrangement is by subject only. The annual cumulation includes an author index.

Social Sciences Index. N.Y.: Wilson, 1974 to date, quarterly. AI3   016

Coverage.   The third index in the Wilson group, this work indexes 265 periodicals in the social sciences. It is the first place to look for articles in economics, environmental science, geography, psychology, sociology, and related subjects. Book reviews are listed in the back of each issue.
How to Find an Article.   Follow the same procedure as for *Readers' Guide* and *Humanities Index.* Indexing is in dictionary form, with authors and subjects interfiled.

The *Social Sciences Index* and the *Humanities Index* were formerly combined into one index, under various names. From 1907 to 1965 it was the *International Index.* From 1965 to March 1974 it was the *Social Sciences and Humanities Index.* Now they are entirely separate indexes that cover different periodicals.

General Science Index. N.Y.: Wilson, 1978 to date, 10/yr.
Z791.G78   016.6

Coverage.   This work indexes close to 90 general science periodicals in the English language at the nontechnical level. All basic scientific subjects are covered, including environment, food and nutrition, medicine and health, and psychology.
How to Find an Article.   Follow the same procedure as for other Wilson indexes. Book reviews are listed in back of each issue.

Technical Articles in Journals

For specialized articles in a narrow subject area, you will want to turn to a subject index. There are hundreds, usually with self-descriptive titles.

Whenever you want to find a subject index, turn to Section Two of this manual, or ask your librarian.

Materials Besides Articles

Some Indexes go beyond periodicals. They tell you where to find newspaper articles, reports, and parts of books. A good example, the one most often used in libraries, is the *Essay and General Literature Index.*

Essay and General Literature Index. N.Y.: Wilson, 1900 to date, semiannual. AI3.E75   080

Coverage.   This book is an index to essays and critical articles collected in books. Periodicals are not indexed. The essays and articles cover many subjects—so many that you can often use this work in conjunction with the *Readers' Guide.* It is particularly good for finding background articles in the humanities. Coverage of critical articles (telling why a certain novel is fine, or what a certain poem means) is excellent; in this respect the work can be used in conjunction with the *Humanities Index.*
Frequency.   The index comes out twice a year, with the second number a cumulated issue. One basic volume covers 1900 through 1933, and there are five- and seven-year cumulations thereafter.
How to Find Material.   The index is a dictionary arrangement of subjects and authors. When you look up work by an author, if it is followed by a subheading "about" what follows is "about" the author. Another subsection may be "about individual works." To find an article buried in a book—so well buried you would not find it otherwise—look under the author that interests you or under a subject heading.

You will find the entry looks different than in the periodical indexes. It will give you the name of the author, subject, or title in bold face. Under that it tells you *in* what book you will find the essay. A typical entry is:

Vonnegut, Kurt
> **about**
Davis R. P. Science fiction themes in Kurt
Vonnegut's work.
In Gibson, R. Q. Science Fiction Reader,
p. 20–40.

The key to watch for is the *In,* which tells you where the essay is found. All the books analyzed are listed with full bibliographical information in the back of the index, but usually you have enough when you have the author and the title. You go to the card catalog and look up the book by Gibson.

Abstracts

Some indexes go one step further and supply you with a summary of the contents of the article. In a regular index, when you find an article entitled "Big changes ahead in 1979 cars," you must figure out from the title what the article is about. How much easier it is when the index publisher tells you about the article—usually in 50 to 150 words. You can then decide whether you need the whole article.

The 50- to 150-word explanation about the article is called an *abstract.* Usually the abstract is short and objective. No opinion is given about the article's value. A typical abstract is shown in Figure 6-1.

There are numerous abstracting services, but most are limited to scientific and technical subjects. A few are considered briefly in Section Two.

HOW TO USE AN INDEX

You look for for information in a periodical index much as you do in the encyclopedia.

Most of the time you will look under subjects. You are not so likely to know the authors or titles of articles. Because subjects are so important in using periodical indexes, Chapter 7 will tell you more about subject headings.

Generally the periodical index subject headings are fairly current. There are many cross-references to help you along, particularly in the Wilson indexes.

Follow the Subject Headings

You may have some subject headings from the encyclopedia. Use them in searching the index. If not, look first under precise subjects—try "football plays,"

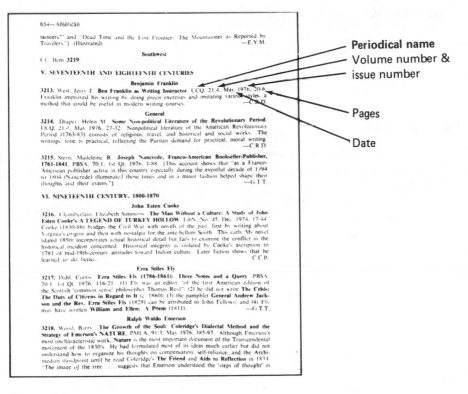

Periodical name

Volume number & issue number

Pages

Date

Figure 6-1

A typical abstract, from *Abstracts of English Studies,* tells you where to find the article and what it contains. You locate these abstracts by means of the index to their volume. Vol. 20, June 1977. No. 10 *Abstracts of English Studies,* Copyright © 1977 by the National Council of Teachers of English. Reprinted by permission of the publisher and the author.

not just "Sports." Watch carefully for cross-references from your words to the terminology used by the index.

When you arrive at a subject heading, write it down. You can use it to search other sources, including the card catalog. Also, you have a record of what you searched in the index.

Begin with the most recent issue of the index and work backward until you have enough material. Stay with your heading. As you search, watch for how the wording of the subject heading may change over time. Be aware that new subject headings may either replace or come before the heading you are using.

Be sure to check for subheadings and subdivisions of the subject. Thanks to having the subject headings spread out on a page, it is easy to see the breakdown. Don't forget to turn the page to see whether more follows.

Learn the Abbreviations

Because the index may list millions of articles, it is necessary to conserve space. Space is saved by using abbreviations—many more than in a card catalog.

Check the abbreviations, particularly for the name of magazines, in the beginning pages of the index (Figure 6-2).

The Entry Form

Nearby is usually a clear explanation of the entry form used in the index. The precise form differs from index to index, but the elements are the same (Figure 6-3).

By subject you would find:

WOLVES (the subject you are looking up)
   Alaskan wolfkill. (the name of the article) *Sci Digest* (the name of the magazine, abbreviated from *Science Digest*) *79:20–39* (the volume number first, then the pages) *My '76* (the month the article was published, May 1976).

By author you would find:

Dessauer, John P. (the author of the article)
   Too many books revisited. (the title) *Pub W* (the name of the magazine, abbreviated from *Publishers Weekly*) *211:41–3* (the volume number and pages) *My 16 '77* (abbreviation for the date of publication, May 16, 1977).

What to Copy from the Index

There is more information in the typical index entry than you really need.[1] In order to find a periodical article, you need to copy just three facts:

1. The name of the magazine. Be sure you understand the abbreviation.
2. The date your article was published—usually the month and year. Be sure you understand the abbreviations.
3. The page numbers where the article appears in the periodical. (You also may want the volume number, if the periodical is in a bound volume in the library.)

It is not necessary, but if you are working with several issues of the index, you may want to copy the name of the index, its date, and where you found

---

[1] *Exception:* You may need additional data if the magazines are locked away and you have to depend upon someone else to find the magazine. The library will have standard call slips for this purpose. Find a slip and be sure you understand what information is needed.

Figure 6-2

Check the abbreviations used in the index. These abbreviations are used by the *Readers' Guide. Readers' Guide to Periodical Literature.* Copyright © 1975, 1976, 1977 by the H.W. Wilson Company. Material reproduced by permission of the publisher.

ABBREVIATIONS OF PERIODICALS INDEXED

For full information, consult pages vi-ix

Aging—Aging
Am Artist—American Artist
Am City & County—American City & County
Am Educ—American Education
Am For—American Forests
*Am Heritage—American Heritage
Am Hist Illus—American History Illustrated
Am Hist R—American Historical Review
Am Home—American Home
Am Imago—American Imago
Am Lib—American Libraries
Am Rec G—American Record Guide
    (Publication suspended with D '72; resumed
    N '76)
Am Scholar—American Scholar
Am West—American West
America—America
American City. See American City & County
Américas—Américas

*Ebony—Ebony
Educ Digest—Education Digest
Engl J—English Journal
Environment—Environment
Esquire—Esquire

Fam Health—Family Health incorporating To-
    day's Health
*Farm J—Farm Journal
Field & S—Field & Stream
Film Q—Film Quarterly
Flying—Flying
Focus—Focus
*For Affairs—Foreign Affairs
Forbes—Forbes
*Fortune—Fortune

ABBREVIATIONS

*	following name entry, a printer's device	Jr	Junior
+	continued on later pages of same issue	jt auth	joint author
Abp	Archbishop	Ltd	Limited
abr	abridged	m	monthly
Ag	August	Mr	March
Ap	April	My	May
arch	architect		
Assn	Association	N	November
Aut	Autumn	no	number
Ave	Avenue		
		O	October
Bart	Baronet		
bibl	bibliography	por	portrait
bibl f	bibliographical foot- notes	pseud	pseudonym
bi-m	bimonthly	pt	part
bi-w	biweekly	pub	published, publisher publishing
bldg	building		
Bp	Bishop	q	quarterly
Co	Company	rev	revised
comp	compiled, compiler		
cond	condensed	S	September
cont	continued	sec	section
Corp	Corporation	semi-m	semimonthly
		Soc	Society
D	December	Spr	Spring
Dept	Department	Sq	Square
		Sr	Senior
ed	edited, edition, editor	St	Street
		Summ	Summer
F	February	supp	supplement
		supt	superintendent
Hon	Honorable		
		tr	translated, transla- tion, translator
il	illustrated, illustra- tion, illustrator		
Inc	Incorporated	v	volume
introd	introduction, intro- ductory		
		w	weekly
		Wint	Winter
Ja	January		
Je	June	yr	year
Jl	July		

14   SOCIAL SCIENCES INDEX

Author

Name of article

Subject

Abbreviation of magazine

Volume number

Pages

Month/Year

See also reference

See reference

Art —cont.
        Themes
   See also
Canada in art
Industrialization in art
Frames in art
       Canada
Dinosaur pie. S. M. Crean. Can Forum 56:4 My '76
      United States
Black American art, 1750-1950; il Crisis 83:316-17 N '76
Art, Australian (aboriginal)
   Two engraved stone plaques of late pleistocene age from Devil's Lair, Western Australia. C. E. Dortch. bibl Archaeol Phy Anthrop Oceania 11:32-44 Ap '76
Art, Roman
   Pompeii: paid for by cigarettes. Economist 261:28 N 20 '76
Art and state
      Canada
Feet of clay planted firm in USA. G. Curnoe. Can Forum 56:9-11 My '76
Invisible country; excerpts from Who's afraid of Canadian culture? S. M. Crean. Can Forum 56:7-14 Je '76
      China
Most unimaginative fare. P. Jones. Far E Econ R 94:56-7 O 1 '76
      Taiwan
Change takes its toll on culture. W. Armbruster. Far E Econ R 93:27-8 Ag 27 '76
      United States
United States—National foundation on the arts and the humanities
Art centers
   Concentration of facilities in new town centres. A. Whittick. il Town & Country Plan 44:440-2 O '76
Art education. See Art—Study and teaching
Art festivals
   Mr Culture gets in on the act. R. Yao. Far E Econ R 94:38 O 15 '76
Art objects, Forgery of. See Forgery of works of art
Art thefts
   Vandals who pilfer priceless relics may not realize the enormity of their crimes but dealers and buyers are the real culprits. F. Celoria. Geog Mag 49:204+ D '76
Arterial catheterization
   Monitoring pulmonary artery pressures. S. L. Woods. il Am J Nursing 76:1765-71 N '76
Artificial satellites in regional planning
   Regional land use classification derived from computer-processed satellite data. P. W. Mausel and others. il maps Am Inst Plan J 42:153-64 Ap '76; Reply with rejoinder. C. Blackmon. 42:440-2 O '76
Artists
   See also
Geographers as artists
Artists, British
   See also
Lowry, L. S.
Morris, W.
Artists, Canadian
   See also
Jeffreys, C. W.
Arts, Decorative. See Arts and crafts
Arts and crafts

Population, warfare, and the male supremacist complex. W. T. Divale and M. Harris. bibl Am Anthrop 78:521-38 S '76
Theory of power relationships in marriage. B. C. Rollins and S. J. Bahr. bibl J Marr & Fam 38:619-27 N '76
Women, horticulture, and society in sub-Saharan Africa. C. S. Lancaster. bibl Am Anthrop 78:539-64 S '76
Work integration, marital satisfaction, and conjugal power. T. D. Kemper and M. L. Reichler. bibl Hum Relat 29:929-44 O '76
Ash, Robert
   Economic aspects of land reform in Kiangsu, 1949-52. China Q no66:261-92; no67:519-45 Je-S '76
Ashanti law. See Law, Ashanti
Ashhab, Naim
   Developing countries and disarmament. World Marx R 19:84-9 Jl '76
Ashmore, Harry S.
   This is Arkansas. Center Mag 9:2-7 N '76
Ashton, Roderick
   Aspects of timing in child development. bibl Child Develop 47:622-6 S '76
   Infant state and stimulation. Develop Psychol 12:569-70 N '76
Asia
   See also
Police—Asia
Smuggling—Asia
Urbanization—Asia
      Defenses
   See also
Military assistance—Asia
      Economic conditions
   See also
Black market—Asia
      Economic relations
        United States
Ties that bind. J. Srodes. Far E Econ R 94:10-11 N 12 '76
      Foreign relations
        Great Britain
Future of the British outlook on Asia. C. Philips. Asian Aff 63:249-54 O '76
        Russia
Moscow stirs the pot. D. Peiris. Far E Econ R 93:10 S 10 '76
        United States
Asia waits for the word from Carter. S. Barber. Far E Econ R 94:10-11 N 12 '76
Carter and the pragmatists. D. Peiris. Far E Econ R 94:14+ N 12 '76
      Politics
Carter and the pragmatists. D. Peiris. Far E Econ R 94:14+ N 12 '76
Peace front in Asia. B. Lhamsuren. World Marx R 19:79-84 Jl '76
Asia, Central
   See also
Central Asia, Soviet
Asia, Southeastern
   See also
Banks and banking—Asia, Southeastern
      Civilization
Ecology, culture, social organization, and state formation in southeast Asia [with discussion] R. L. Winzeler. bibl Cur Anthrop 17:623-40 D '76
   See also
Pottery—Asia, Southeastern

Figure 6-3

The primary elements to look for in a periodical index. (Example is from the *Social Sciences Index.*) *Social Sciences Index.* Copyright © 1977 by the H.W. Wilson Company. Material reproduced by permission of the publisher.

the entry. You will have a running record of what you've looked at, and a way to refer back to the index if you need more information.

Turn back to the two examples of periodical index entries—the one on wolves and the one by John Dessauer. Here is what you would need to write down to find the articles. Notice how little you need.

Wolves
    Science Digest (name of the magazine), May, 1976 (date the article was published) p. 20 (beginning page)
Dessauer
    Publishers Weekly, May 16, 1977, p. 41

You might want to add after each of these notes RG (*Readers' Guide to Periodical Literature*), June 10, 1977, to tell you where you found the two articles.

COMPUTER SEARCHES

In many medium to large libraries, you don't have to go to all this work: the computer can search some indexes for you.

The advantage of a computer-assisted search is that it is fast, efficient, more timely than the printed index, and more comprehensive.

In simple terms, here is how a computer search works. An index or abstract has been transferred to a magnetic tape or its equivalent. The tape is called a "data base." The data base is "searched" by the computer, much in the same way you would search an index. This search is done at a tremendous speed, which saves you countless hours of work. The librarian carries out the computer search for you. In the end, you get a printed listing of articles—much the same kind of list you would have if you had manually searched the index and laboriously copied down the references to articles.

Sometimes the list will include abstracts, sometimes not. It depends on whether the abstracts are available, or whether you request them.

Not all indexes or abstracts are available for a computer search. However, the number so available is increasing each month, so it will pay you to inquire. There should be signs or notices giving information on the availability of a computer-assisted search. Should you find no notices, ask the reference librarian.

Once you receive the list you are back to the point you would be at if you had searched the index yourself. You still must find the articles.

HOW TO FIND THE PERIODICAL

Now you have the name, date, and page numbers of two periodical articles. Fine, but where do you find them?

Signs and floor plans should point you in the right direction. If you don't know where the library keeps the periodicals—both current and back issues—ask the librarian.

Now you have to find your title. Ask the librarian how to do it. In your library, the periodicals may be listed in alphabetical order by title in the card catalog. They may be in a separate catalog or computer printout. Or they simply may be listed on sheets posted near the indexes, the catalog, or the magazines. Find out which system your library uses.

On the list of titles you will find several new bits of information. How long the library has been taking the periodical is indicated by a beginning date. "Vol. 1, No. 1, 1970+," means the library has the *first volume* (vol. 1) and the *first issue* (no. 1). The + sign indicates that the library has all the succeeding issues. Sometimes the symbol will read "Vol. 5, No. 1, 1975+," which means you are out of luck if you are looking for a title before 1975. (Notations do differ somewhat. Another form to indicate continuation is a dash—May 1969—.)

```
FLM     Zwink, Monika, 1942-
BF          Locus of control as predictor of
637     traditional and feminist respondents'
I5      perceived influence in same and mixed
Z85x    gender interview / by Monika Zwink.
        1977.
            xii, 142 leaves : ill.
            Thesis--University of Colorado.
            Bibliography: leaves [109]-117.
            Microfilm copy of typescript.  Ann
        Arbor, Mich.  : Xerox University
        Microfilms, 1977.      -- 1 reel ; 35mm.

            1. Interviewing--Evaluation.  I. Title
```

Figure 6-4

A catalog card showing that what you need is on microfilm. Note: In this library periodicals are arranged by the Library of Congress classification system (not in alphabetical order by title), hence the call number.

The periodical may be available in the library only on microform. This fact is indicated clearly on the listing (Figure 6-4). If you don't know where or how the microform is arranged, ask the librarian.

You now know the library has the periodicals you want. Where are they in the library?

If only the title and indication of how many issues the library has is given, you are safe to assume the periodicals are kept in alphabetical order by title. Go right to the shelves.

Larger libraries tend to use call numbers. Look for a call number after the title in a list, or in the upper left-hand corner of a catalog card. (See pp. 18–20 for an explanation of the call number system.) In that case, you look for the call number on the shelves. When the number you have matches up with the number on the magazines, you are almost home.

All you have to do now is to find the exact issue. If it is current, you should find the loose copy on the shelves. If it is not on the shelves, the library may keep it in a reading room. Ask the librarian.

If the magazine is not current, it is likely to be in a bound volume. The volumes are on the shelf in chronological order, usually clearly marked with year and volume number. (When you are working with many back issues, it may pay you to jot down the volume number from the periodical index.)

If not in a bound volume, the periodical may be available only on microform in the library. Check back: The catalog list should tell you.

When you can't find the bound volumes or the indication of microform, but the list indicates your library has the periodical, don't give up: ask the librarian for help.

The Problems

This whole procedure works, but it can be frustrating. How do you handle typical problems?

Problem 1: The periodical issue you are looking for is not on the shelves. Probably it is in another part of the library.[2]

Solution: Double check. Go back to the card catalog to see whether you are really looking in the right place.

Problem 2: The periodical you seek is being bound into a volume, and is not on the shelf.

Solution: Go to the librarian to find out when the bound volume will be returned to the library.

Problem 3: The periodical is so current that it is not on the shelves.

Solution: If the library has magazine racks, displays, and so on, be sure to check there first for current issues.

Problem 4: Sometimes you will find the bound volume and discover that the article you want has disappeared. Someone has cut it out. Vandalism of this type is a problem in any library.

Solution: Report the missing part of the volume to the librarian who may be able to order the missing article quickly from another library or another source in the library.

Problem 5: For one reason or another the article you want still is missing.

Solution: Visit other libraries. They may have your article. In a large library, there is probably a list of magazines available in other libraries. If you can't find the list, ask the librarian.

Providing you have time, ask the librarian to order the magazine article for you on interlibrary loan. This process may not take long, so it is always worth checking.

When all else fails, double back and try to find a substitute article.

---

[2] Libraries usually agree on the call number assigned to a periodical. The trouble comes in how they tell you where the periodical is actually located. For example, one library explains its abbreviations like this: "Mic" means the title is on microfilm and houses in the Microforms Area; "Ext" designates hard copy of a title at the branch or extension library. There are other prefixes for other forms and locations. Another library explains: Notations like "Holdings listed in central serials record" refer to a record of all issues of each periodical held in the library. The actual magazine, however, is in the periodical room, or in a branch library. Each library has its own unique system. Save yourself. Ask for help from the librarian.

Chapter **7**

What to Look Up

By now you know your way around the "big three" reference forms—the card catalog (Chapter 3), the encyclopedia (Chapter 5), and the index (Chapter 6). To use them all, you just look up an author, title, or subject. Only one puzzle remains—How do you know the right word to look up? This chapter will help you solve that puzzle.

The Author

The best way—when you are using an index or a catalog—is to look under the name of an authority on your subject. But how do you know who wrote, say, on the pros and cons of a peace treaty with the Soviet Union? How can you find out who is an expert on dancing, jazz, marriage, the women's movement, or anything else?

You will find names of authors who write material you need in lists of readings at the end of encyclopedia articles, in footnotes to magazine articles, in your textbook, in class notes, and in many other places. The more you become involved with the subject the more names of experts you will gather.

The Title

Let's say you can't run down an expert in your field. You could look under the title of a book or article by that author. The catch is that you rarely will know the title, even of a popular book.

Therefore, although card catalogs and indexes allow you "entrance" by the title, that approach to finding information rarely is used.

The Subject

Chances are, then, you will look for most information by subject. Instead of looking up Joe Dokes, author of a book on whaling, you are more likely simply to look under "Whales." You are less likely to look up *Dokes and the Whale*, the title of his book.

Simple as it sounds, trying to find information by subject can be the most frustrating of all. Why? Well, let's begin by looking up some local history.

SUBJECT HEADINGS

How do you find out what book or magazine has material on local history?

The answer is the subject heading.

Some indexer or cataloger reads the book or the article and decides that it is about local history, among other things. So before the book or magazine is shelved, it gets the subject heading "Local history." This heading will crop up when you look for the book in a card catalog, or when you look for the article in a periodical index. There may be several other books and articles under the same subject heading.

Subject headings, then, are an effort to analyze a book, article, record, film, or any form of information by its topics. They make it possible to bring like things together in the index, card catalog, and encyclopedia.

The same book or article might appear three or four times more under other subject headings that describe other aspects of the information—for example, "Economic history," "Church history," or "Constitutional history." Each heading offers you a separate way into the same information.

How does the indexer choose the order of words in the subject heading? Why not "History—Local" instead of "Local history" or "History—Economic" instead of "Economic history"? Why not, in fact, "History of money" instead of "Economic history," or . . . ?

The indexer knows national and international rules that govern what words to use and in what order. The indexer turns also to lists of standard subject headings to decide such questions.

The catch in this system is that the indexer assumes *you* will look under the same words, in the same order. That's not always the case.

Different Words, Different Order

Fortunately, most subject headings are in the language and in the order you are likely to use in everyday speech, or in discussing a technical subject with its own special jargon.

You should not have much trouble with the card catalog or the periodical index—particularly the latter. Periodical indexes are more flexible about subject heading words and order than the average card catalog.

Still, in any reference work, sooner or later you and the person who assigned the subject headings are going to be at odds. The indexer is going to be using a different term or a different order of terms than you use or even know. The two of you literally are using a different language to explain the same subject.

You're back in the situation discussed in Chapter 2, when you couldn't make your question clear to the librarian. The two of you were using different words to describe the elusive question. You solved the problem by talking over the question with the librarian. There's no chance to use that approach with an indexer or a cataloger.

For example, you are looking for something on "American authors." You look in the card catalog. Nothing there. Why? Because the cataloger knows the rule that says it should be "Authors—American."

You want something on "Trucks." Nothing there, because the cataloger prefers "Motor—Trucks." How about hunting for a "Job"? You will have to use the cataloger's subject heading, "Applications and positions." If you look up "Movies," you will find nothing. It's under "Motion pictures."[1]

Trying to guess the exact wording of the subject heading is confusing. Even more confusion arises when the subject you are looking for is buried as a subheading. For example, if you want to find a book on the CIA, you often can't just look under "CIA." You must turn to "United States—Central Intelligence Agency." You learn to look for history books under the name of the country first, but then you want an art book about art in the U.S. No, it's *not* "United States—Art and society." The correct heading is "Art and society— United States."

How to Find Your Heading

There are several fairly simple ways to solve the problem of confusing subject headings.

---

[1] I'm indebted to Sanford Berman, head cataloger of the Hennepin County Library, Edina, Minnesota, for these and other sterling examples throughout this section. He is a pioneer in begging for sanity in subject headings.

Find a Cross-reference.   The first solution is to look carefully at the index or catalog cards. Usually you are going to find a *cross-reference* appears on a separate line in most indexes and on a separate card in most card catalogs.

One type of cross-reference refers you from the word you used to the word the indexer or cataloger used. For example, you look up "Town planning," and the cross-reference reads: "see City planning." Or you try to find something under "Oriental rugs" and you find a cross-reference to the proper terminology: "see Rugs and carpets—Oriental."

The "see" cross-reference solves most of your problems about trying to outguess the cataloger or indexer.

There is another, even more useful type of cross-reference. It sends you to related areas and subjects. For example, if you look under "City planning," a legitimate subject heading, you will find several books or articles. Then comes a line or card "see also Community Development, Housing," and so on. When you turn to these subject headings you will find more material and possibly even another "see also" reference to other related topics.[2]

Find a Synonym.   If you still can't find your subject heading, and there is no librarian nearby, you can still puzzle out the missing subject heading for yourself.

Try to think of a *synonym*—a similar word. For example, you look up movies. There is *no* cross-reference that reads "see Motion pictures." Try to think of similar words for movies. It might be "Films" (no), "Cinema" (no), "Flicks" (no—slang terms are never used), or "Motion pictures" (yes!).

Be More Specific.   Remember the rule of indexing and cataloging: you will find a subject under the most specific subject heading. Be as specific as possible. For example, don't look for "Flowers" under "Botany." Look under "Flowers," the specific term. Don't look under "Insects" when you want "Flies." Don't look under "Automobiles" when you want "Automobile racing."

Remember to look for subheadings under the major heading. For example, there was nothing under "Automobile," but if you jump over a couple of pages in an index, or through a few cards in the catalog card drawer, you find the subheading "Automobile racing."

Play with the Order.   Try reversing the order of two or three words. For example, if you find nothing under "French authors," try the correct "Authors, French."

Catalogers and indexers put almost everything about United States history under that heading, with scores of subheadings and divisions. So always look

---

[2] Catalogers and indexers sometimes use shorthand abbreviations for "see" and "see also" references: *sa* or *xx* mean "see also," *x* means "see."

under "U.S.—History" as a start, *not* under American Revolutionary War or Civil War. However, it is *not* "U.S.—Natural history." It's "Natural History—U.S."[3]

Figure 7-1

In the insert is the entire entry for "Jazz" in *Sears List of Subject Headings,* 10th ed. The vast number of other possible subject headings is suggested in the more expansive listing in *Library of Congress Subject Headings,* 8th ed. The notations *sa* and *xx* mean "see also"; X means "see." Notice the detailed descriptive notes to help you find material under "Jazz ensembles" and "Jazz quintets." *Sears List of Subject Headings,* 10th Ed. Copyright © 1972 by the H.W. Wilson Company. Material reproduced by permission of the publisher.

Jazz music
 See also Blues (Songs, etc.)
 x Soul music; Swing music
 xx Dance music; Music
Jez *See Au~~~~ 7

Jazz dance
 xx Dancing
Jazz emsembles
 sa Suites (String quartet with jazz emsemble)
Jazz ensemble with chamber orchestra (*M1040-1041*)
 sa Concertos (Jazz ensemble with chamber orchestra)
 Monologues with music (Jazz ensemble with chamber orchestra)
 xx Chamber-orchestra music

 Concertos (Jazz ensemble with chamber orchestra)
 Jazz ensembles
 Scores (*M1040*)
Jazz ensemble with orchestra (*M1040-1041*)
 sa Concertos (Jazz ensemble)
 xx Concertos (Jazz ensemble)
 Jazz ensembles
Jazz ensembles (*M900-949, M960-985*)
 Here are entered single jazz compositions for ten or more solo instruments, also collections of jazz compositions for any number or combination of solo instruments
 sa Choruses, Sacred (Mixed voices) with jazz ensemble
 Clarinet with jazz ensemble
 Concertos (Clarinet with jazz ensemble)
 Concertos (Jazz ensemble)
 Concertos (Jazz ensemble with chamber orchestra)
 Concertos (Percussion with jazz ensemble)
 Dance-orchestra music
 Jazz ensemble with chamber orchestra
 Jazz ensemble with orchestra
 Monologues with music (Jazz ensemble)
 Percussion with jazz ensemble
 Piano with jazz ensemble
 Suites (Jazz ensemble)
 x Ensembles (Music)
 xx Dance-orchestra music
Jazz music (*Indirect*) (*ML3561*)
 sa Blues (Songs, etc.)
 Instrumentation and orchestration (Dance orchestra)
 Ragtime music
 Jazz quintets, Jazz septets, *and similar headings, and various headings for instrumental music followed by the qualifying adjective* (Jazz), e.g. Piano music (Jazz); *also subdivisions* Methods (Jazz) *and* Studies and exercises (Jazz) *under names of instruments or groups of instruments,* e.g. Saxophone Studies and exercises (Jazz); Wind instruments Methods (Jazz)
 x Be bop music
 Bebop music
 Soul music
 Swing music

 xx Dance music History and criticism
 Music
 Music History and criticism 20th century
 Interpretation (Phrasing, dynamics, etc.) (*MT75*)
 Juvenile literature (*ML3930*)
 Pictorial works
 Terminology (*ML108*)
Jazz musicians
 xx Musicians
 Biography
 Correspondence, reminiscences, etc.
  See Musicians Correspondence, reminiscences, etc.
 Juvenile literature
 Portraits
  See Musicians Portraits
Jazz nonets
 xx Instrumental music
Jazz octet with orchestra (*M1040-1041*)
 sa Concertos (Jazz octet)
 Jazz octets
 xx Concertos (Jazz octet)
 Jazz octets
 Orchestral music
Jazz octets
 sa Concertos (Jazz octet)
 Jazz octet with orchestra
 xx Concertos (Jazz octet)
 Jazz octet with orchestra
Jazz quartet with orchestra (*M1040-1041*)
 sa Concertos (Jazz quartet)
 xx Concertos (Jazz quartet)
 Jazz quartets
 Orchestral music
Jazz quartets
 sa Concertos (Jazz quartet)
 Jazz quartet with orchestra
 xx Instrumental music
 Quartets (Piano, percussion, vibraphone, double bass)
Jazz quintet with orchestra (*M1040-1041*)
 sa Concertos (Jazz quintet)
 xx Concertos (Jazz quintet)
 Jazz quintets
Jazz quintets
 sa Concertos (Jazz quintet)
 Jazz quintet with orchestra
 xx Instrumental music
 Jazz music
Jazz septets
 xx Instrumental music
 Jazz music
Jazz sextets
 xx Instrumental music
Jazz trio with orchestra (*M1040-1041*)
 sa Concertos (Jazz trio)
 xx Concertos (Jazz trio)
 Jazz trios
 Orchestral music
Jazz trios
 sa Concertos (Jazz trio)
 Jazz trio with orchestra
 Suites (Jazz trio)
 xx Instrumental music

Ask for Help.   There are logical rules for all of these variations in subject headings. Sometimes, though, they work more for the benefit of the indexer and the cataloger than of the user. Few people learn the finer rules. Fortunately, the liberal use of "see" and "see also" references makes most rules more academic than meaningful. The only real rule to remember: if you are lost in the rules, ask the librarian for help.

SUBJECT HEADING LISTS

There's still another solution to the subject heading dilemma. Try to use the lists the indexer or cataloger used to assign those original, elusive subject headings.

There are two lists you should find in book form near the reference desk or the card catalog. If not, ask the librarian. The correct order and wording used in the card catalog modifications comes from one of these two works:[3]

1. *Sears List of Subject Headings,* 11th ed. N.Y.: Wilson, 1977. Z695.S43   025.3   An alphabetical list of subject headings used in most small to medium-sized libraries. You will find two useful features: It refers you from the improperly worded or ordered heading you look under to the proper heading, and it includes numerous "see also" references to help you in running down a subject.

2. *Library of Congress Subject Headings,* 8th ed. Washington, D.C.: U.S. Government Printing Office, 1975. Z695.U47   025.3   A work from which most of *Sears* is drawn. It is used in large libraries. It is many times larger than *Sears* and includes thousands more subject headings, "see" references, and "see also" references (Figure 7-1).

FILING RULES

Even if you approach a catalog or an index knowing the right title, author, or subject, you should know something about how these words are filed.

Except in some specialized indexes or catalogs, the entries are in alphabetical order. The key work to look for is the first word in the index entry, at the top of the catalog card.

There are five simple exceptions to the first-word approach:

1. When a title or subject begins with an article such as "the" or "an," the article is ignored. Thus "The Dream of Dreams" is filed under "Dream," not "The."

---

[3] However, many libraries and even more publishers have their own subject heading authority lists that differ in part or even radically from *Sears* or *Library of Congress.* In that case the library or publisher should use numerous cross-references. When they have not, once more, ask the librarian for help.

2. Abbreviations are treated as if they were spelled out—"Mr." is filed as "Mister." Ditto for numbers—"One, Five," not "1, 5."

3. Whether a name is spelled MacElroy or McElroy, the catalog treats it as if there were an "a." A series of entries might read "MacColley, McEnery, Machinery, McNeil."

4. Libraries tend to file catalog cards on a word-by-word basis rather than a letter-by-letter basis. Letter by letter, "Newark" would come before "New York." Word by word, "New York" comes before "Newark," because each word is a separate unit.

5. When authors have exactly the same name, the oldest one comes first. John Smith born in 1675 is first in the catalog drawer. He is followed by John Smith of 1900 and John Smith of 1945.

Librarians and publishers have hundreds of other filing rules, but you need only remember the basic filing rules just listed. Beyond that, read the topmost word on the card first and keep thumbing through the cards in alphabetical order. When you are looking at an index, keep scanning the whole page or even several pages.

Books About a Writer

When you are interested in reading about authors, it's good to know one further filing rule. When you look up a book by Kurt Vonnegut, you find his *Cat's Cradle* and *Slaughterhouse-Five* in that order under his last name. Now if you want to read something *about* Vonnegut, you have to keep going until you've finished the file of books *by* him. Books written about an author always come after books the author wrote.

You may not find any books about the author. Don't quit. Probably your library has a divided card catalog.

Divided Catalogs and Indexes

For convenience and efficiency, some indexes and catalogs are divided. The author cards are in one section, the title cards in another section, and the subject cards in a third section.

There are variations. Some catalogs and indexes, for example, combine the author and title entries, but have a separate place for the subjects.

By thumbing through an index you can soon see what method is used. Be careful. Some indexes that combine authors and titles in one alphabetical list may seem to be only an author index. The reason is that they use only *some* titles and all the authors.

A card catalog can be another matter. It is harder to tell at a glance whether it is divided. People who are accustomed to the dictionary catalog (so called because the author, title, and subject cards are in a single catalog in alphabetical order) may not find an author or a subject—and quit.

Don't make that mistake. Many large libraries have divided catalogs. Make it your business to find out before you use the catalog. There are usually signs to indicate which catalog is which.

Failure? Never!

When you can't find what you want, don't count yourself a failure.

There is a good chance the card catalog, index, or other reference book failed you. The ports of entry were too clogged for you to navigate.

The answer: Ask for help from the librarian.

Chapter **8**

Biography

Almost all of us are interested in what other people are doing, especially if they are famous or infamous. Biography is among the most popular kinds of reading. At least two national magazines (*People* and *Us*) have built impressive circulations telling you about other people.

Almost every subject can be approached through the study of the life of a leader in that field. Many experienced researchers use biography as the starting point of their studies. When you must do research in political science, history, literature, or science, a good place to begin is with a leading person's life. You often can write a paper or deliver a talk about that person and thereby cover your subject in a fascinating and informative way.

You may have less ambitious need for biography. You probably only want to know someone's dates, famous actions, nationality, or present address. There are biographical reference works for all of these questions.

TWO TYPES OF BIOGRAPHICAL SOURCES

There are thousands of biographical reference works, but it is not hard to select the right kind for your purposes. They fall into two basic types—biographical dictionaries and essay-type sources.

Biographical dictionaries include only brief data about an individual, and they tend to concentrate on living persons. An example is *Who's Who in America.* You use these sources to find facts like a person's full name, occupation, and age.

This kind of reference work is of little value to you when you are writing a paper or delivering a talk. Certainly, it will help you with dates and current data about the individual, but the information is really too brief for expository purposes.

Essay-type sources may devote many pages to an individual. The essay gives you background and an overview of the person's achievements. Some sources are concerned with only living persons, some with only dead persons, and some, such as the *Encyclopaedia Britannica* or *Americana,* with both.

Works of either type often are limited in other ways. For example, some works only tell you about people of a given country, profession, or time period.

WHICH BIOGRAPHICAL SOURCE?

Let's take a look at the most basic, general, biographical reference works.

If you want specialized works, such as those that deal only with the lives of authors, scientists, artists, or teachers turn to Section Two.

Biographical Dictionaries About the Living

Who's Who in America. Chicago: Marquis Who's Who Inc., 1899 to date, every two years. E663.W56   920.03

Probably the most famous biographical source in a library, *Who's Who in America* lists approximately 75,000 people. You can use this work for basic data about a prominent person in the U.S.—birth date, education, employment, and often address. Or you can use it to check on an individual whom you want as a guest speaker or who is interviewing you for a job.

There are literally scores of "Who's Who's" for almost every country and profession, including *Who's Who of American Women* and *Who's Who in Finance and Industry.* Useful as they are to librarians, they are about the last place you should go for lengthy information.

If you can't find the person you are seeking in *Who's Who in America,* there are numerous alternative sources. The best alternative, one you may even wish to consult first, is described next.

Biographical Dictionaries Master Index. Detroit: Gale, 1976 to date, biennial. 3 vols. Z5305.WU5   920.073

This work, as the title suggests, is a "master index" to 53 biographical dictionaries such as *Who's Who in America, American Men and Women of Science,* and *Black American Authors.*

When you look up a person's name, there is a reference to the source where you will find short, biographical data about the person (Figure 8-1). There are over 800,000 names listed, so the odds are that you will find your person. Emphasis is on the United States.

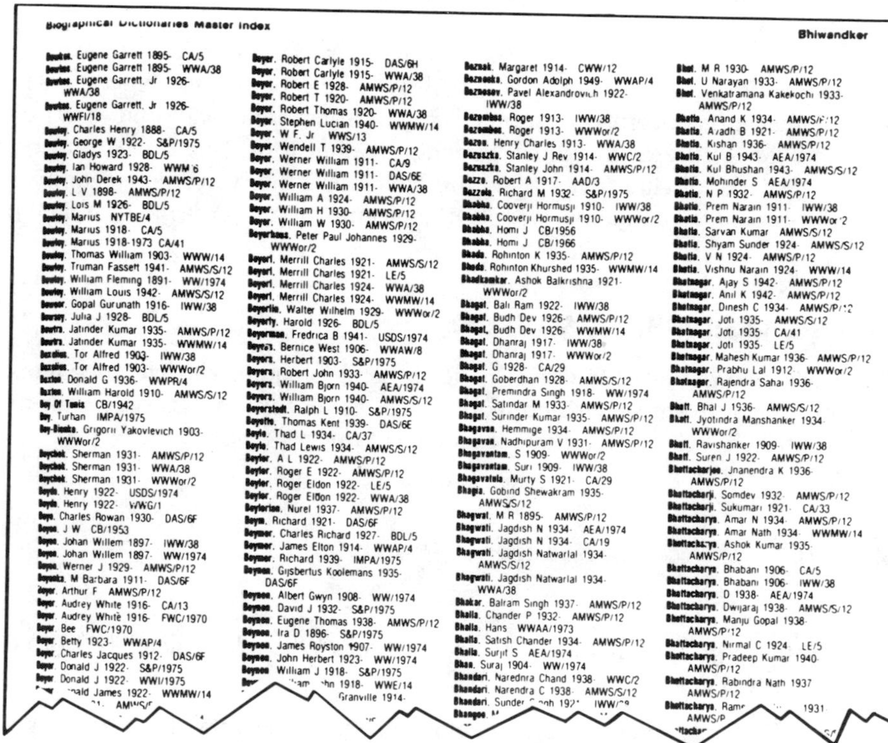
Biographical Dictionaries Master Index
Bhiwandker

Bowles. Eugene Garrett 1895- CA/5
Bowles. Eugene Garrett 1895- WWA/38
Bowles. Eugene Garrett, Jr 1926- WWA/38
Bowles. Eugene Garrett, Jr 1926- WWFI/18
Bowley. Charles Henry 1888- CA/5
Bowley. George W 1922- S&P/1975
Bowley. Gladys 1923- BDL/5
Bowley. Ian Howard 1928- WWM/6
Bowley. John Derek 1943- AMWS/P/12
Bowley. L V 1898- AMWS/P/12
Bowley. Lois M 1926- BDL/5
Bowley. Marius NYTBE/4
Bowley. Marius 1918- CA/5
Bowley. Marius 1918-1973 CA/41
Bowley. Thomas William 1903- WWW/14
Bowley. Truman Fassett 1941- AMWS/S/12
Bowley. William Fleming 1891- WW/1974
Bowley. William Louis 1942- AMWS/S/12
Bowser. Gopal Gurunath 1916- IWW/38
Bowsey. Julia J 1928- BDL/5
Bowtra. Jatinder Kumar 1935- AMWS/P/12
Bowtra. Jatinder Kumar 1935- WWMW/14
Boxelius. Tor Alfred 1903- IWW/38
Boxelius. Tor Alfred 1903- WWWor/2
Boxton. Donald G 1936- WWPR/4
Boxton. William Harold 1910- AMWS/S/12
Boy Of Tunis CB/1942
Boy. Turhan IMPA/1975
Boy-Bianko. Grigorii Yakovlevich 1903- WWWor/2
Boychok. Sherman 1931- AMWS/P/12
Boychok. Sherman 1931- WWA/38
Boychok. Sherman 1931- WWWor/2
Boyde. Henry 1922- USDS/1974
Boyde. Henry 1922- WWG/1
Boye. Charles Rowan 1930- DAS/6F
Boyen. J W CB/1953
Boyen. Johan Willem 1897- IWW/38
Boyen. Johan Willem 1897- WW/1974
Boyen. Werner J 1929- AMWS/P/12
Boyenka. M Barbara 1911- DAS/6F
Boyer. Arthur F AMWS/P/12
Boyer. Audrey White 1916- CA/13
Boyer. Audrey White 1916- FWC/1970
Boyer. Bee FWC/1970
Boyer. Betty 1923- WWAP/4
Boyer. Charles Jacques 1912- DAS/6F
Boyer. Donald J 1922- S&P/1975
Boyer. Donald J 1922- WWI/1975
Boyer. ...nald James 1922- WWMW/14
...1- AMWS/...

Boyer. Robert Carlyle 1915- DAS/6H
Boyer. Robert Carlyle 1915- WWA/38
Boyer. Robert E 1928- AMWS/P/12
Boyer. Robert T 1920- AMWS/P/12
Boyer. Robert Thomas 1920- WWA/38
Boyer. Stephen Lucian 1940- WWMW/14
Boyer. W F, Jr WWS/13
Boyer. Wendell T 1939- AMWS/P/12
Boyer. Werner William 1911- CA/9
Boyer. Werner William 1911- DAS/6E
Boyer. Werner William 1911- WWA/38
Boyer. William A 1924- AMWS/P/12
Boyer. William H 1930- AMWS/P/12
Boyer. William W 1930- AMWS/P/12
Boyerhaus. Peter Paul Johannes 1929- WWWor/2
Boyerl. Merrill Charles 1921- AMWS/S/12
Boyerl. Merrill Charles 1921- LE/5
Boyerl. Merrill Charles 1924- WWA/38
Boyerl. Merrill Charles 1924- WWMW/14
Boyerlin. Walter Wilhelm 1929- WWWor/2
Boyerty. Harold 1926- BDL/5
Boyerman. Fredrica B 1941- USDS/1974
Boyers. Bernice West 1906- WWAW/8
Boyers. Herbert 1903- S&P/1975
Boyers. Robert John 1933- AMWS/P/12
Boyers. William Bjorn 1940- AEA/1974
Boyers. William Bjorn 1940- AMWS/S/12
Boyerstedt. Ralph L 1910- S&P/1975
Boyette. Thomas Kent 1939- DAS/6E
Boyle. Thad L 1934- CA/37
Boyle. Thad Lewis 1934- AMWS/S/12
Boyler. A L 1922- AMWS/P/12
Boyler. Roger E 1922- AMWS/P/12
Boyler. Roger Eldon 1922- LE/5
Boyler. Roger Eldon 1922- WWA/38
Boylerian. Nurel 1937- AMWS/P/12
Boym. Richard 1921- DAS/6F
Boymer. Charles Richard 1927- BDL/5
Boymer. James Elton 1914- WWAP/4
Boymer. Richard 1939- IMPA/1975
Boymen. Gijsbertus Koolemans 1935- DAS/6F
Boynean. Albert Gwyn 1908- WW/1974
Boynean. David J 1932- S&P/1975
Boynean. Eugene Thomas 1938- AMWS/P/12
Boynean. Ira D 1896- S&P/1975
Boynean. James Royston 1907- WW/1974
Boynean. John Herbert 1923- WW/1974
Boynean William J 1918- S&P/1975
...iam ...hn 1918- WWE/14
...Granville 1914-

Boznak. Margaret 1914- CWW/12
Boznocka. Gordon Adolph 1949- WWAP/4
Boznosov. Pavel Alexandrovich 1922- IWW/38
Bozombos. Roger 1913- IWW/38
Bozombos. Roger 1913- WWWor/2
Bozon. Henry Charles 1913- WWA/38
Bozuszka. Stanley J Rev 1914- WWC/2
Bozuszka. Stanley John 1914- AMWS/P/12
Bozzo. Robert A 1917- AAD/3
Bozzola. Richard M 1932- S&P/1975
Bhabha. Cooverji Hormusji 1910- IWW/38
Bhabha. Cooverji Hormusji 1910- WWWor/2
Bhabha. Homi J CB/1956
Bhabha. Homi J CB/1966
Bhada. Rohinton K 1935- AMWS/P/12
Bhada. Rohinton Khurshed 1935- WWMW/14
Bhadkamkar. Ashok Balkrishna 1921- WWWor/2
Bhagat. Bali Ram 1922- IWW/38
Bhagat. Budh Dev 1926- AMWS/P/12
Bhagat. Budh Dev 1926- WWMW/14
Bhagat. Dhanraj 1917- IWW/38
Bhagat. Dhanraj 1917- WWWor/2
Bhagat. G 1928- CA/29
Bhagat. Goberdhan 1928- AMWS/S/12
Bhagat. Premindra Singh 1918- WW/1974
Bhagat. Satindar M 1933- AMWS/P/12
Bhagat. Surinder Kumar 1935- AMWS/P/12
Bhagavan. Hemmige 1934- AMWS/P/12
Bhagavan. Nadhipuram V 1931- AMWS/P/12
Bhagavantam. S 1909- WWWor/2
Bhagavantam. Suri 1909- IWW/38
Bhagavatula. Murty S 1921- CA/29
Bhagia. Gobind Shewakram 1935- AMWS/S/12
Bhagwat. M R 1895- AMWS/P/12
Bhagwati. Jagdish N 1934- AEA/1974
Bhagwati. Jagdish N 1934- CA/19
Bhagwati. Jagdish Natwarlal 1934- AMWS/S/12
Bhagwati. Jagdish Natwarlal 1934- WWA/38
Bhakar. Balram Singh 1937- AMWS/P/12
Bhalla. Chander P 1932- AMWS/P/12
Bhalla. Hans WWAA/1973
Bhalla. Satish Chander 1934- AMWS/P/12
Bhalla. Surjit S AEA/1974
Bhan. Suraj 1904- WW/1974
Bhandari. Narednra Chand 1938- WWC/2
Bhandari. Narendra C 1938- AMWS/S/12
Bhandari. Sunder ...ngh 192... IWW/...
Bhangoo. ...

Bhat. M R 1930- AMWS/P/12
Bhat. U Narayan 1933- AMWS/P/12
Bhat. Venkatramana Kakekochi 1933- AMWS/P/12
Bhatia. Anand K 1934- AMWS/P/12
Bhatia. Avadh B 1921- AMWS/P/12
Bhatia. Kishan 1936- AMWS/P/12
Bhatia. Kul B 1943- AEA/1974
Bhatia. Kul Bhushan 1943- AMWS/S/12
Bhatia. Mohinder S AEA/1974
Bhatia. N P 1932- AMWS/P/12
Bhatia. Prem Narain 1911- IWW/38
Bhatia. Prem Narain 1911- WWWor/2
Bhatia. Sarvan Kumar AMWS/S/12
Bhatia. Shyam Sunder 1924- AMWS/S/12
Bhatia. V N 1924- AMWS/P/12
Bhatia. Vishnu Narain 1924- WWW/14
Bhatnagar. Ajay S 1942- AMWS/P/12
Bhatnagar. Anil K 1942- AMWS/P/12
Bhatnagar. Dinesh C 1934- AMWS/P/12
Bhatnagar. Joti 1935- AMWS/S/12
Bhatnagar. Joti 1935- CA/41
Bhatnagar. Joti 1935- LE/5
Bhatnagar. Mahesh Kumar 1936- AMWS/P/12
Bhatnagar. Prabhu Lal 1912- WWWor/2
Bhatnagar. Rajendra Sahai 1936- AMWS/P/12
Bhatt. Bhal J 1936- AMWS/S/12
Bhatt. Jyotindra Manshanker 1934- WWWor/2
Bhatt. Ravishanker 1909- IWW/38
Bhatt. Suren J 1922- AMWS/P/12
Bhattacharjee. Jnanendra K 1936- AMWS/P/12
Bhattacharji. Somdev 1932- AMWS/P/12
Bhattacharji. Sukumari 1921- CA/33
Bhattacharya. Amar N 1934- AMWS/P/12
Bhattacharya. Amar Nath 1934- WWMW/14
Bhattacharya. Ashok Kumar 1935- AMWS/P/12
Bhattacharya. Bhabani 1906- CA/5
Bhattacharya. Bhabani 1906- IWW/38
Bhattacharya. D 1938- AEA/1974
Bhattacharya. Dwijaraj 1938- AMWS/S/12
Bhattacharya. Manju Gopal 1938- AMWS/P/12
Bhattacharya. Nirmal C 1924- LE/5
Bhattacharya. Pradeep Kumar 1940- AMWS/P/12
Bhattacharya. Rabindra Nath 1937- AMWS/P/12
Bhattacharya. Ram... 1931- AMWS/P...

Figure 8-1

Part of a typical page from *Biographical Dictionaries Master Index.* After each name comes the date of birth, an abbreviation for the source where you will find the biography, and the page in that source. From *Biographical Dictionary Master Index,* edited by Dennis La Beau. Copyright 1975 by Gale Research Company.

A drawback, at least in smaller libraries: you may find the name only to discover the library does not have the biographical dictionary indexed. In this case, ask the librarian for help. The librarian may be able to get the information from another library—even over the phone when there is a rush.

If you can't find anything about your person in these two sources, check similar biographical dictionaries on the shelf near *Who's Who in America.* Check also that the person you are looking up is alive, and that you have the proper spelling of the name.

Finally, is the person from the United States, or apt to be in the limelight there? If not, you may have to approach the search through international versions of *Who's Who,* such as *Who's Who in Australia.*

When all these checkpoints are covered, and you still can't find anything, the most likely source of help is your librarian. The librarian can refer you to even more specialized biographical dictionaries, particularly those in subject areas.

Essay-Type Sources About the Living

When you want essays, articles, and other lengthy sources of information about a living person, turn first to *Current Biography.*

Current Biography. N.Y.: Wilson, 1940 to date, monthly.
C100.C8   920.03

Current Biography features essays two pages or longer on people in the news. The information is accurate, objective, and easy to follow. Each year about 170 to 200 international personalities are featured. Individual monthly issues are arranged alphabetically by name, and there is an excellent annual index. Every few years there is a cumulative index to the whole set. This way you can look up people who have had some claim to fame since 1940.

Current Biography has several other useful features. Each of the reports includes a picture of the person. A listing of biographical references that follows the article can be used for additional searching. The annual index not only includes names, but features an index of professions and occupations so you can look up, for example, a scientist, a lawyer, or an artist.

When you don't find the name you are looking for in a single issue, or in an annual cumulation, be sure to check the cumulative indexes. It's possible the sketch appeared several years ago. When you don't find enough, or you find nothing about your individual, the next place to look is the *Encyclopaedia Britannica* (Micropaedia) or the *Americana.* Neither is strong on living Americans (unless they happen to be presidents) but they at least will indicate to you whether the person is truly still living and the person's nationality.

Let's say you still find nothing, or not enough. In that case you can try one of the next two sources in the order you prefer.

Biography Index. N.Y.: Wilson, 1947 to date, quarterly.
Z5301.B5   016.92

This work indexes material about people, both living and dead, that has appeared in some 2000 periodicals and books. You look up a name, and you will find references to articles, essays, or books about the person (Figure 8-2).

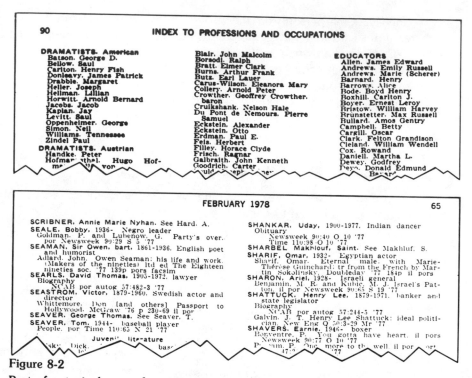

Figure 8-2

Part of a typical page from *Biography Index* and a page from the index to professions and occupations in the back. *Biography Index* Copyright © **1978** by the H.W. Wilson Company. Material reproduced by permission of the publisher.

This index is particularly useful for biography because it looks at so many different possible sources. Note, too, that when you have to look up a profession or occupation that an appended index lists people in this fashion.

The New York Times Biographical Service. New York: Arno Press, 1970 to date, monthly. CT120.N45   920.02

Here once again you will find people famous both in the U.S. and abroad, both living and dead. However, the sketches concentrate on living U.S. citizens.

Unlike *Biography Index,* this source is self-contained. It is like *Current Biography* in that each monthly issue features sketches of individuals—sketches that have appeared the previous month in *The New York Times.*

Each issue has its own index. Also, there is an annual index. Once again, be sure to check earlier issues when you find nothing or not enough.

If you want still more about a living person, you have four major resources left.

Check the card catalog, the *Readers' Guide to Periodical Literature,* (especially current issues), and specialized biographical sources and indexes (many of them are listed in the subject areas in the second part of this manual). And by all means check with your librarian for additional clues.

Essay-Type Sources About The Dead

When you are sure the person you are seeking information on is dead, the problem is much easier. Normally history has had time to evaluate the individual, and you are likely to find too much rather than too little.

When you are looking only for data such as birth and death dates, chief claim to fame, or nationality, turn to *The Encyclopaedia Britannica* (Micropaedia) or the *Americana* or any good encyclopedia. When you want fuller information, the following sources are best.

Webster's Biographical Dictionary, rev. ed. Springfield, Mass.: Merriam, 1974. CT103.W4   920.02

This work lists both the living and the dead, but most of the focus is on the famous dead. It is international in scope and covers all periods. There are about 40,000 names. Only brief data is given about each individual.

If you don't find what you want here, look on the shelf next to *Webster's*. There are scores of these types of biographical dictionaries, and the library will have at least two or three, perhaps even dozens.

For more detailed information, a good place to start is the *Britannica* (Macropaedia) or the *Americana*. Beyond them are numerous sources. The next one is the most famous and most often used.

Encyclopedia of World Biography. N.Y.: McGraw-Hill, 1973. 12 vols. CT103.M27   920.02

Here there are about 5000 sketches of people from all countries and times. Most of the entries are short, but for more important personages they may run several pages. There are good illustrations.

Written for younger people, the essays are easy to understand. They not only trace a person's life, but evaluate it.

Look at the index, which considers those 5000 people in terms of places, ideas, professions, and so on.

Most of the people highlighted here will be found in the *Britannica* or the *Americana,* sometimes in more, but often in less detail. Among the three encyclopedias, you normally will find enough.

Dictionary of American Biography. N.Y.: Scribner's, 1974. 11 vols. and Supplements. E176.D563   920.07

Dictionary of National Biography. London: Oxford, 1938. 21 vols. and Supplements. DA28.D48   920.03

Notable American Women 1607–1950. Cambridge, Mass.: Harvard University Press, 1971. 3 vols. CT3260.N57   920.72

These three sets are basic biographical sources for the U.S. (8), England (9), and women in the U.S. (10).

They share much in common. Each features long, scholarly essays, often with critical and evaluative comments about the role of the person in history. Each includes valuable bibliographies for further reading. Each includes only the famous dead.

Notable American Women came along because the other two sets ignored women—or included them only as the "wives of." Supplements for the U.S. and English sets now pay considerably more attention to famous women.

When you fail to find enough, or anything, try these steps:

a. Consult other sets in the vicinity. There are scores of one-volume and multivolume works that highlight the activities of the famous, now dead.

b. Turn to *Biography Index*, which includes references in books and magazines to both the living and the dead.

c. Try specialized biographies, many of which are listed in the subject areas in the second part of this manual.

d. Check the card catalog.

e. Ask your librarian for additional clues.

SHORTCUTS

More than likely you already know something about the person. Here are some shortcuts to getting more.

For the most part you will want an overview of the subject, which you can get easily in any standard encyclopedia—*if* the person is fairly famous and probably dead. If not, skip the encyclopedia articles and check the name in *Biography Index* or the *Readers' Guide to Periodical Literature*.

When you are looking for a single biography, it may be simplest to go straight to the biography section (if your library uses the Dewey system) and browse.

When you are looking for a person in a subject area like art or science, it is easiest to check the standard biographical sources in that area first. Many of them are described in the second section of this manual.

When you are looking for a biography in a subject area, and don't know the name of a leading plumber, Ohio artist, or New York librarian, check the subject approach in *Biography Index* and *Current Biography*.

There are numerous collections of short biographical sketches (many analyzed in *Biography Index*), but your library won't have them all. Try starting at the other end: look under some of these subject headings in the card catalog: "Biography," "United States—Biography," "Presidents—United States,"

"Scientists," "Poets," "Sports—Biography." A general rule is to look under the occupation, profession, or country.

Who is Jane Doe or John Smith? When you know absolutely nothing about a person's claim to attention, you should turn to the index in *Americana* or *Britannica* (Micropaedia), which will not only identify the person, but give you background and possibly a bibliography for additional places to look. Not there? See *Webster's Biographical Dictionary*.

When all else fails, try the card catalog. It's possible someone has written about your missing person, or that the person has written a book. Also try any of the author sources, such as *Contemporary Authors* (see p. 133), and any periodical index, but begin with the *Readers' Guide to Periodical Literature* and then move to the *Humanities Index, Social Science Index,* and *General Science Index.*

The person may use a *pseudonym* (an assumed name). If so, you may be looking under the wrong name. Check the name you have in a book of pseudonyms (see Chapter 11).

Still nothing? The time has come to talk to your librarian, who has many other ways of helping you find the name.

Chapter **9**

Short, Quick Answer Sources

Many questions require only a short, quick answer, which can be found in a single source. For example: What is the population of New York City? Who is the head of the CIA? How far is it from here to Washington, D.C.? What's the address of my Senator?

The librarian often will answer such ready reference questions. Trained in knowing just where to look, the librarian may save you hours of searching.

But at times you want to find the answer yourself. There are no rigid rules about where you find answers. Just make yourself familiar with some common types of ready reference books—almanacs, yearbooks, handbooks and manuals, directories, and geographical sources.

ALMANACS

Two of the best grab bag information sources are the encyclopedia and the almanac. If you are looking for some odd type of fact (the average age of people who live in the Northeast, or the wheat production for 1970s in Ohio), turn to the encyclopedia index. It is particularly important to use the index (or Micropaedia for the *Britannica*).

68

Equally useful, and even more so for a *current* fact, is the general almanac. Start with the best-known example, *The World Almanac.*

The World Almanac. N.Y.: Newspaper Enterprise Association, 1868 to date, annual. A467.N5W7   317.3

Now over a hundred years old, *The World Almanac* is as well known in the U.S. as an encyclopedia or a phone book.

Within the several hundred pages you find summaries and charts with useful data and statistics on everything from economics to sporting events. Thanks to an excellent index you can wind your way through the thousands of facts without any great difficulty. Even zip codes and advice on filling out your income tax form are included.

About 30 percent of the data is updated each year. It is generally accurate, as a good deal of the information comes from various government agencies. For example, the Department of Labor is the source of facts on employment, cost of living, and primary depressed areas.

When you don't find what you need in either the encyclopedias or in *The World Almanac,* try the other almanacs. They will be on the shelf near *The World.* In fact, many libraries have special sections for current almanacs and many of the other titles discussed in this chapter.

Among the other good almanacs are the *Information Please Almanac,* the *CBS News Almanac,* and the best-selling *The People's Almanac.* The last is more like a one-volume encyclopedia than a standard almanac, and it can be extremely useful for out-of-the-way facts.

YEARBOOKS

Still can't find the fact? You may be looking in the wrong type of reference book. You might be better off looking in a yearbook.

In Chapter 5 you learned about the yearbooks that encyclopedia publishers put out. These books update the basic sets, although they can be used independently. Encyclopedia yearbooks have their own indexes, and they generally concentrate on summarizing the past year's major events and personalities.

An encyclopedia yearbook is a good backup for the almanac. It also expands your information. For example, the almanac will tell you who won the World Series in 1968. The encyclopedia yearbook is likely to add description, commentary, and background information.

Besides the encyclopedia yearbooks, many yearbooks appear in specific fields. One of the basic, most used sources is *Statesman's Year-Book.*

Statesman's Year-Book. N.Y.: St. Martin's, 1964 to date, annual. JA51.S7   310.5

POLAND 1257

Gierek government is restructuring economic policy in the light of the recommendations of an expert commission as to methods (reported April 1972). The commission proposed strengthening the rôle of central planning (not in greater control of detail but in attention to strategy and the use of scientific techniques), reorganizing investment policy and increasing the autonomy of enterprises by the use of economic instruments, relating the income of each workforce to the profitability of the enterprise. The former three-tier hierarchy of industry (ministries–industrial associations–enterprises) is being modified to include specializing combines and large enterprises ('big economic organizations') containing 'inner units'. By 1975 these proposals had been extended to firms producing two-thirds of the country's output.

GNP grew by 10% during the 1971–75 plan. The current plan is running from 1976 to 1980. Under it, national income is scheduled to rise by 7% per annum, and industrial and agricultural production are expected to rise by 48–50%, and 16–19%, by 1980 respectively.

AGRICULTURE AND FORESTRY. In 1975 there were 19·2m. hectares of agricultural land, of which 15·2m. were in private hands, 0·3m. in co-operatives, 3·3m. in state farms. Private holdings average 5·3 hectares, and may not exceed 50 hectares. 14·8m. hectares were arable, 0·3m. orchards, 2·5m. meadows, 1·6m. pasture lands; 8·6m. hectares were forests (predominantly coniferous); 103,600 hectares were afforested in 1975, and 24·2m. cu. metres of timber gained.

Collectivization has been largely abandoned (there were only 1,120 co-operatives in 1975) but remains a long-term aim of the Government which makes use of economic incentives to foster the formation of new collective farms. Existing co-operatives are encouraged to specialize and merge with others. Farmers, on retiring, are encouraged to turn over their private plots to the State in exchange for a pension. During 1971–75, 120,000 farms were taken over in this way. A new approach is being tried with 'agricultural circles' (35,600 with 2·8m. members in 1975). In 1975 there were 3,660 state farms.

	Area (1,000 hectares)			Yield (1,000 metric tons)		
Crops	1973	1974	1975	1973	1974	1975
Wheat	1,962	2,022	1,842	5,607	6,414	5,211
Rye	3,416	3,138	2,792	8,263	7,677	6,271
Barley	1,083	1,230	1,335	3,160	3,914	3,652
Oats	1,272	1,182	1,291	3,211	3,242	2,932
Potatoes	2,678	2,684	2,581	51,917	48,635	46,456
Sugar-beet	445	440	496	13,664	12,971	15,339

Livestock (1975): 13m. cattle (6m. cows), 21·3m. pigs, 3m. sheep, 2·2m. horses, 99·8m. poultry. Milk production in 1975 was 15,900m. litres. Tractors in use in 1975: 520,700 (in 15-h.p. units).

FISHERIES. In 1975 the fishing fleet had 130 deep-sea vessels totalling 196,100 GRT. The catch was 648,000 metric tons.

In 1966 Poland joined the Fisheries Convention of 1964, extending the fishing limits from 3 to 12 miles.

INDUSTRY. Production in 1975 (and 1974) (in 1,000 metric tons): Coke, 18,300 (18,100); pig-iron, 8,206 (8,213); crude steel, 15,007 (14,566); rolled steel, 11,085 (10,558); cement, 15,500 (18,500); sulphuric acid (100%), 3,410 (3,319); nitrogenous fertilizers, 1,533 (1,457); phosphoric fertilizers, 829 (824); aluminium, 103 (102); electrolytic copper, 249 (195); lead, 76·2 (71·6); zinc, 243 (233); crude oil, 553 (550); salt, 3,513 (3,295); sugar, 1,699 (1,467); electricity, 97,200m. kwh. (91,600m.); natural gas, 5,963m. cu. metres (5,729m.). In 1975, 83 ships over 100 DWT were built (1,023,000 DWT), 164,000 cars and 64,900 lorries.

Output of light industry in 1975 (and 1974): Cotton fabrics, 928m. metres (885); woollen fabrics, 125m. metres (117); silk and synthetic fibres, 180m. metres (187); shoes, 162m. pairs (157); household glass, 44,800 metric tons (45,900); paper, 981,000 metric tons (969,000).

MINING. Poland is a major producer of coal (reserves of some 71,000m. metric tons) and sulphur. Copper reserves are estimated at 10m. metric tons. There is

Figure 9-1

A typical page from *The Statesman's Year-Book.* From *The Statesman's Year-Book,* edited by John Paxton, © St. Martin's Press, Inc., Macmillan & Co., Ltd. and by permission of Macmillan, London and Basingstoke.

Despite the awesome title, this work is no more than an annual overview of the economic, political, and cultural status of some 166 nations. There's a section on international organizations and a large section on the United States.

Coverage is arranged by continent. Then countries are listed alphabetically. Information given for each country includes population, type of government, religion, education, and agriculture (Figure 9-1).

Now this same type of information is found in most encyclopedias, so why use the *Statesman's Year-Book*? Because it is published yearly, the data on magnesium production is more up-to-date than the data in an encyclopedia a few years old. Also, the yearbook is compact. You only have one volume, not 12 or 24 to go through.

Like almanacs, numerous yearbooks cover specific countries. They will be near the *Statesman's Year-Book*.

Not all yearbooks have that word in their title. For example, here is another basic yearbook:

U.S. Bureau of the Census. Statistical Abstract of the United States.

Washington, D.C.: U.S. Government Printing Office, 1879 to date, annual.
HA202   317.3

This publication is written, financed, and published by the government. You can use it to update the almanac, the encyclopedia yearbooks, and the *Statesman's Year-Book* when you need statistical information on almost any aspect of life in the United States—from the number of people employed in the previous year to the amount of aspirin consumed.

You get an overview of 35 major aspects of life, such as education and agriculture. Usually you find relatively easy statistical data in tabular form (Figure 9-2).

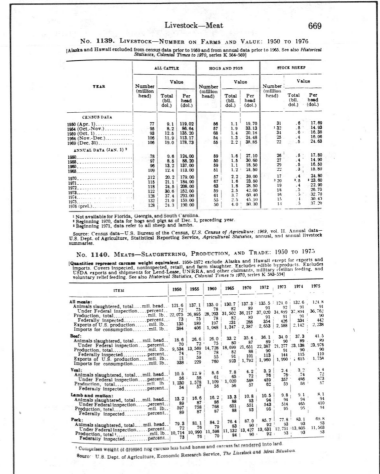

Figure 9-2

A typical page from *Statistical Abstract of the United States.*

Publishers of other almanacs draw upon the *Statistical Abstract*. You will find, for example, that the *World Almanac* and the encyclopedias often use the *Statistical Abstract* as a source of data.

HANDBOOKS AND MANUALS

Almanacs and yearbooks tend to be fairly general. When you want specific information, you should turn to a handbook or a manual.

The difference between the two forms is slight. A manual tends to tell you how to do something, whereas a handbook is normally a mass of facts built around a single subject.

When you have a task—from looking up a formula for a chemical reaction to repairing a shower—there is probably a handbook or a manual on the subject.

This category can be stretched to include many sources that are not quite yearbooks or almanacs. Here is the best example:

Guinness Book of World Records. N.Y.: Sterling, 1955 to date, annual.
AG243.G87   032

This work comes out annually, so it is a yearbook. It includes miscellaneous data on everything from the tallest man to the shortest poem, so it is an almanac. However, it probably comes closest to being a handbook because there is a central theme: world records—and fun.

Fun should be stressed. Not many reference works qualify for this descriptor, but this most famous of all reference books is purchased not so much to settle arguments as to be enjoyed.

There are now over 30 million copies in print. The volume of sales is a record in itself.

Of more direct use are the standard handbooks and manuals, many of which you know: *Emily Post's Etiquette,* a manual of some importance for many people; *Famous First Facts,* a version of Guinness that sticks to firsts in the U.S.; and *Robert's Rules of Order,* which tells you how to conduct a meeting.

There are hundreds more. Among them you may find two government titles useful.

U.S. Department of Labor. Occupational Outlook Handbook. Washington, D.C.: U.S. Government Printing Office, 1949 to date, biennial.
HF5381.U62   331.7

Here you will find close to 700 objective descriptions of as many types of work. Each is an illustrated essay that clearly indicates the future market for employment, the rates of pay, chances for advancement, where the jobs are located, and more.

Updated every two years, it is relatively useful. The basic job descriptions are accurate, but the information on opportunities for employment is much less reliable.

U.S. National Archives. United States Government Manual. Washington, D.C.: U.S. Government Printing Office, 1935 to date, annual. JK421.UN34   353

This source is where you turn when you want a profile of a government organization such as the Supreme Court or National Archives (Figure 9-3). For each, a brief history and description is given. The manual also contains names and addresses (and often phone numbers) of the leading people in each of the government organizations. It is a good source for up-to-date material to augment what you find, for example, in an encyclopedia.

DIRECTORIES

Most directories, no matter how detailed or technical, do much the same thing as your telephone directory. By definition, a directory is a list of persons or organizations, systematically arranged, usually in alphabetical order.

You turn to a directory when you want up-to-date phone numbers, addresses, names of people who are in charge of this or that, names of companies who manufacture a product, names of doctors in your community, and so on.

There are scores of directories, but let's consider only one:

(Your City) Directory. Detroit: Polk.

There are over 800 city directories, so you can substitute any city or community you wish as "Your City." Most are published by Polk, as they have been since about 1870.

They are updated every year or so, and are a type of phone book. Here, you can look up a person, company, or organization by name *and* by street, phone number, or business.

When you look up the name of a street, the directory lists everyone living on that street. Also, you will find what these people do for a living, whether they own their homes, and how many members are in the family.

Normally you must have a name to get a phone number. In many city directories there is a reverse system whereby if you have the phone number, you can find who has the phone. This feature is useful when you want to know what unnamed company is behind a blind advertisement.

Less useful is the listing, as in the yellow pages of your phone book, of the community's primary business and government organizations.

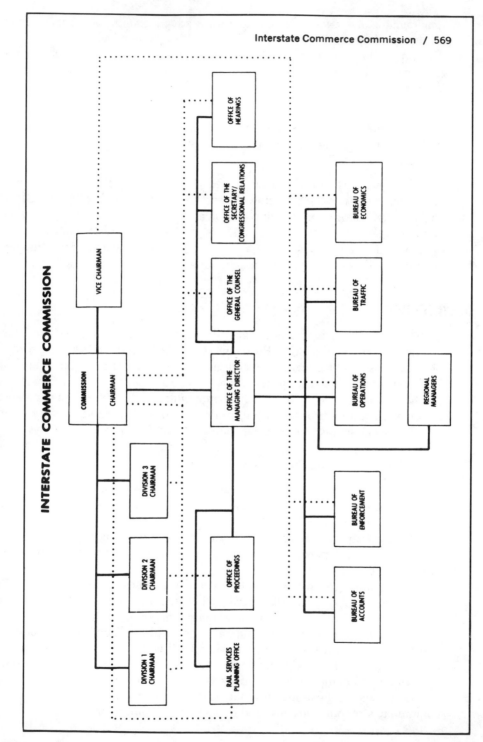

Figure 9-3   A typical page from *United States Government Manual.*

To give you an idea of how many other directories there are, consider the *Guide to American Directories.* Frequently revised, the 1975 edition includes names of 5200 directories for industries, professions, and businesses.

In a large library you can almost be sure to find a directory for your needs. If you can't find one easily, ask the librarian.

GEOGRAPHICAL AIDS

The best-known geographical sources are the familiar atlas and the road maps you find in service stations.

Atlases

All libraries have a section of atlases. Some include maps for the whole of the world, some for only a special part of the world. Some concentrate on industry or history.

The usual atlas is easy enough to master. Turn to the index and look up the place you are seeking. You are given the page number of the map and the grid square where that feature—city, river, mountain—is located.

There are scores of atlases, and the average library has the better ones. But before you use even the best title, check the date. Several dates are usually on the back of the title page; look for the last date. It is not always representative of when the atlas was revised, but at least it gives you a point of reference.

Dates are important. Borderlines change, names of towns and cities change, and so do railroads, airline patterns, and climate.

The next two books are the best general atlases.

The Times Atlas of the World: Comprehensive 5th Edition. London: Times Newspapers Limited, 1975. G1019.B395   912

Frequently revised, this atlas has large-scale, multiple maps, which many consider works of art for their fine colors and ease of use. There is an exhaustive 200,000-name index.

National Geographic Atlas of the World, 4th ed. Washington, D.C.: National Geographic Society, 1975. G1019.N28   912

Also frequently revised, this atlas emphasizes the United States and North America, with numerous insets for major cities. The maps are good to excellent and easy to read. There is an impressive 140,000-name index.

Any of the standard Rand McNally or Hammond atlases you are likely to find in a library are good. These companies are among the world's largest map and atlas publishers. Both have solid reputations for fine work, and usually their name is part of the name of the atlas.

Gazeteers

Sometimes you want not an atlas, but only the location of a city, a river, or some other place. Then you should turn either to an encyclopedia or to a gazeteer.

A gazeteer essentially is the exhaustive index to an atlas, without the maps. It is a dictionary of geographical locations, which will give other information too. A good gazeteer is:

Webster's New Geographical Dictionary, rev. ed. Springfield, Mass.: Merriam, 1972. G103.W45   910

Here you will find about 50,000 alphabetically arranged names. Location is given as well as vital data on population or characteristics that set off the place from others of its type. Most of the entries are brief—a line or even less. However, when you look up large cities you may find more data, including information on primary industries (Figure 9-4).

Figure 9-4

A typical page from a gazeteer, *Webster's New Geographical Dictionary.* By permission, from Webster's New Geographical Dictionary © 1977 by G.&C. Merriam Co., Publishers of the Merriam-Webster Dictionaries.

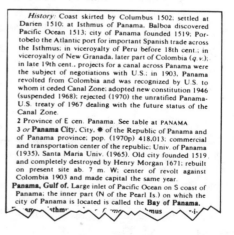

Webster's is not only more convenient than the average atlas, but it also provides pronunciation—a feature not always found in the atlas index.

Next to *Webster's* you may find an old standard in many libraries. This work is the *Columbia-Lipincott Gazeteer of the World,* which hasn't been thoroughly revised since 1952. Therefore it is dangerous to use when checking on countries, but safe enough for out-of-the-way place names. It has 130,000 entries.

None of these gazeteers comes up to the 200,000 listings in *The Times Atlas.* When you get stuck, turn to *The Times* index for help.

WHICH QUICK ANSWER SOURCE?

You now know a few of the best quick answer sources. Suppose, though, you must choose from unfamiliar titles covering the same general material. Which title should you pick?

Here are four guidelines.

You should look for the *most recent* title. You will use most of these reference works to update an encyclopedia. Therefore, to see you have the latest edition available, always look on the back of the title page for the latest date.

Second, choose the one with the *best index.* The index is particularly important when you are trying to dig out facts from a handbook, manual, or almanac. (Directories are in well defined order and do not often require an index.)

Third, pick the one which is *easiest to understand.* You may not always have this choice, but when you do it's a good idea to pick up the reference work that is going to give you the least amount of difficulty.

Most important: try to pick the title that *answers your question* most precisely. It takes a bit of experience, although even a beginner realizes an almanac is a better source of information on Pulitzer Prize winners than a city directory. The more you practice finding the information for yourself, the better you will get at choosing the right source.

Chapter **10**

Dictionaries

You turn to a dictionary for many reasons, not only to check spelling, definition, or pronunciation. There are dictionaries for foreign languages, for professions, for subjects, for slang, for just about everything and everyone. You will find many of them in your library.

DESK OR COLLEGE DICTIONARIES

At home you probably have at least one short, hard-cover dictionary of the desk or college type. A good example:

The American Heritage Dictionary of the English Language, New College Edition. Boston: Houghton Mifflin, 1976. PE1625.A54   423

First published in 1969, this dictionary has some 155,000 entries. (The average desk dictionary has between 130,000 and 180,000 entries). The coverage of modern words is good to excellent. More important, the definitions are clear, concise, and almost always complete. You don't have to refer to other words in the dictionary to understand the definition.

The format is good, and it is one of the few dictionaries that has up-to-date illustrations. Equally good are the symbols that make it clear how to pronounce a word.

Some take exception to this dictionary's rather peculiar way of evaluating whether or not a word is good English. A panel discusses the matter and votes. At least by this method you can tell whether a majority believes the word is proper English for conversation or for writing. Not all dictionaries can be relied upon to give you correct usage information.

When it comes to selection of a desk dictionary from among scores that are as good or almost as good, it is more a matter of personal taste than objective measurement. For example, *The New York Times* has adopted as its official desk dictionary *Webster's New World Dictionary of the American Language* (N.Y.: Collins-World, 2nd ed., 1972). On the other hand, that old standby, *Webster's New Collegiate Dictionary,* is by far the best-selling of all the college dictionaries. Any of these desk dictionaries sells for around $10.

A fine guide to quality in all types of dictionaries is Kenneth Kister's *Dictionary Buying Guide* (N.Y.: Bowker, 1977). You can rely upon the author's analysis and advice.

UNABRIDGED DICTIONARIES

For an unabridged dictionary—one with over 250,000 entries—the natural and the single best choice is *Webster's.*

Webster's Third New International Dictionary of the English Language. Springfield, Mass.: Merriam, 1961. PE1625.W36   423

This dictionary has the most words—some 450,000. Issued in 1961, it is frequently revised, and new words and new definitions are added. It is the official dictionary for most courts of law and government organizations. In a word (no pun intended), it is the place to look for the authoritative definition.

The unabridged has many advantages besides the number of words. For example, it contains numerous quotations to show you how the words have been and should be used.

On the other hand, it is of little value for pronunciation. The symbols are too complicated. And it does not tell you whether a word is acceptable for usage in writing or speech. If anything, it tends to equate everyday use with good use.

Note one important feature about this and other Merriam Webster: the oldest definition comes first.

There is a limited number of unabridged dictionaries. The only one to come close to *Webster's* in number of words is the now outdated *Funk & Wagnalls New Standard Dictionary,* which has 458,000 entries. However, of this number, about 70,000 are proper names.

The *Funk & Wagnalls* has not been revised thoroughly since 1913. Minor revisions are made, but the dictionary is quite outdated.

Some people claim that the *Random House Dictionary of the English Language* (N.Y.: Random House, 1966) is an unabridged work. Well, yes and no. It does boast 260,000 entries, or about 100,000 more than most desk dictionaries. Still, it has almost 200,000 fewer than *Webster's Third International*. Suffice to say it is a good to excellent dictionary that you can use with confidence.

HISTORICAL DICTIONARIES

One unabridged dictionary is unlike all the rest.

The Oxford English Dictionary. Oxford: Clarendon, 1933. 13 vols. Supplements, 1972, 1977. PE1625.N53   423

Certainly the most famous English language dictionary, this work is not the place to go to find a current definition. It is the place to trace the history of a word. The whole purpose of the massive set, including the two relatively recent supplements, is to show you how the English language developed.

Arrangement is alphabetical, and definitions are given in historical order. Then dated quotations show how the word developed over the years. Variations on a word may take not just a column or two, but many pages, and the quotations can run into the hundreds.

There are over 500,000 words and at least two million supporting quotations. When you want to discover how the term "red tape" was first used, or the variations on the word "set" (which march over 20 full pages), this is your dictionary.

The *OED* (as it is called) is not just a dictionary. It is an institution, a cultural heritage that is as well known and as loved as any work in the English language.

DICTIONARIES OF SYNONYMS

Another type of dictionary should be in your personal collection, along with the desk dictionary—a book of synonyms.

Webster's New Dictionary of Synonyms. Springfield, Mass.: Merriam, 1973. PE1591.W4   423.1

When you are writing a paper or letter, giving a speech, or working a crossword puzzle, you often need a new word, a substitute or a synonym. A good place to look is this work, which lists synonyms in alphabetical order. The

7500 main entries not only explain the difference between synonyms but give you extensive quotations to illustrate the difference.

For example, you will find under "vigorous" synonyms such as "energetic," "strenuous," "lusty," and "nervous." Each one of these words has a definite, slightly different meaning, shown in a column of quotations. The importance of differentiating here is enormous. It is one thing to say "I am vigorous," quite another to say "I am lusty," or "I am nervous"!

You may have heard about *Roget's Thesaurus*. First issued in 1852, it has been continually republished since then by various publishers, under various names, although usually with "Roget" in the title. A *thesaurus* differs from a standard dictionary of synonyms in giving words in groups rather than word by word. Grouping words according to ideas is useful, but only for advanced writers. Most people find the average dictionary of synonyms easier to follow. A modification of Roget, with words listed in alphabetical order and cross-references to other words and ideas, is *Webster's Student's Thesaurus* (Springfield, Mass.: Merriam, 1978).

In closing, you may wish to know that there are dictionaries for crossword puzzle fans. Some of them are in libraries, but if you are a true fanatic you will either avoid all such dictionaries as unfair help or have a wide selection of them in your home. One of the best is *The New York Times Crossword Puzzle Dictionary*.

section two
A Key to Library Sources

HOW TO USE THIS SECTION

The purpose of this section is to lead you directly to useful reference sources. Don't try to read through it. When you have a reference problem, go right to the part you need.

Into what general subject area does your question fall—humanities, science, or social sciences? Each has a separate chapter, divided into more specific subjects, such as literature, medicine, or psychology. Find the area you want by means of the index or the table of contents.

Introducing your subject area are three or four quick guides. They might be all you need. First, the most *basic sources* are described. You can just glance at their names and numbers, and go straight to the reference shelves. Second, the *classification numbers* for the general subject are given. You can use them to go straight to the regular shelves. Third comes a summary of typical *subject headings*. As you learned in Chapter 7, information is not always filed under the words you would expect. You can use these headings to go straight to the card catalog. Finally, in some chapters you will find an *outline by form* of the titles to be discussed in the rest of the chapter.

After these quick guides comes the heart of each area: a chart of questions and sources of answers. Turn to the chart for your subject. Find a subsection where your question might fit. For example, in the chart on art, you might need the subsection on biographies of artists.

Now find a sample question similar to yours. Opposite the question will be the names of reference sources, in approximate order of importance, that meet your needs.

After each chart you will find brief descriptions of almost all those sources,[1] and their classification numbers. These titles are in alphabetical order. Under some of them are descriptions and numbers of related titles, substitutes that might help you just as much.

So once you find a recommended source on the shelf, don't be in a hurry. Look around for similar titles near it. They may meet your particular needs even better.

This section, especially its charts, should enable you to approach any question, even the trickiest-seeming research, with more confidence. The more you practice using it, the more experienced you will get at looking things up.

Remember, though, that there are many other approaches and sources to which the librarian can steer you. So at the risk of repetition, each chart ends with the advice, "See the librarian." Even when you have grown quite self-reliant in the library, if you use this book along with the librarian's friendly help, you will do best of all.

---

[1] A few of the sources were described in Section One or elsewhere in Section Two. The Title Index will tell you their classification numbers and the pages on which they are described.

Chapter **11**

The Humanities

Art and Music

This section will help you find information in the fine arts: architecture, painting, sculpture, drawing, photography, and music. It does not include applied arts such as antiques, ceramics, and costumes. The emphasis here is on visual arts and music in the United States.

BASIC GUIDES

For information in these fields these seven works are the most basic guides:

1. *Guide to Reference Books* (see p. 29) in the fine arts section, pp. 375–392 and the music section, pp. 413–428. (Applied arts are discussed on pp. 393–401.) Z1035.1S43   011

2. *Guide to Art Reference Books* (Chamberlin, Mary). Chicago: American Library, 1959. Tells you where to find basic titles in the fine arts. "Chamberlin," as it is known, includes annotations for about 2500 titles, and you will find

almost anything you need here. It is now dated, but at this writing (1978) is in the process of revision. Z5931.C45   016.7

3. *Fine Arts: A Bibliographic Guide* (Donald Ehresmann). Littleton, Colo.: Libraries Unlimited, 1975. While hardly up to the standards of Chamberlin, this book still is useful title until a new Chamberlin is issued. Z5931.E47   016.7

4. *Music Reference and Research Materials* (Vincent Duckles), 3rd ed. N.Y.: Free Press, 1974. Lists close to 2000 items with detailed indexes. Basic to the field. ML113.D83   016.78

5. *Information on Music* (Guy Marco). Littleton, Colo.: Libraries Unlimited, 1975. The first of a multiple-volume guide. ML113.M33   016.78

6. *The Humanities: A Selective Guide to Information Sources* (Robert Rogers). Littleton, Colo.: Libraries Unlimited, 1974. A discursive approach with annotated listings of basic titles. Sections on visual and performing arts. Z5579.R63   016.0013

7. *Photographic Literature* (Albert Boni). Dobbs Ferry, N.Y.: Morgan and Morgan, 1962. Supplement, 1972. Lists close to 15,000 books, pamphlets, and periodical articles on most aspects of photography. Dated, but still the basic guide to the field. Z7134.B6   016.77

CLASSIFICATION NUMBERS

Dewey Decimal System

If your library uses the Dewey Decimal classification system, you will find arts in the 700s. The basic divisions are:

720 Architecture
730 Sculpture
740 Drawing
750 Painting
760 Graphic arts
770 Photography
780 Music

Library of Congress System

If your library uses the Library of Congress classification system, you will find most arts in the N section. N alone covers the visual arts in general; NA is architecture, and ND is painting. TR is photography. M is the music section.

Note: No matter which of the classification systems is used, be sure to *check the oversize sections.* Many art books, larger in size than normal books, are shelved separately. This is indicated, too, on the catalog card.

SUBJECT HEADINGS

Generally titles in this field are filed under the main subject and subdivided by country: "Art—French," "Art—Chinese," "Music—Spanish," and so on. Look also for subdivisions by time: "Architecture—Modern," "Sculpture—20th century," and so on. For biography look under the name of the artist, photographer, composer, or musician.

OUTLINE OF SOURCES BY FORM

1. Biographical sources
   Ewen, *Great Composers*
   International Who's Who in Music
   Allgemeines Lexikon der Bildenden kunstler (Thieme)
   Who's Who in American Art
2. Directories
   American Art Directory
3. Encyclopedias, yearbooks, handbooks, and dictionaries
   The Book of World Famous Music
   Encyclopedia of World Art
   Dictionary of Music and Musicians (Grove)
   Harvard Dictionary of Music
   A History of Architecture
   McGraw-Hill Dictionary of Art
   Oxford Companion to Art
4. Indexes and abstracts
   Art Index
   Cumulated Index of Record Reviews
   Index of Reproductions of American Paintings
   Music Index
   Photo-Lab Index

CHART 1: QUESTIONS AND SOURCES OF ANSWERS IN ART AND MUSIC

Art — General Information

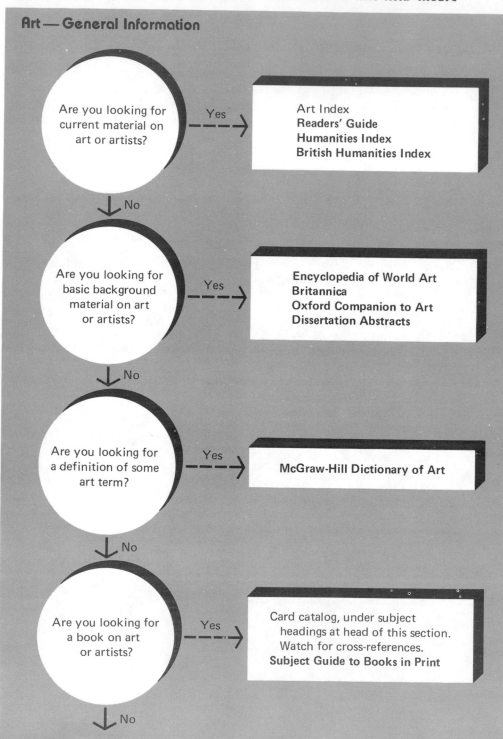

Are you looking for current material on art or artists?

Yes →
- Art Index
- Readers' Guide
- Humanities Index
- British Humanities Index

↓ No

Are you looking for basic background material on art or artists?

Yes →
- **Encyclopedia of World Art**
- **Britannica**
- **Oxford Companion to Art**
- **Dissertation Abstracts**

↓ No

Are you looking for a definition of some art term?

Yes →
- **McGraw-Hill Dictionary of Art**

↓ No

Are you looking for a book on art or artists?

Yes →
Card catalog, under subject headings at head of this section. Watch for cross-references.
Subject Guide to Books in Print

↓ No

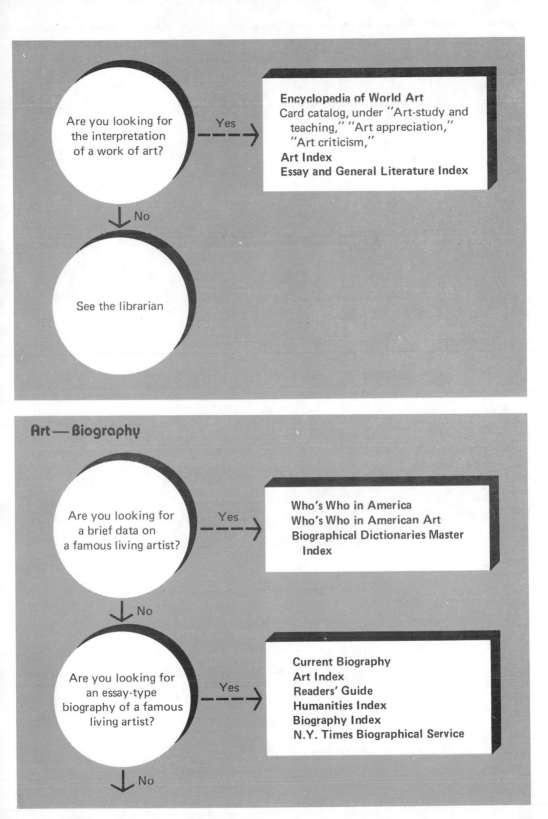

Are you looking for
the interpretation
of a work of art?

Yes

Encyclopedia of World Art
Card catalog, under "Art-study and
teaching," "Art appreciation,"
"Art criticism,"
Art Index
Essay and General Literature Index

No

See the librarian

Art — Biography

Are you looking for
a brief data on
a famous living artist?

Yes

Who's Who in America
Who's Who in American Art
**Biographical Dictionaries Master
Index**

No

Are you looking for
an essay-type
biography of a famous
living artist?

Yes

Current Biography
Art Index
Readers' Guide
Humanities Index
Biography Index
N.Y. Times Biographical Service

No

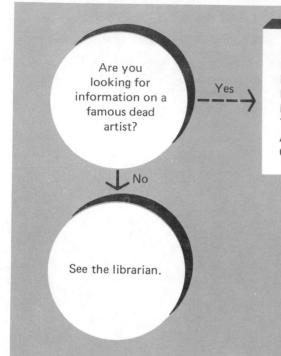

Are you looking for information on a famous dead artist?

Yes → Dictionary of American Biography
Britannica
Dictionary of National Biography
Encyclopedia of World Art
Biography Index
Thieme, **Allgemeines Lexikon**
Art Index
Card catalog, under name of artist

No ↓

See the librarian.

Art — Miscellaneous

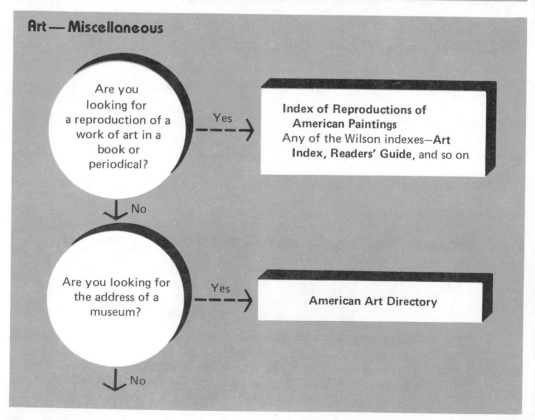

Are you looking for a reproduction of a work of art in a book or periodical?

Yes → **Index of Reproductions of American Paintings**
Any of the Wilson indexes—**Art Index, Readers' Guide**, and so on

No ↓

Are you looking for the address of a museum?

Yes → **American Art Directory**

No ↓

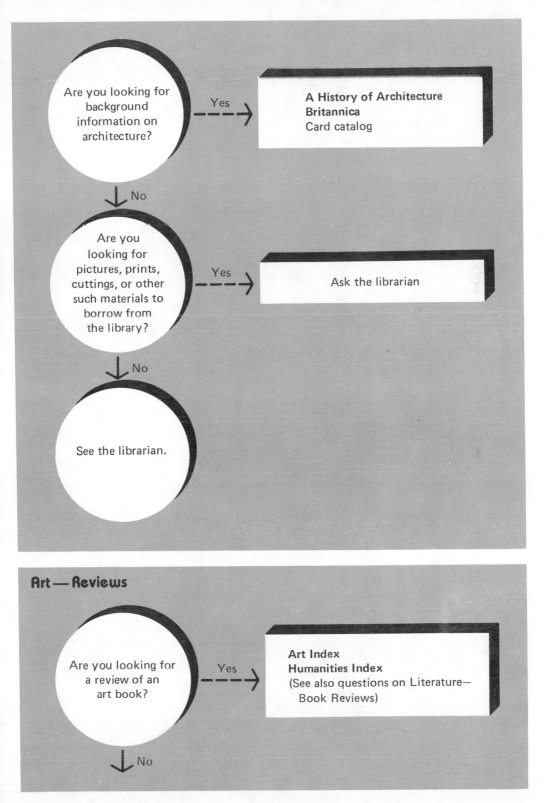

Are you looking for background information on architecture?

Yes → A History of Architecture
Britannica
Card catalog

No ↓

Are you looking for pictures, prints, cuttings, or other such materials to borrow from the library?

Yes → Ask the librarian

No ↓

See the librarian.

Art — Reviews

Are you looking for a review of an art book?

Yes → **Art Index**
Humanities Index
(See also questions on Literature—
Book Reviews)

No ↓

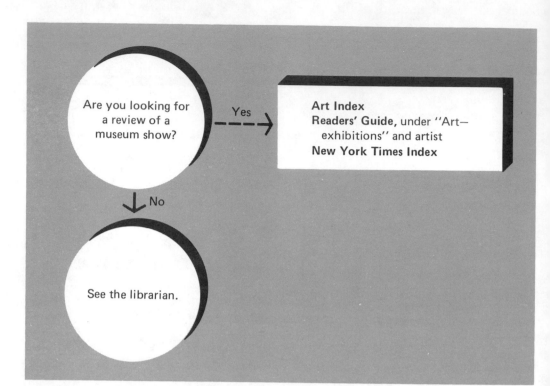

Are you looking for a review of a museum show?

Yes → Art Index
Readers' Guide, under "Art—exhibitions" and artist
New York Times Index

No ↓

See the librarian.

Music—General Information

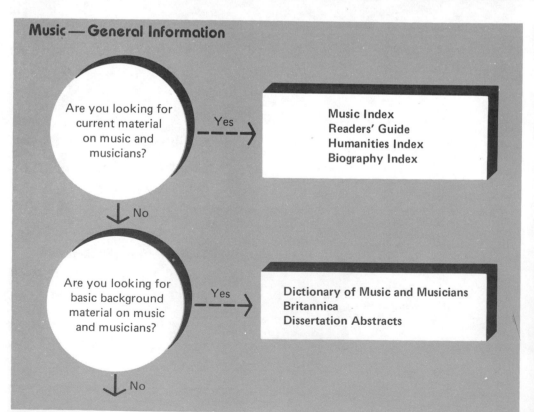

Are you looking for current material on music and musicians?

Yes → Music Index
Readers' Guide
Humanities Index
Biography Index

No ↓

Are you looking for basic background material on music and musicians?

Yes → Dictionary of Music and Musicians
Britannica
Dissertation Abstracts

No ↓

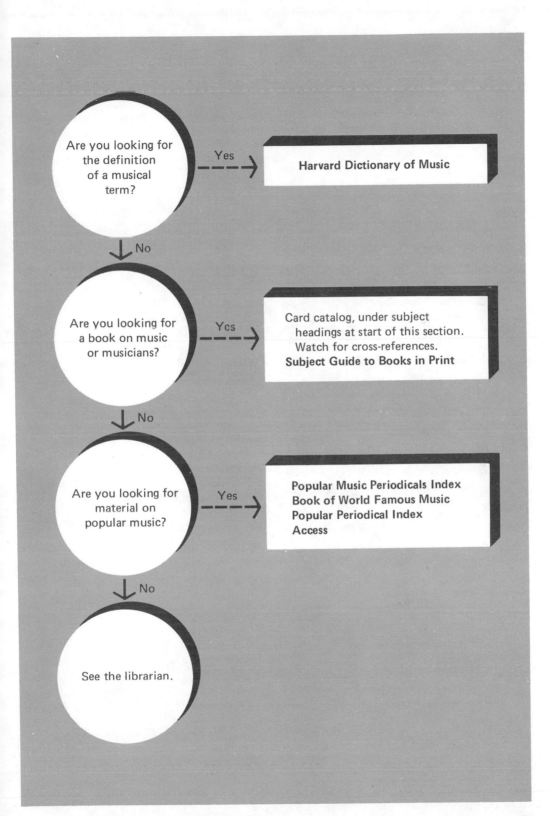

Are you looking for the definition of a musical term?

Yes → **Harvard Dictionary of Music**

No ↓

Are you looking for a book on music or musicians?

Yes → Card catalog, under subject headings at start of this section. Watch for cross-references. **Subject Guide to Books in Print**

No ↓

Are you looking for material on popular music?

Yes → **Popular Music Periodicals Index**
Book of World Famous Music
Popular Periodical Index
Access

No ↓

See the librarian.

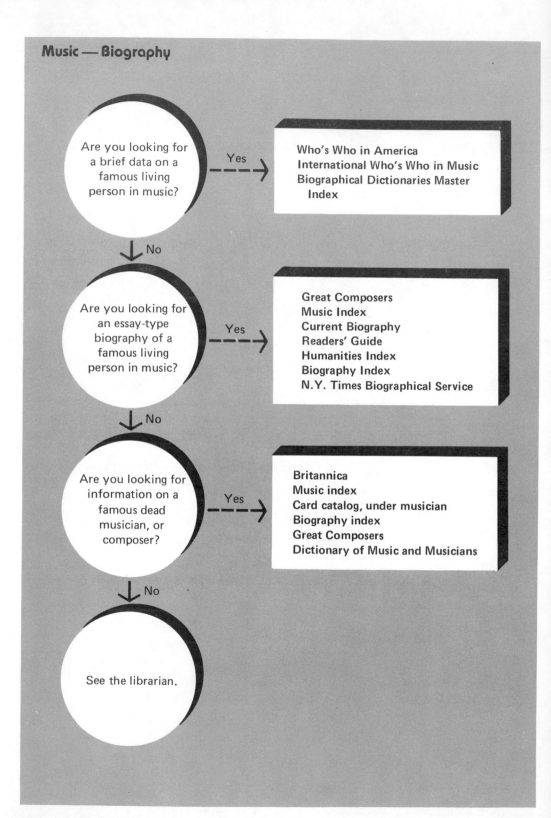

Are you looking for a brief data on a famous living person in music?

Yes →

Who's Who in America
International Who's Who in Music
Biographical Dictionaries Master
Index

No ↓

Are you looking for an essay-type biography of a famous living person in music?

Yes →

Great Composers
Music Index
Current Biography
Readers' Guide
Humanities Index
Biography Index
N.Y. Times Biographical Service

No ↓

Are you looking for information on a famous dead musician, or composer?

Yes →

Britannica
Music index
Card catalog, under musician
Biography index
Great Composers
Dictionary of Music and Musicians

No ↓

See the librarian.

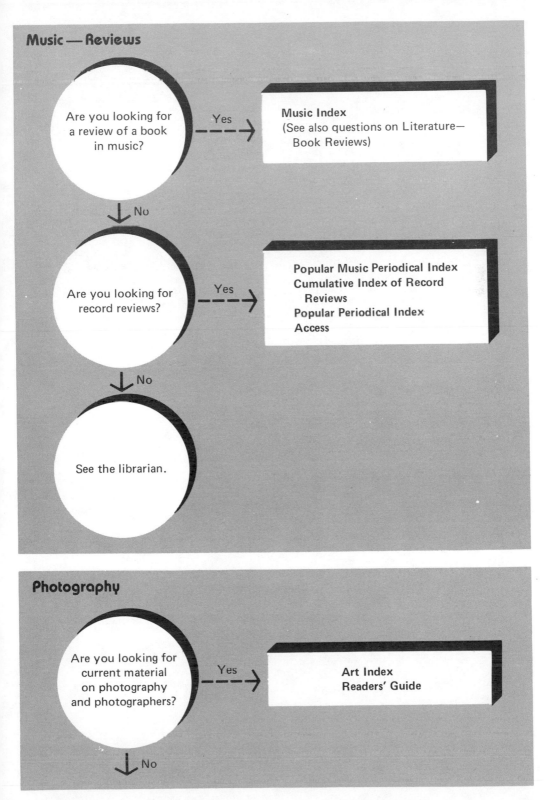

Music — Reviews

Are you looking for a review of a book in music?

— Yes → **Music Index** (See also questions on Literature— Book Reviews)

↓ No

Are you looking for record reviews?

— Yes → **Popular Music Periodical Index**
Cumulative Index of Record Reviews
Popular Periodical Index
Access

↓ No

See the librarian.

Photography

Are you looking for current material on photography and photographers?

— Yes → **Art Index**
Readers' Guide

↓ No

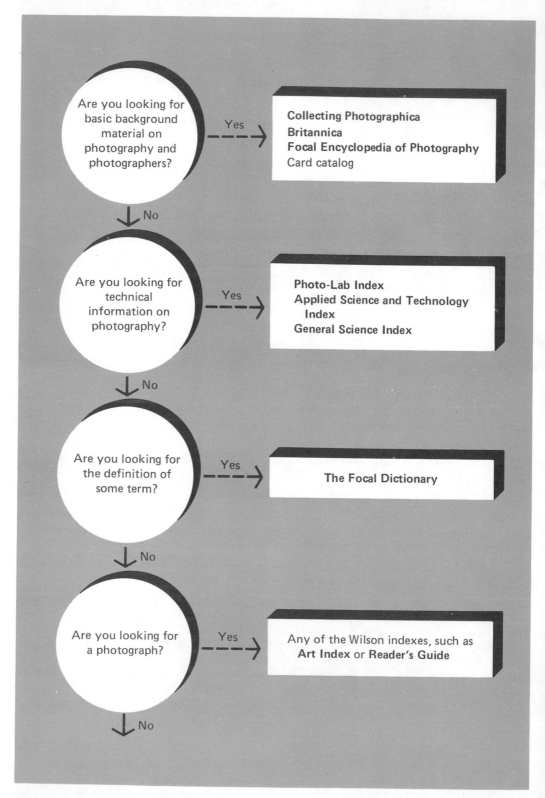

Are you looking for basic background material on photography and photographers? — Yes → Collecting Photographica / Britannica / Focal Encyclopedia of Photography / Card catalog

No ↓

Are you looking for technical information on photography? — Yes → Photo-Lab Index / Applied Science and Technology Index / General Science Index

No ↓

Are you looking for the definition of some term? — Yes → The Focal Dictionary

No ↓

Are you looking for a photograph? — Yes → Any of the Wilson indexes, such as Art Index or Reader's Guide

No ↓

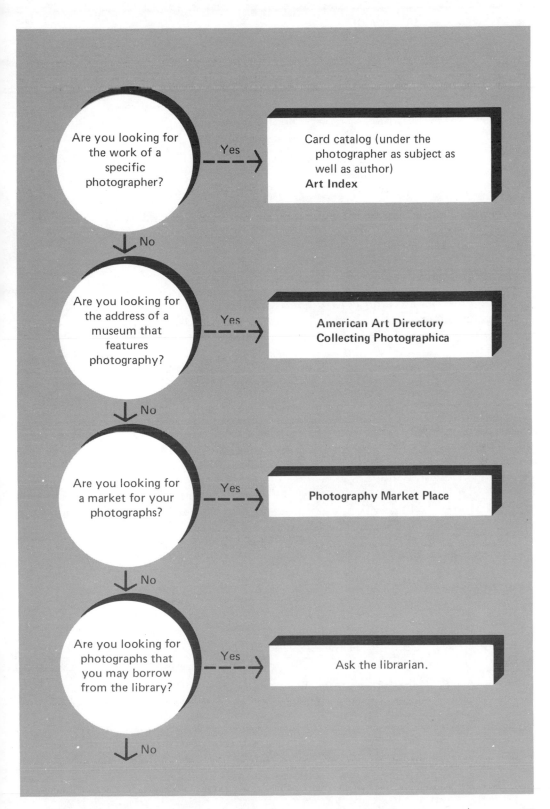

Are you looking for the work of a specific photographer? — Yes → Card catalog (under the photographer as subject as well as author) **Art Index**

No ↓

Are you looking for the address of a museum that features photography? — Yes → **American Art Directory** **Collecting Photographica**

No ↓

Are you looking for a market for your photographs? — Yes → **Photography Market Place**

No ↓

Are you looking for photographs that you may borrow from the library? — Yes → Ask the librarian.

No ↓

See the librarian.

DESCRIPTIONS OF SOURCES

Allgemeines Lexikon der Bildenden Kunstler   (Thieme, Ulrich). Leipzig: Seeman, 1907–1950. 37 vols. By far the most comprehensive and best known of the essay-type biographical reference works for artists. Usually called "Thieme," it has both short and long articles on artists from throughout the world and from all time periods up to the 20th century. The catch is that it is in German, as is the work which brings this up through the 20th century: Vollmer, Hans. *Allgemeines Lexikon der Bildenden Kunstler des XX Jahrhunderts.* Leipzig: Seeman, 1952–1962. 6 vols. N40.T4   927

American Art Directory.   N.Y.: Bowker, 1898 to date, triennial. A geographical listing of some 3000 museums, art schools, organizations, and so on in the U.S. N50.A54   705.8

Art Index.   N.Y.: Wilson, 1929 to date, quarterly. Tells you where to find articles in about 150 periodicals that have to do with art. Turn here too for material on archeology, photography, landscape design, and related subjects. Z5937.A78   016.7

Related Titles

RILA: International Repertory of the Literature of Art.
Williamstown, Mass.: Clark Library, 1973 to date, semiannual. A major abstracting service still being developed, which includes books as well as periodicals. Z5937.R16   016.7

Art Bibliographies Modern.   Santa Barbara: ABC-Clio, 1973 to date, semiannual. Abstracts of material from over 500 periodicals, books, and related materials. Z5937.C55   016.7

The Book of World Famous Music   (J. J. Fuld). N.Y.: Crown, 1971. Source of information about best-known musical compositions from classic to popular, with emphasis on the latter. ML113.F8   016.78

Related Title

Popular Music: An Annotated Index of American Popular Songs (Nat Shapiro). N.Y.: Adrian, 1964. 6 vols. Arranged by year, then by title, each volume lists major American popular songs from 1920. ML120.U5S5 784.02

Collecting Photographica (Gilbert, George). N.Y.: Hawthorn Books, 1976. A guide to sources of photographica, including photographic museums, a bibliography, and addresses of major dealers in photographs and photographic equipment. Assumes some knowledge of collecting and the field. The basic guide of its type. TR6.5G654 770.75

Related Title

Collectors' Guide to Nineteenth-Century Photographs (Welling, William). N.Y.: Macmillan, 1976. Prices and explains old photographs. Amply illustrated. TR6.5W44 770.75

Cumulated Index of Record Reviews. Washington: Music Lib. Assn., 1950 to date, annual. Tells you where to find reviews of primarily classical recordings in about 30 U.S. and European periodicals. ML156.C8 781.973

Related Titles

Annual Index to Popular Music Record Reviews. Metuchen, N.J.: Scarecrow, 1972 to date, annual. ML156.9A75 789.9

Records in Review. N.Y.: Scribner's, 1958 to date, annual. Reprint of reviews which appear in *High Fidelity* magazine. ML156.9H5 789.913

Encyclopedia of World Art. N.Y.: McGraw-Hill, 1959–1968. 15 vols. Basic set that covers all major aspects of art from the beginning through the 1950s. Excellent lengthy articles. The concluding section of each volume includes black and white illustrations. N31.E48 703

Great Composers: 1300–1900 (Ewen, David). N.Y.: Wilson, 1966. A standard essay-type biographical source, one of many by Ewen. There are about 200 biographies, with portraits of most of the composers. ML390.E833 780.92

Related Titles

Composers Since 1900 (Ewen, David). N.Y.: Wilson, 1969. ML390.E833 780.92

Popular American Composers   (Ewen, David). N.Y.: Wilson, 1962.
Supplement, 1972. ML390.E845   927.8

Baker's Biographical Dictionary of Musicians.   N.Y.: Schirmer,
1965. ML105.B16   927.8

Dictionary of Music and Musicians   (Grove, George), 5th ed. N.Y.: St.
Martin's, 1955. 9 vols. Supplement, 1961. A classic that covers the whole field
from biographies to musical history. (It does not give opera plots.) A new edition
is scheduled in 1978 or 1979. ML100.G8863   780.3

Related Titles

New Oxford History of Music.   London: Oxford, 1954. 10 vols.
Covers the history of music from its beginnings through the 1950s.
ML160.N44   780.9

New Kobbe's Complete Opera Book.   N.Y.: Putnam, 1976. Includes
plots and describes the music. MT95.K52   782.1

Harvard Dictionary of Music   (Willi Apel), 2nd ed. Cambridge: Harvard,
1969. Basic dictionary-encyclopedia that not only defines terms, but includes
some long essays. No biographical material. Includes opera plots, songs, and
so on. ML100.A64   780.3

A History of Architecture on the Comparative Method.   (Banister
Fletcher), 17th ed. N.Y.: Scribner's, 1961. History from ancient times through
the middle of the 20th century. Profusely illustrated. NA200.F63   720.9

Index to Reproductions of American Paintings   (Lyn Smith). Metuchen,
N.J.: Scarecrow, 1977. Tells you where to find paintings reproduced in some

Related Titles

Catalogue of Color Reproductions of Paintings, 1960 to 197–.
N.Y.: Unipub, various dates. A basic listing that is useful, as well, for telling
you where the original paintings are located. NE1860.A2   759

Sculpture Index   (Clapp, Jane). Metuchen, N.J.: Scarecrow, 1970. 2
vols. Locates work; gives dimensions and other data. Tells where to find
reproductions in some 950 books and sources. NB36.C55   730.16

Index to Reproductions of American Paintings   (Monro, Isabel).
N.Y.: Wilson, 1948. Supplement, 1964. ND205.M57   759.13

Index to Reproductions of European Paintings, 1956. Lists by artist, title, and usually by subject paintings in over 1000 sources. ND45.M6   016.759

International Who's Who in Music (formerly *Who's Who in Music*). N.J.: Rowman & Littlefield, 1935 to date. Data approach to information on the world figures in music. Seven appendixes (from orchestras to major concert halls and opera houses) make this source particularly useful. ML106.G7   927.8

McGraw-Hill Dictionary of Art. N.Y.: McGraw-Hill, 1969. 5 vols. Like a small encyclopedia; many of the definitions are article length. Contains biographical sketches. N33.M23   703

Related Titles

A Visual Dictionary of Art. Greenwich, Conn.: N.Y. Graphic Society, 1974. About 4500 entries with a stress on painting and sculpture. N33.V56   703

Dictionary of Arts and Artists (Peter Murray). Baltimore: Penguin, 1972. A useful dictionary with a stress on Western art. N31.M8   703

Music Index. Detroit: Information service, 1950 to date, monthly. Tells you where to find information in about 300 periodicals. Includes book reviews. Primarily useful for material on classical music, although some popular approaches are considered. ML118.M84   780

Related Titles

Popular Music Periodicals Index. Metuchen, N.J.: Scarecrow, 1975 to date, annual. A subject and author approach to over 60 periodicals that cover popular music. ML118.P66   780

RILM. International Repertory of Music Literature. Flushing, N.Y.: RILM abstracts, 1967 to date, quarterly. Includes abstracts of periodical articles, books, dissertations, catalogs, and so on, with author-subject index. ML1.I83   780

Oxford Companion to Art. Oxford: Clarendon, 1970. An encyclopedia approach to the fine arts in the typical "companion" format. The visual arts are stressed. N33.09   703

Related Titles

Oxford Companion to the Decorative Arts. Oxford: Clarendon, 1975. NK30.093   745

Phaidon Dictionary of Twentieth-Century Art.   London: Phaidon, 1973. N6490.P46   709

Photography Market Place,   2nd ed. N.Y.: Bowker, 1977. A basic listing, with full addresses and other information, of picture buyers, technical services, career opportunities, equipment sources, and so on. TR12.P52   380.1

Related Title

Artist's and Photographer's Market.   Cincinnati: Writer's Digest, 1976 to date, annual. Describes about 3600 markets for photographs, as well as illustrations, cartoons, and other visual art forms. N8600.A78   380.1

Photo-Lab Index.   Dobbs Ferry, N.Y.: Morgan and Morgan, 1939 to date, annual. The basic manual for serious (not amateur) photo enthusiasts. Answers thousands of questions about technical aspects. Divided between photographic materials and general facts by subject area.

Related Titles

The Focal Dictionary of Photographic Technologies   (Spenser, Douglas).Englewood Cliffs, N.J.: Prentice-Hall, 1973. A basic source of information for both beginners and experts.

Focal Encyclopedia of Photography.   N.Y.: Focal Press, 1965. 2 vols. Somewhat dated, but basic for history and technology aspects of photography.

Who's Who in American Art.   N.Y.: Bowker, 1935 to date, biennial. Data on about 9000 individuals—not only artists. N6536.W5   927

Related Titles

Who's Who in Art.   London: Art Trade Press, 1927 to date, biennial. Primarily British artists and those in related fields. N40.W6   709.2

Index of Artists   (Mallet, Daniel). N.Y.: Bowker, 1935. A self-contained data approach to artists of the world, but emphasizing Americans. Also lists where you may find more information. Numerous works update this title. Look on the shelf near Mallet. N40.M3   927

Literature

This section will help you find information about authors, book reviews, plots, quotations, various literary forms, and other aspects of literature. The emphasis is on U.S. and English literature.

BASIC GUIDES

The four most basic guides to literature are listed below. Turn to them in about the order listed.

1. *Guide to Reference Books* (see p. 29) The literature section is extensive, pp. 293–374.

2. *Selective Bibliography for the Study of English and American Literature* (Richard Altick), 5th ed. N.Y.: Macmillan, 1975. A general guide to the basic reference works you are likely to be using in literature. Z2001.A4X   016.8207

3. *Literary Research Guide* (Margaret Patterson). Detroit: Gale, 1976. One of the best guides, with over 15,000 critical annotated entries and a fine index. Z6511.P37   016.0168

4. *A Concise Bibliography for Students of English* (Arthur Kennedy and Donald Sands), 5th ed. Stanford: Stanford University Press, 1972. Classified bibliography of titles, without annotations. Much used by undergraduates. Good index. Z2011.K35   016.82

CLASSIFICATION NUMBERS

Dewey Decimal System

If your library uses the Dewey Decimal system, you will find literature in the 800s. Fiction has no call number; it is shelved in the fiction section by author. The basic breakdown is:

808.8 Collections of poetry, drama, and so on.
809   History and criticism
810   American literature (the subdivisions for other literatures are the same)
    811 American poetry
    812 American drama
    813 American fiction
    814 American essays
    815 American speeches
    816 American letters
    817 American satire and humor
    818 Miscellany
820   English literature
830   German literature
840   French literature
850   Italian literature
860   Spanish literature
870   Latin literature
880   Greek literature
890   Other

Library of Congress System

If your library uses the Library of Congress system, you will find literature in the P section. You will find fiction in the same place where you find material about the author. The P section also includes language. You primarily will be involved with PR (English literature) and PS (U.S. literature). Romance literature is PQ, German, PT. Again a logical breakdown is evident within each of the letter combinations.

SUBJECT HEADINGS

Generally begin looking up "Literature" or the name of the form, such as "Poetry." Literature of a particular country is listed under the name of the country; for example, "Japanese literature."

For works *by* an author, look under the author's last name. Works *about* an author come after works by the author. If the catalog is divided (Chapter 3), works about the author are in a separate subject catalog.

Here are some representative headings:

Your Term	Subject headings
Book reviews	"Book reviews"
Criticism	"Literature—Stories, plots, etc."
	"American literature—History and criticism"
	"Poetry—History and criticism"
Plots	"Plots—Drama"
	"Literature—Stories, plots, etc."
	"Poetry—Stories, plots, etc."
Plays	"Drama"
	"Drama—History and criticism"
	"American drama"
Poetry	"Poetry—Collections"
	"American poetry—History and criticism"
Short stories	"Short stories"
	"Science fiction"
Speeches	"Orations"
	"Speeches, addresses, etc."

OUTLINE OF SOURCES BY FORM

1. Bibliographies
   Articles on American Literature
   Blanc, *Bibliography of American Literature*

      Fiction Catalog
      MLA International Bibliography
      New Cambridge Bibliography of English Literature
2. Biography
      American Authors and Books
      Author series such as H. W. Wilson publications
      Authors: Critical and Biographical References
      Celebrity Register
      Contemporary Authors
      Contemporary Novelists
      Contemporary Poets
      Index to Literary Biography
      Junior Book of Authors
3. Book reviews, criticism, plots, and so on
      The American Novel
      Book Review Digest
      Book Review Index
      Contemporary Literary Criticism
      Current Book Review Citations
      Dramatic Criticism Index
      Masterplots
      The New York Times Book Review
      Plot Summary Index
      Poetry Explication
      Twentieth Century Short Story Explication
4. Encyclopedias, yearbooks, handbooks, and dictionaries
      Cambridge History of American Literature
      Cambridge History of English Literature
      Cassell's Encyclopedia of World Literature
      Literary History of the United States
      McGraw-Hill Encyclopedia of World Drama
      Oxford Companion to American Literature
      Oxford Companion to English Literature
      Princeton Encyclopedia of Poetry and Poetics
      Reader's Encyclopedia
5. Indexes and abstracts
      Abstracts of English Studies
      Dissertation Abstracts
      Granger's Index to Poetry
      Play Index
      Short Story Index
      Speech Index
6. Quotations
      Bartlett
      Stevenson
7. Writing
      Writer's Market

CHART 2: QUESTIONS AND SOURCES OF ANSWERS IN LITERATURE

Authors — Biographies

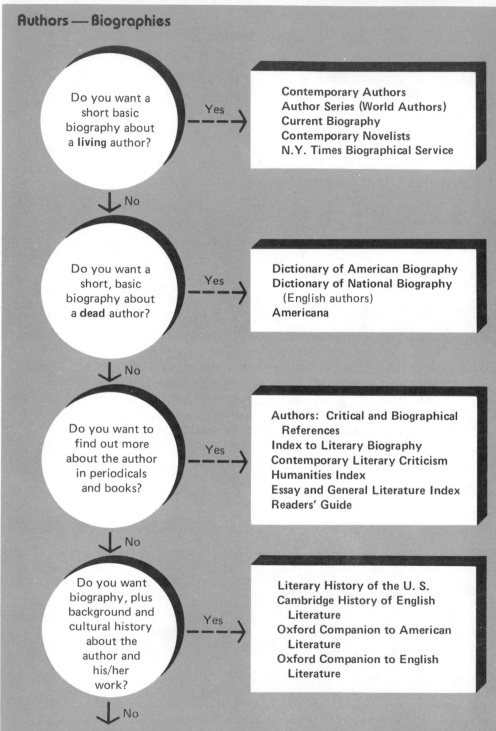

Do you want a short basic biography about a living author? — Yes →
- Contemporary Authors
- Author Series (World Authors)
- Current Biography
- Contemporary Novelists
- N.Y. Times Biographical Service

No ↓

Do you want a short, basic biography about a dead author? — Yes →
- Dictionary of American Biography
- Dictionary of National Biography (English authors)
- Americana

No ↓

Do you want to find out more about the author in periodicals and books? — Yes →
- Authors: Critical and Biographical References
- Index to Literary Biography
- Contemporary Literary Criticism
- Humanities Index
- Essay and General Literature Index
- Readers' Guide

No ↓

Do you want biography, plus background and cultural history about the author and his/her work? — Yes →
- Literary History of the U. S.
- Cambridge History of English Literature
- Oxford Companion to American Literature
- Oxford Companion to English Literature

No ↓

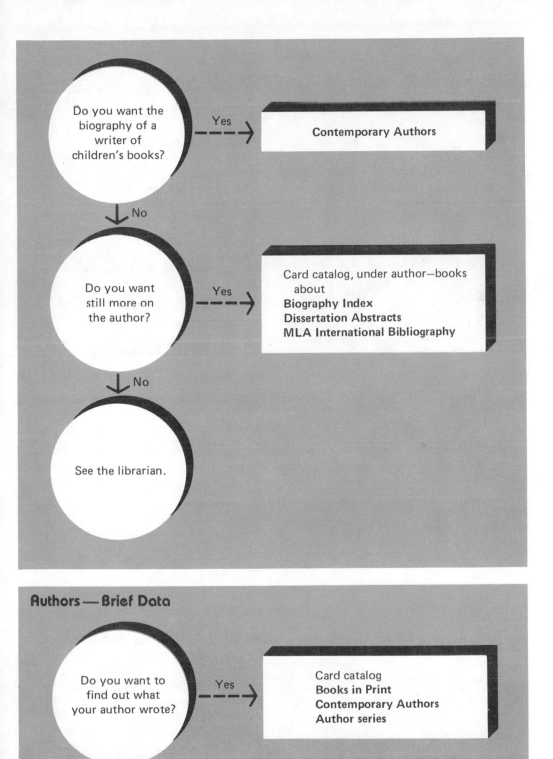

Do you want the biography of a writer of children's books?

Yes → Contemporary Authors

↓ No

Do you want still more on the author?

Yes → Card catalog, under author—books about
Biography Index
Dissertation Abstracts
MLA International Bibliography

↓ No

See the librarian.

Authors — Brief Data

Do you want to find out what your author wrote?

Yes → Card catalog
Books in Print
Contemporary Authors
Author series

↓ No

109

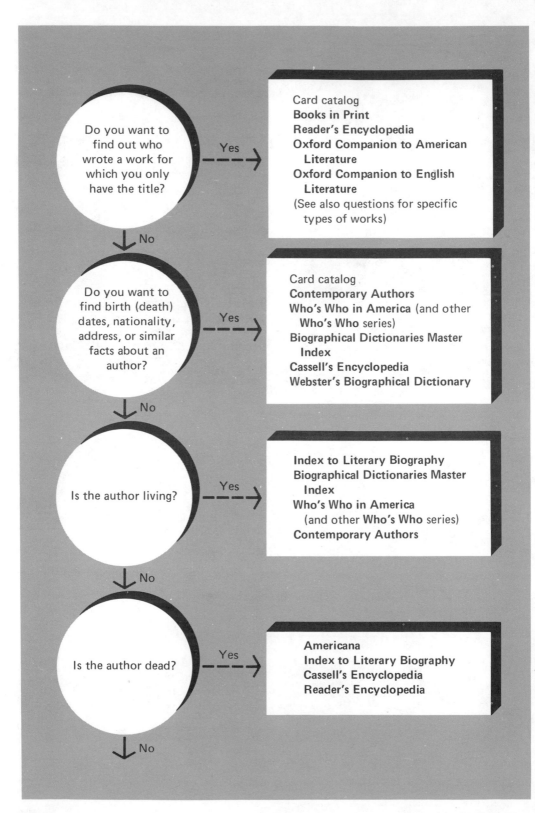

Do you want to find out who wrote a work for which you only have the title?

Yes →

Card catalog
Books in Print
Reader's Encyclopedia
Oxford Companion to American Literature
Oxford Companion to English Literature
(See also questions for specific types of works)

No ↓

Do you want to find birth (death) dates, nationality, address, or similar facts about an author?

Yes →

Card catalog
Contemporary Authors
Who's Who in America (and other **Who's Who** series)
Biographical Dictionaries Master Index
Cassell's Encyclopedia
Webster's Biographical Dictionary

No ↓

Is the author living?

Yes →

Index to Literary Biography
Biographical Dictionaries Master Index
Who's Who in America (and other **Who's Who** series)
Contemporary Authors

No ↓

Is the author dead?

Yes →

Americana
Index to Literary Biography
Cassell's Encyclopedia
Reader's Encyclopedia

No ↓

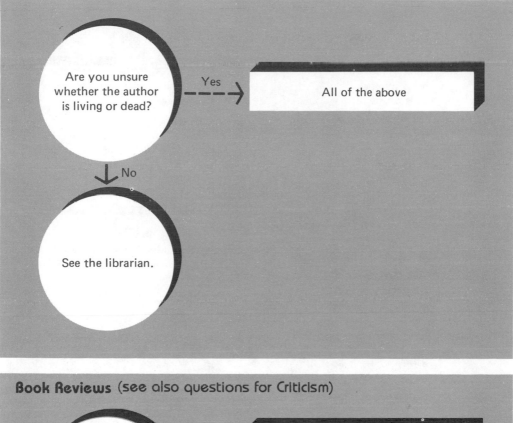

Are you unsure whether the author is living or dead?

Yes → All of the above

No ↓

See the librarian.

Book Reviews (see also questions for Criticism)

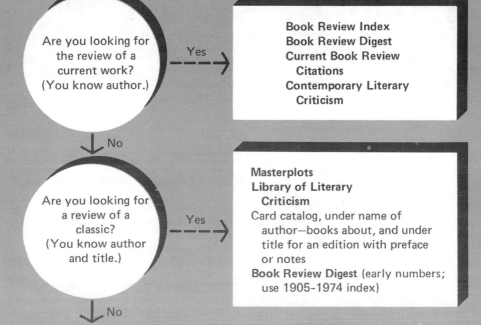

Are you looking for the review of a current work? (You know author.)

Yes →
Book Review Index
Book Review Digest
Current Book Review Citations
Contemporary Literary Criticism

No ↓

Are you looking for a review of a classic? (You know author and title.)

Yes →
Masterplots
Library of Literary Criticism
Card catalog, under name of author—books about, and under title for an edition with preface or notes
Book Review Digest (early numbers; use 1905-1974 index)

No ↓

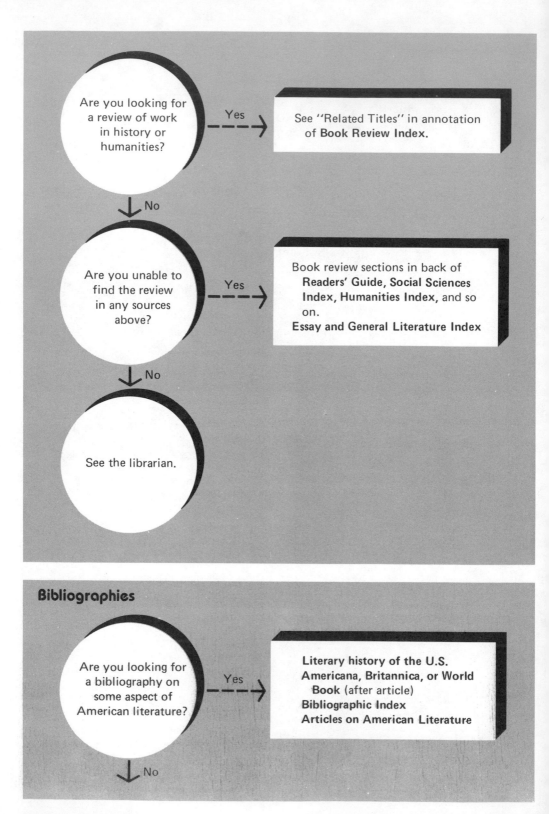

Are you looking for a review of work in history or humanities?

Yes → See "Related Titles" in annotation of **Book Review Index.**

No ↓

Are you unable to find the review in any sources above?

Yes → Book review sections in back of **Readers' Guide, Social Sciences Index, Humanities Index,** and so on.
Essay and General Literature Index

No ↓

See the librarian.

Bibliographies

Are you looking for a bibliography on some aspect of American literature?

Yes → **Literary history of the U.S.
Americana, Britannica, or World Book** (after article)
**Bibliographic Index
Articles on American Literature**

No ↓

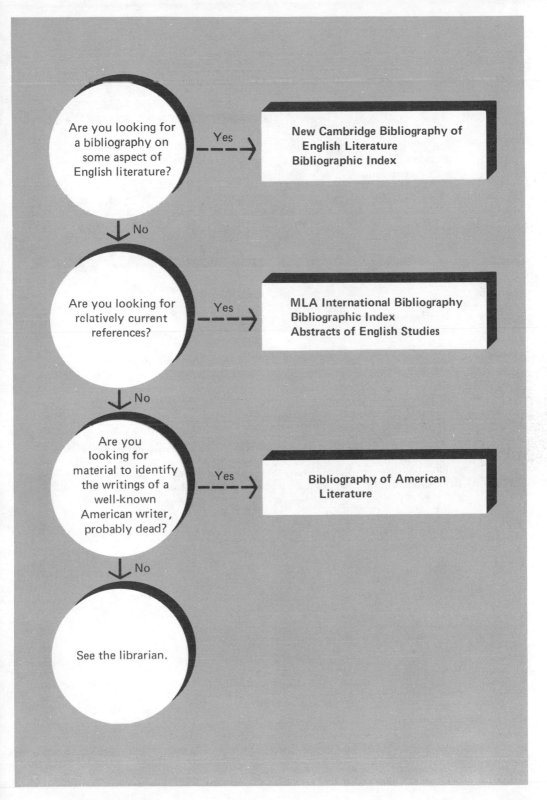

Are you looking for a bibliography on some aspect of English literature?

Yes → New Cambridge Bibliography of English Literature
Bibliographic Index

No ↓

Are you looking for relatively current references?

Yes → MLA International Bibliography
Bibliographic Index
Abstracts of English Studies

No ↓

Are you looking for material to identify the writings of a well-known American writer, probably dead?

Yes → Bibliography of American Literature

No ↓

See the librarian.

113

Criticism, Plots, Synopses (see also questions on Novels, Plays, Short Stories, and Poetry)

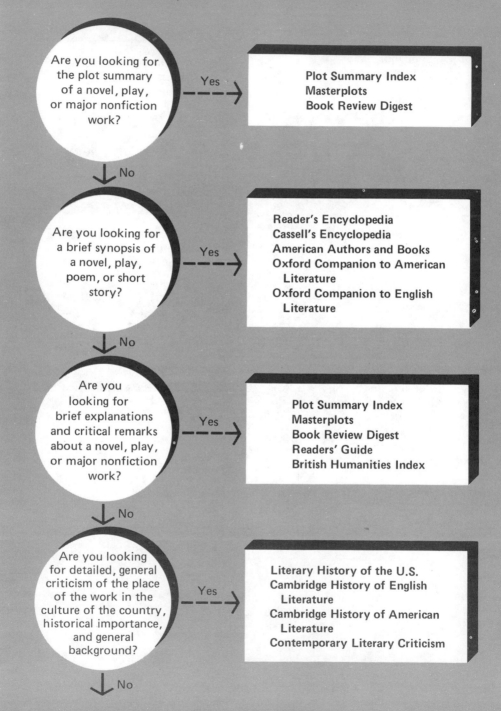

Are you looking for the plot summary of a novel, play, or major nonfiction work?

Yes → Plot Summary Index
Masterplots
Book Review Digest

No ↓

Are you looking for a brief synopsis of a novel, play, poem, or short story?

Yes → Reader's Encyclopedia
Cassell's Encyclopedia
American Authors and Books
Oxford Companion to American
  Literature
Oxford Companion to English
  Literature

No ↓

Are you looking for brief explanations and critical remarks about a novel, play, or major nonfiction work?

Yes → Plot Summary Index
Masterplots
Book Review Digest
Readers' Guide
British Humanities Index

No ↓

Are you looking for detailed, general criticism of the place of the work in the culture of the country, historical importance, and general background?

Yes → Literary History of the U.S.
Cambridge History of English
  Literature
Cambridge History of American
  Literature
Contemporary Literary Criticism

No ↓

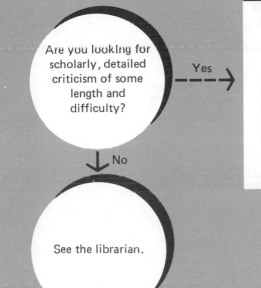

Are you looking for scholarly, detailed criticism of some length and difficulty?

Yes ----→ Card catalog, under author—books about or under "Literature—history and criticism" "Poetry—history and criticism," and so on.
Essay and General Literature Index
Humanities Index
MLA International Bibliography
Abstracts of English Studies
Contemporary Literary Criticism
Authors: Critical and Biographical References

↓ No

See the librarian.

Novels

Are you looking for critical comments on an older, well-known novel?

Yes ----→ **American Novel**
Library of Literary Criticism
The English Novel
Book Review Digest (older volumes)
Humanities Index
Essay and General Literature Index

↓ No

Are you looking for critical comments on a recent novel?

Yes ----→ **Book Review Digest**
Book Review Index
Contemporary Literary Criticism
The Contemporary Novel

↓ No

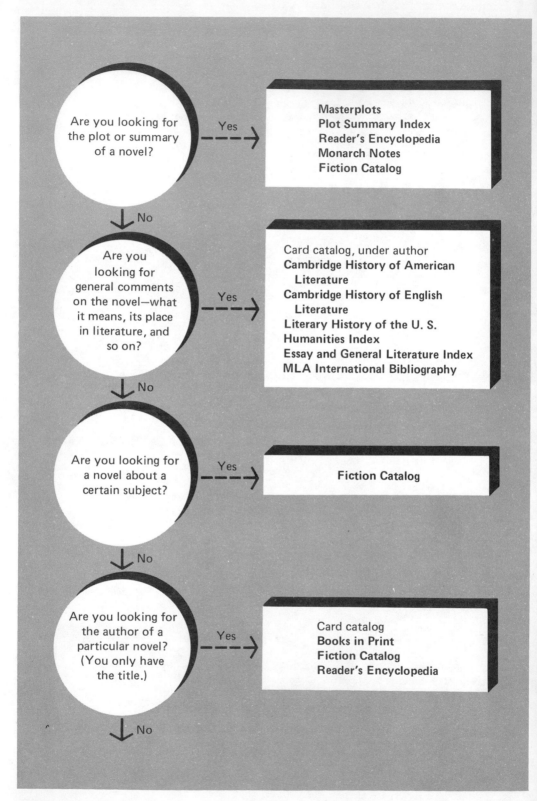

Are you looking for the plot or summary of a novel?

Yes →
Masterplots
Plot Summary Index
Reader's Encyclopedia
Monarch Notes
Fiction Catalog

↓ No

Are you looking for general comments on the novel—what it means, its place in literature, and so on?

Yes →
Card catalog, under author
Cambridge History of American Literature
Cambridge History of English Literature
Literary History of the U. S.
Humanities Index
Essay and General Literature Index
MLA International Bibliography

↓ No

Are you looking for a novel about a certain subject?

Yes →
Fiction Catalog

↓ No

Are you looking for the author of a particular novel? (You only have the title.)

Yes →
Card catalog
Books in Print
Fiction Catalog
Reader's Encyclopedia

↓ No

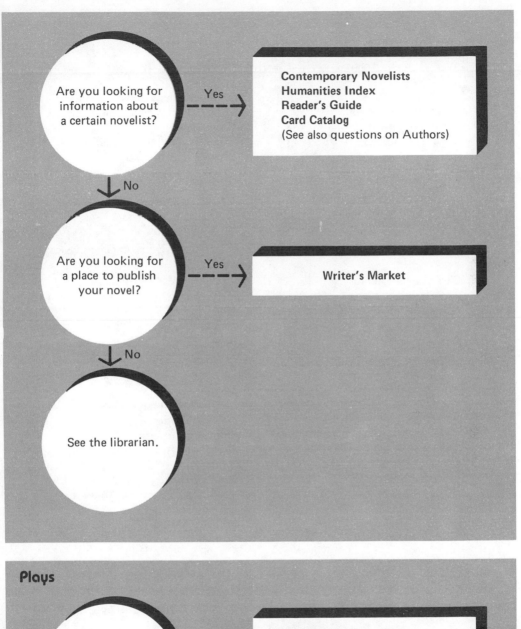

Are you looking for information about a certain novelist?

Yes →

Contemporary Novelists
Humanities Index
Reader's Guide
Card Catalog
(See also questions on Authors)

No ↓

Are you looking for a place to publish your novel?

Yes →

Writer's Market

No ↓

See the librarian.

Plays

Are you looking for critical comments on an older, well-known play?

Yes →

Dramatic Criticism Index
Library of Literary Criticism
Drama Criticism
N.Y. Times Theatre Reviews
Essay and General Literature Index
Humanities Index

No ↓

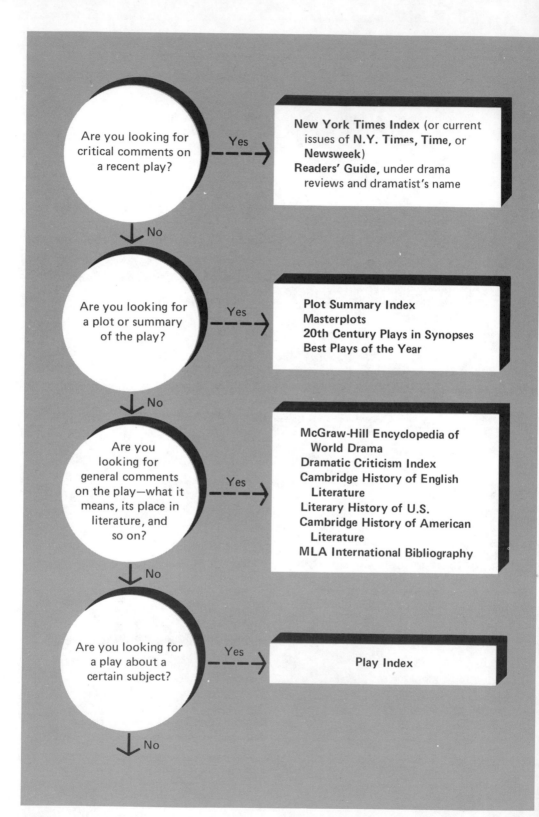

Are you looking for critical comments on a recent play? — Yes → New York Times Index (or current issues of N.Y. Times, Time, or Newsweek)
Readers' Guide, under drama reviews and dramatist's name

No ↓

Are you looking for a plot or summary of the play? — Yes → Plot Summary Index
Masterplots
20th Century Plays in Synopses
Best Plays of the Year

No ↓

Are you looking for general comments on the play—what it means, its place in literature, and so on? — Yes → McGraw-Hill Encyclopedia of World Drama
Dramatic Criticism Index
Cambridge History of English Literature
Literary History of U.S.
Cambridge History of American Literature
MLA International Bibliography

No ↓

Are you looking for a play about a certain subject? — Yes → Play Index

No ↓

118

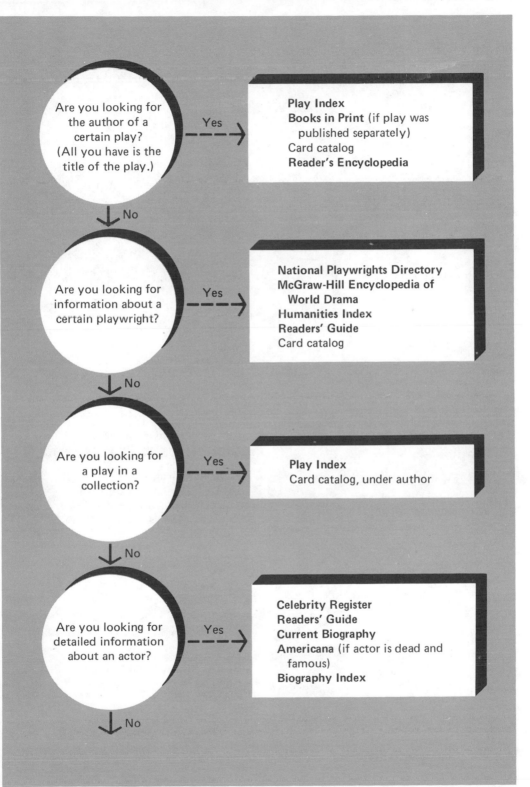

Are you looking for the author of a certain play? (All you have is the title of the play.) — Yes →

Play Index
Books in Print (if play was published separately)
Card catalog
Reader's Encyclopedia

No ↓

Are you looking for information about a certain playwright? — Yes →

National Playwrights Directory
McGraw-Hill Encyclopedia of World Drama
Humanities Index
Readers' Guide
Card catalog

No ↓

Are you looking for a play in a collection? — Yes →

Play Index
Card catalog, under author

No ↓

Are you looking for detailed information about an actor? — Yes →

Celebrity Register
Readers' Guide
Current Biography
Americana (if actor is dead and famous)
Biography Index

No ↓

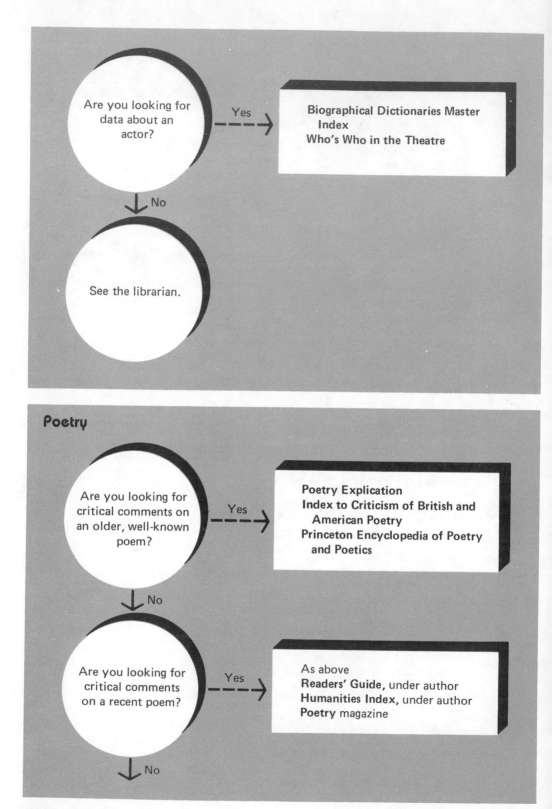

Are you looking for data about an actor?

Yes → Biographical Dictionaries Master Index
Who's Who in the Theatre

No ↓

See the librarian.

Poetry

Are you looking for critical comments on an older, well-known poem?

Yes → Poetry Explication
Index to Criticism of British and American Poetry
Princeton Encyclopedia of Poetry and Poetics

No ↓

Are you looking for critical comments on a recent poem?

Yes → As above
Readers' Guide, under author
Humanities Index, under author
Poetry magazine

No ↓

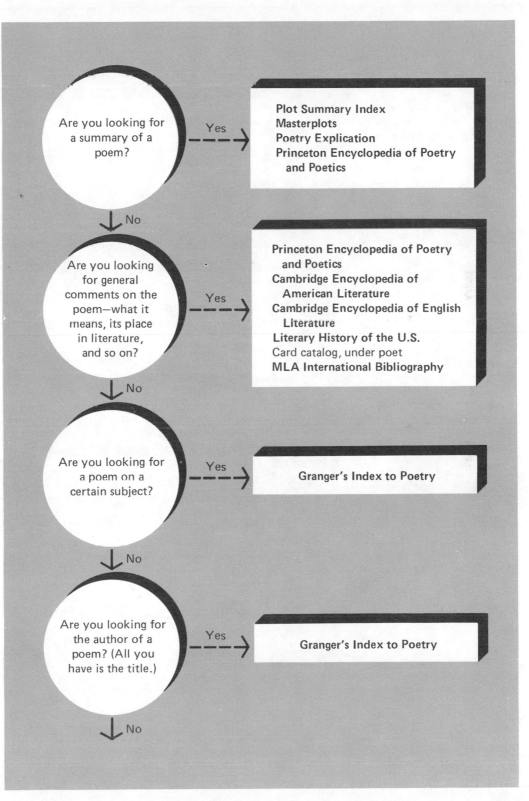

Are you looking for a summary of a poem?

Yes →

Plot Summary Index
Masterplots
Poetry Explication
Princeton Encyclopedia of Poetry and Poetics

No ↓

Are you looking for general comments on the poem—what it means, its place in literature, and so on?

Yes →

Princeton Encyclopedia of Poetry and Poetics
Cambridge Encyclopedia of American Literature
Cambridge Encyclopedia of English Literature
Literary History of the U.S.
Card catalog, under poet
MLA International Bibliography

No ↓

Are you looking for a poem on a certain subject?

Yes →

Granger's Index to Poetry

No ↓

Are you looking for the author of a poem? (All you have is the title.)

Yes →

Granger's Index to Poetry

No ↓

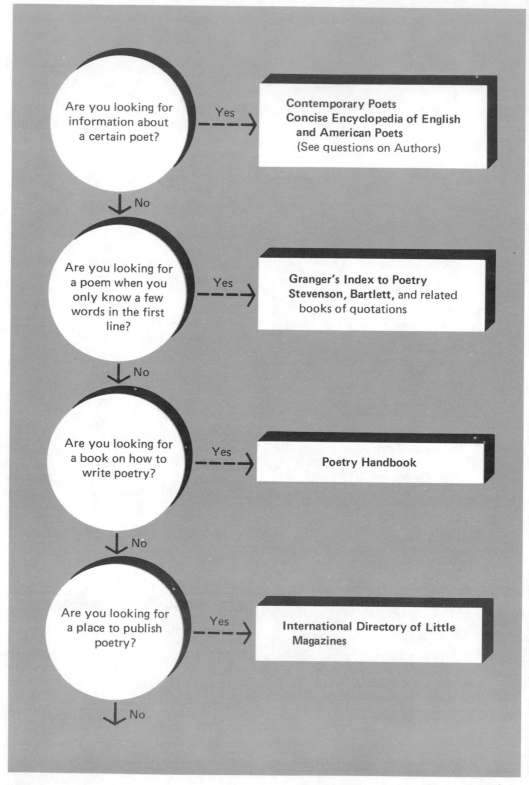

Are you looking for information about a certain poet?

Yes → **Contemporary Poets**
Concise Encyclopedia of English and American Poets
(See questions on Authors)

↓ No

Are you looking for a poem when you only know a few words in the first line?

Yes → **Granger's Index to Poetry**
Stevenson, Bartlett, and related books of quotations

↓ No

Are you looking for a book on how to write poetry?

Yes → **Poetry Handbook**

↓ No

Are you looking for a place to publish poetry?

Yes → **International Directory of Little Magazines**

↓ No

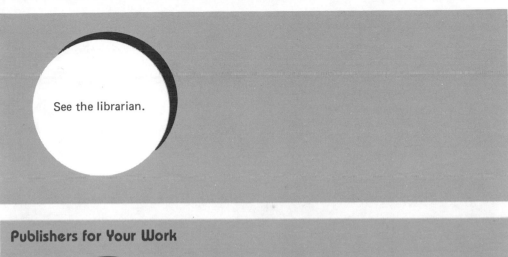

See the librarian.

Publishers for Your Work

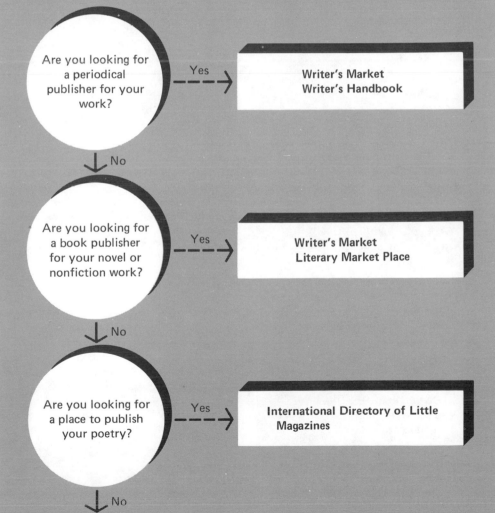

Are you looking for a periodical publisher for your work?

Yes → Writer's Market
Writer's Handbook

No

Are you looking for a book publisher for your novel or nonfiction work?

Yes → Writer's Market
Literary Market Place

No

Are you looking for a place to publish your poetry?

Yes → International Directory of Little Magazines

No

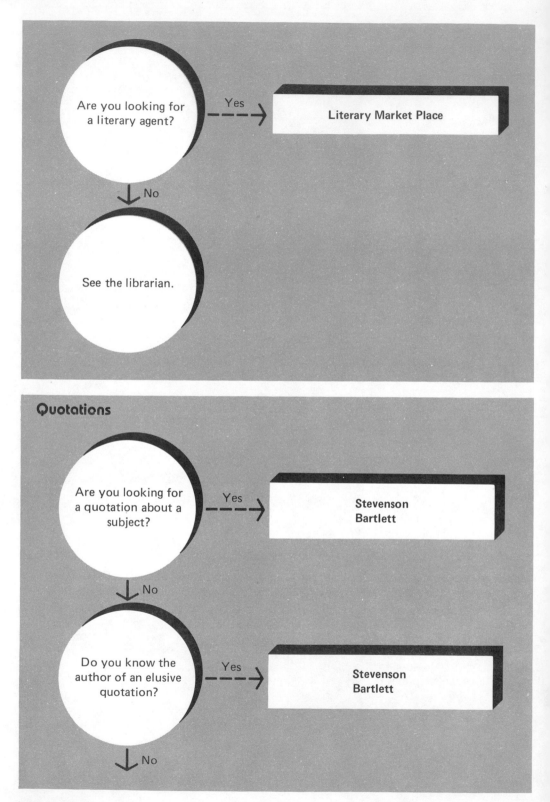

Are you looking for a literary agent?

Yes → **Literary Market Place**

No ↓

See the librarian.

Quotations

Are you looking for a quotation about a subject?

Yes → **Stevenson**
Bartlett

No ↓

Do you know the author of an elusive quotation?

Yes → **Stevenson**
Bartlett

No ↓

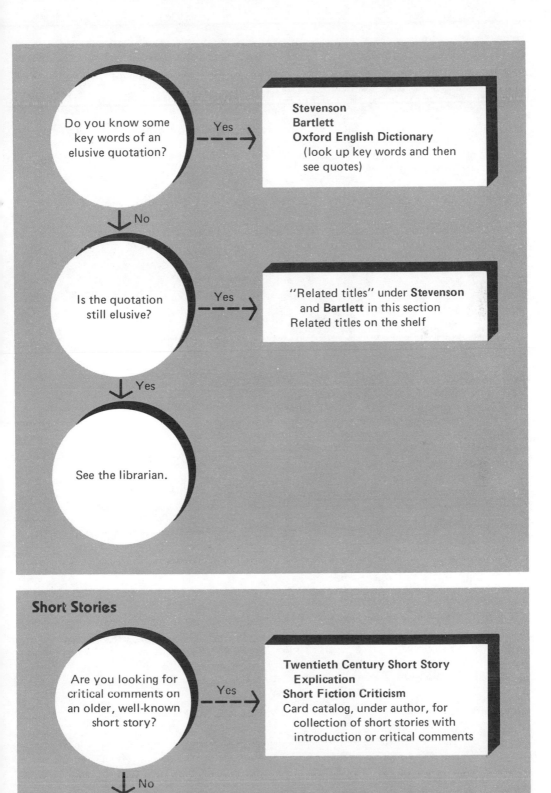

Do you know some
key words of an
elusive quotation?

Yes →

Stevenson
Bartlett
Oxford English Dictionary
   (look up key words and then
   see quotes)

↓ No

Is the quotation
still elusive?

Yes →

"Related titles" under **Stevenson**
  and **Bartlett** in this section
Related titles on the shelf

↓ Yes

See the librarian.

Short Stories

Are you looking for
critical comments on
an older, well-known
short story?

Yes →

Twentieth Century Short Story
  Explication
Short Fiction Criticism
Card catalog, under author, for
  collection of short stories with
  introduction or critical comments

↓ No

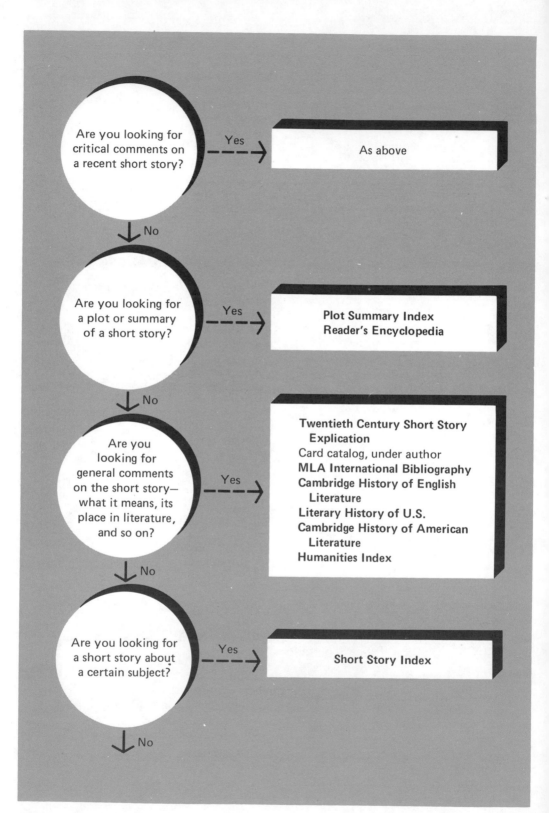

Are you looking for critical comments on a recent short story? — Yes → As above

No ↓

Are you looking for a plot or summary of a short story? — Yes → **Plot Summary Index**
Reader's Encyclopedia

No ↓

Are you looking for general comments on the short story— what it means, its place in literature, and so on? — Yes → **Twentieth Century Short Story Explication**
Card catalog, under author
MLA International Bibliography
Cambridge History of English Literature
Literary History of U.S.
Cambridge History of American Literature
Humanities Index

No ↓

Are you looking for a short story about a certain subject? — Yes → **Short Story Index**

No ↓

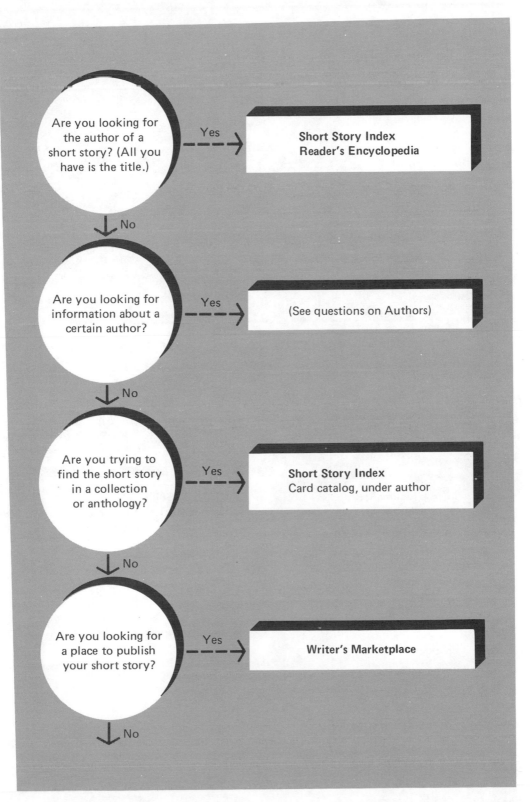

Are you looking for the author of a short story? (All you have is the title.) — Yes → **Short Story Index**
Reader's Encyclopedia

No

Are you looking for information about a certain author? — Yes → (See questions on Authors)

No

Are you trying to find the short story in a collection or anthology? — Yes → **Short Story Index**
Card catalog, under author

No

Are you looking for a place to publish your short story? — Yes → **Writer's Marketplace**

No

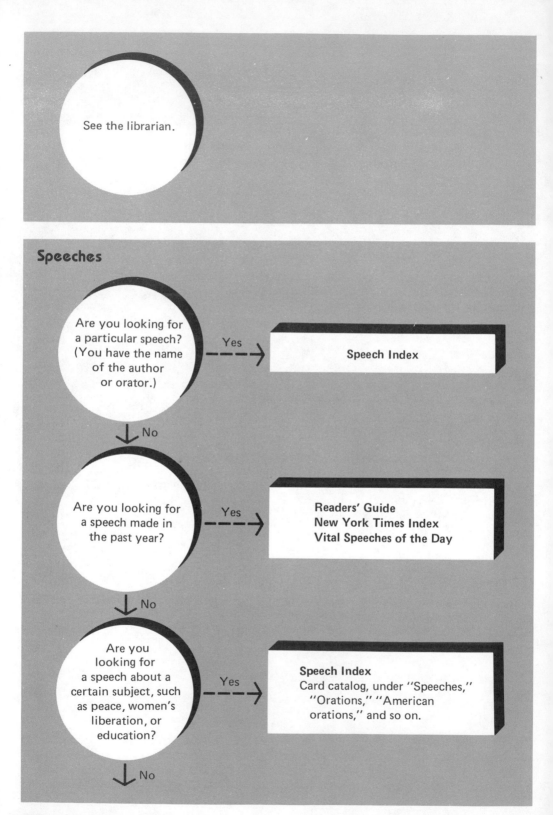

See the librarian.

Speeches

Are you looking for a particular speech? (You have the name of the author or orator.) — Yes → Speech Index

No

Are you looking for a speech made in the past year? — Yes → Readers' Guide / New York Times Index / Vital Speeches of the Day

No

Are you looking for a speech about a certain subject, such as peace, women's liberation, or education? — Yes → **Speech Index** / Card catalog, under "Speeches," "Orations," "American orations," and so on.

No

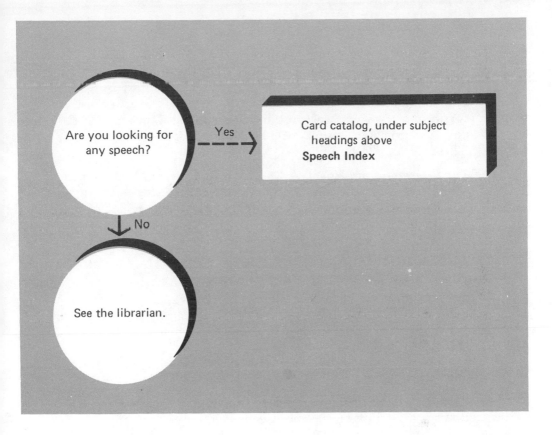

DESCRIPTIONS OF SOURCES

Abstracts of English Studies.   Urbana, Ill.: National Council of Teachers of English, 1958 to date. 9/yr. Tells you where to locate articles on all aspects of English literature in some 1500 journals. Each item is abstracted. NE25.A16   016.4

American Authors and Books   (William Burke). N.Y.: Crown, 1972. Self-contained short entries on authors, and titles with brief synopses and plots. Material listed in alphabetical order and limited to the United States. Z1224.B87   920.03

The American Novel: A Checklist of Twentieth Century Criticism   (Donna Gerstenberger). Denver: Swallow, 1961–1971. 2 vols. Arranged alphabetically by novelist. Lists criticism published about novelists and their work in a wide variety of sources. Be sure to check both volumes. The first covers criticism written between 1789 and 1959, the second between 1960 and 1968. Z1231.F4G4   016.81

Related Titles

The English Novel, 1578–1956: A Checklist of 20th Century Criticism. Denver: Swallow, 1959. Again arranged by author. Tells you where to find criticism in both books and periodicals. Z2014.F4B4   016.82

The Contemporary Novel: A Checklist of Critical Literature on the British and American Novel since 1945 (Irving Adelman). Metuchen, N.J.: Scarecrow, 1972. Arranged by author. Z1231.F4A34   016.82

The Continental Novel: A Checklist of Criticism in English, 1900–1966. Metuchen, N.J.: Scarecrow, 1968. Z5916.K4   016.80

Articles on American Literature (Lewis Leary). Durham, N.C.: Duke University Press, 1954, 1970. Tells you where to find material in periodicals and other bibliographies. Supplements the *MLA International bibliography.* Z1225.L492   016.8109

Related Titles

Bibliography of Bibliographies in American Literature. N.Y.: Bowker, 1970. Lists bibliographies by author, genre, and so on in books and in periodicals. Z1225.A1N5   016.016

See also *Literary History of the United States* (p. 135).

Author Series. A catch title for a series of individual works published by the H. W. Wilson Company of New York. They offer *self-contained* biographical material—usually one or two pages—on an author. Most essays include some criticism, and sometimes comments by the author. Each ends with a bibliography of works by and about the author. For contemporary authors, *see*

World Authors, 1950–1970.   1975. PN771.W86   920.03

Twentieth Century Authors.   1942. PN771.K86   920.03

Supplement.   1955. PN771.K86   920.03

For authors who generally wrote before the 20th century, see

American Authors, 1966–1900.   1938. PS21.K8   920.03

European Authors, 1000–1900.   1967. PN451.K8   920.03

British Authors Before 1800.   1952. PR451.K9   920.03

British   Authors   of   the   Nineteenth   Century.   1936.
PR451.K81936   920.03

Note: This series is indexed in *Biographical Dictionaries Master Index* and
in *Index to Wilson Author Series* (N.Y.: Wilson, 1976).

Authors: Critical and Biographical References   (Richard Combs). Metuchen, N.J.: Scarecrow, 1971. Tells you where to find critical and biographical
material about some 1500 authors in 500 or so books. Most of the emphasis
is on current criticism. PN524.C58   016.809

Related Title

American Writers: A Collection of Literary Biographies.   N.Y.:
Scribner's, 1974. 4 vols. About 100 essays with critical remarks about
writers and their places in literature. Bibliographies. PS129.A55   810

Familiar Quotations   (Bartlett, John), 14th ed. Boston: Little, Brown, 1968.
Arranged under name of author chronologically by earliest to latest author.
Index gives you entrance to quotation by subject, by key words in the quotation,
and by author. PN6081.B27   808.88

Related Title

Oxford Dictionary of Quotations,   2nd ed. N.Y.: Oxford, 1953.
Arranged by author, with detailed index. Standard title.
PN6081.09   808.88

Bibliography of American Literature   (Blanck, Jacob). New Haven: Yale,
1955–1973. 6 vols. Describes the works of about 300 U.S. writers from beginning of Federal period to those who died before the end of 1930. Arranged
alphabetically by author. Does not include periodical articles. Z1225.B55
016.01

Book Review Digest.   N.Y.: Wilson, 1905 to date, monthly. Tells you where
to find reviews in about 75 periodicals. Gives numerous self-contained excerpts
from reviews. You may use the excerpts without looking up the reviews. Cumulated index covers 1905 to 1974. Z1219.C95   028.1

Book Review Index.   Detroit: Gale, 1965 to date, bimonthly. Tells you
where to find reviews in about 300 periodicals. Listed alphabetically by author.
No title or subject index. Z1035.A1B6   028.1

Related Titles

Index to Book Reviews in the Humanities.   Detroit: Thomson, 1960 to date, annual. Includes art, biography, drama, literature. Z1035.A1I63   028.1

Index to Book Reviews in Historical Periodicals.   Metuchen, N.J.: Scarecrow, 1972 to date, annual. Lists reviews by author of book. Separate title index. Z6205.B75   016.909

Cambridge History of American Literature.   N.Y.: Putnam, 1917–1921. 4 vols. History up to about 1900. Dated, but important, particularly for early period. PS88.C3   810.9

Cambridge History of English Literature.   N.Y.: Putnam, 1907–1933. 15 vols. History up to the end of 19th century. Similar in purpose to American version. PR83.C22   820.9

Related Title

Literary History of England   (A. C. Baugh), 2nd ed. N.Y.: Appleton, 1967. A basic title, now dated, which traces history through 1939 in detailed essays. Bibliographic supplement. PR83.B3   820.9

Cassell's Encyclopedia of World Literature,   2nd ed. London: Cassell, 1973. 3 vols. Self-contained and in two parts. The first volume includes essays on history, themes, forms, and so on. The next two volumes are alphabetical by author; a few listings of literary works give plots and synopses. PN41C3 803

Related Titles

Columbia Dictionary of Modern European Literature.   N.Y.: Columbia, 1947. Biographies and survey articles of the literature. PN41.C6   803

Encyclopedia of World Literature in the 20th Century.   N.Y.: Ungar, 1967–1971. 3 vols. Biographies and survey articles. Volume 4 is index and supplement. PN774.U33   803

The Penguin Companion to World Literature.   N.Y.: McGraw-Hill, 1969–1971. 4 vols. Covers the U.S., England, the Orient, and Europe in separate volumes. PN41.P44   803

Celebrity Register.   N.Y.: Simon & Schuster, 1973. There is a photograph of each celebrity, a biographical sketch, and an essay that is long on what makes a celebrity, but sometimes short on fact. CT120.I46   920

Contemporary Literary Criticism.   Detroit: Gale, 1973 to date. Tells you where to find critical articles in books and periodicals about contemporary literature and authors. You may use it as a self-contained source, since it gives up to five excerpts of critical remarks. PN771.O59   809

Contemporary novelists   (James Vinson). N.Y.: St. Martin's, 1972. Brief biographical data followed by a bibliography of the author's work, the author's own comments, and a sometimes lengthy essay on the author by a contemporary scholar. PR737.V5   920.03

Contemporary Poets of the English Language.   Chicago: St. James, 1970. An extensive listing of major and minor poets with short biographical information. Z2014.P7C63   920

Related Title

> ***The concise encyclopedia of English and American***
> ***Poets***   (Stephen Spender). N.Y.: Hawthorn, 1963. Primarily
> biographical sketches, with some background about poetry.
> PR502.C8   821.003

Crowell's Handbook of Classical Literature   (Lillian Feder). N.Y.: Crowell, 1964. Dictionary of names, mythology, titles, and so on with summaries of classics. PA31.F4   880.3

Related Title

> ***Oxford Companion to Classical Literature.***   Oxford: Clarendon,
> 1937. Basic. Covers writers, subjects, institutions, and other aspects of
> Greek and Roman culture. DE5.H3   880.3

Contemporary Authors.   Detroit: Gale, 1962 to date, quarterly. Biographical data on current authors of every variety—including novelists, poets, playwrights, textbook writers, and journalists. Emphasis is on facts and career data. More important writers have an added essay on their work and place in literature. This is the place to look for current writers, particularly the popular and less famous. Z1224.C6   920.03

Current Book Review Citations.   N.Y.: Wilson, 1976 to date, monthly. Tells you where to find reviews in about 2000 periodicals. Reviews are listed alphabetically by author. No title or subject index. Often takes longer to list a review than the similar *Book Review Index.* Monthly issues have annual cumulation. Z1035.A1C86   016.0281

Dissertation Abstracts, International.   Ann Arbor, Mich.: University Microfilms, 1938 to date, monthly. Abstracts of dissertations completed in over 240 universities, not only in literature but also in most other fields—from mathematics to fine arts. First turn to the multiple-volume index set, which is divided by subjects. If you find a dissertation you think you could use, be sure to write down the full information, including the page number where you got the title, and take it to the librarian. The library may be able to borrow or purchase the dissertation on microfilm for your use. Z5055.U5A53   808

Dramatic Criticism Index   (Paul Breed). Detroit: Gale, 1972. Tells you where to find critical material about plays in about 600 books and 200 periodicals. Z5781.B8   016.8092

Related Titles

Drama Criticism   (Arthur Coleman). Denver: Swallow, 1966–1971. 2 vols. Interpretations from 1940 to mid-1960s of English, U.S., classical, and continental plays. Z1231.D7C6   016.8092

A Guide to Critical Reviews   (James Salem). Metuchen, N.J.: Scarecrow, 1966– various dates. Cites reviews of staged productions, not essays on history of plays. In this respect differs from other works listed here. Z1035.A1S3   016.8092

The New York Times Theater Reviews, 1920–1970.   N.Y.: N.Y. Times, 1971. 10 vols. Chronological reprinting of reviews with several indexes, including titles and names. PN1581.N4   792

American Drama Criticism: Interpretations.   Hamden, Conn.: Shoe String, 1967. Supplement, 1976. An index of criticism, listed by playwright. Supplement covers writings from 1969 to 1975. Z123.D7   016.792

Fiction catalog,   9th ed. N.Y.: Wilson, 1977. Annual supplements. Tells you where to find novels by author, by subject, and by form. Each entry gives you a summary of the plot and sometimes critical remarks in 100 to 300 words. Z519.W6   016.823

Related Titles

Historical Fiction   (Hannah Logasa), 9th ed. Ocean City, N.J.: McKinley, 1968. A classified list by subject with an author and title index. Some nonfiction. Z5917.H6L82   016.823

American Historical Fiction   (Arthur Dickinson), 3rd ed. Metuchen, N.J.: Scarecrow, 1971. Chronological arrangement with brief annotations. Author, title, and subject indexes. PS374.H5D5   016.813

Granger's Index to Poetry, 6th ed. N.Y.: Columbia, 1973. Tells you where to find a poem in one or more of 500 collections of poetry. A combined title and first-line index is followed by an author and subject index. A supplement, covering 1970-1977, was published in 1978. PN1021.G7 808.81

Index to Literary Biography. Metuchen, N.J.: Scarecrow, 1975. 2 vols. Tells you where to find biographical material on some 8000 authors of all countries and times. Indexes 50 works of both essay and data type. Z6511.H38 016.809

Library of Literary Criticism. N.Y.: Ungar, various dates. Excerpts from various critical reviews, essays, and so on about authors and their works. Includes novels, plays, nonfiction, and poetry. The extracts tend to be long; you may use them by themselves or to locate further criticism. Coverage is limited to U.S. and English writers. PR83.M73 820.9

Related Titles

> *Modern American Literature* (Dorothy Curley), 4th ed. N.Y.: Ungar, 1969. 3 vols. Supplement, 1976. 1 vol. PS221.C8 810.9
>
> *Modern British Literature* (Ruth Temple). N.Y.: Ungar, 1966. 3 vols. PR473.T4 820.9
>
> *Twentieth Century British Literature.* N.Y.: Ungar, 1968. Z2013.3T4 820.9

Literary History of the United States (Robert Spiller), 4th ed. N.Y.: Macmillan, 1974. 2 vols. One of the definitive histories of American literature. Each chapter is written by an expert and is complete through the 1960s. Covers not only authors and literature, but related areas such as cultural and historical activities. The second volume is a bibliography with a detailed index. Unfortunately little of this work has been updated since the 1963 edition. PS88.L522 810.9

MLA International Bibliography of Books and Articles on the Modern Languages and Literatures. Chicago: Modern Language Association, 1921 to date, annual. Tells you where to find critical material about authors, linguistics, literature, forms, periods of literature, and so on. Arranged by form and national literatures. The first volume includes England and the U.S. Z7006.M64 016.4

McGraw-Hill Encyclopedia of World Drama. N.Y.: McGraw-Hill, 1972. 4 vols. Survey of about 300 major world dramatists. Emphasis is on biography

and U.S. and English playwrights. Also includes criticism, plots, and synopses.
PN1625.M3   809.203

Related Titles

> ***Modern World Drama***   (Myron Matlaw). N.Y.: Dutton, 1972. Summary
> articles, authors, synopses, and drama in individual countries.
> PN1851.M36   809.203
>
> ***The Oxford Companion to the Theatre.***   N.Y.: Oxford, 1967. Covers
> all countries and periods of history. Emphasis on popular drama and
> actors. PN2035.H3   792.03

Masterplots   (Frank Magill), rev. ed. Englewood Cliffs, N.J.: Salem Press,
1976. 12 vols. Self-contained, basic title to find type of work, outline of setting,
characters, critique, summary of the plot or content, and "further critical evaluation of the work." Quite detailed; some descriptions run two or more pages.
Arranged by title with index by author. Covers 2000 basic titles with emphasis
on classics. PN44.M33   808.9
Note: Over the years this work has undergone many changes of format, names,
and publisher. See also *Masterpieces of World Literature in Digest Form* and
various other editions of *Masterplots*.
   Since 1954 there has been a *Masterplots Annual Volume*. Englewood
Cliffs, N.J.: Salem Press, 1954 to date. This volume includes 100 "outstanding"
books published in U.S., both fiction and nonfiction.

Related Titles

> ***Thesaurus of Book Digests***   (Hiram Haydn). N.Y.: Crown, 1949.
> Arranged by title with concise digest of world classics from ancient times to
> present. PN44.H38   808.8
>
> ***Reader's Digest of Books***   (Helen Keller). N.Y.: Macmillan, 1929.
> Primarily for works published before 1917. Short synopses of both fiction
> and nonfiction, from many countries and times. PN44.K4   808.8
>
> ***20th Century Plays in Synopses***   (Evert Sprinchorn). N.Y.: Crowell,
> 1965. Summaries, act by act, of U.S., English, and European plays.
> PN6112.S68   808.82
>
> ***Cyclopedia of Literary Characters***   (Frank Magill). N.Y.: Harper,
> 1964. Arranged by title of work. Gives main characters with brief
> descriptions. Author and character index. PN44.M3   803
>
> ***The New Theatre Handbook and Digest of Plays***   (Bernard Sobel),
> 8th ed. N.Y.: Crown, 1959. Includes, by title, digests of plays up to the
> 1950s. All periods and countries covered. Also has terms, biographies,
> and other entries. PN1625.S6   792.03

Monarch Literature Notes. N.Y.: Simon & Schuster, various dates. Self-contained series that you rarely find in a library, but you will discover in almost any bookstore. The 35- to 75-page paperback gives you the plot, background information, and criticism on a wide number of novels taught in basic English courses. Also, special notes are given over to an author. Many teachers frown on the use of these aids, but they are widely sold and just as widely known. You should use them with caution. PQ2603.E37

Related Title

> **Cliff Notes.** N.Y.: Cliff Publishing Co., various dates. Similar to the *Monarch Notes.* Various series include the *Cliff Notes, Twayne's U.S. Author Series,* and *Cliff Keynote Reviews.* PN44.C33   808

New Cambridge Bibliography of English Literature. London: Cambridge University Press, 1969–1975. 5 vols. Lists thousands of sources of information on English literature from the years 600 to 1950. The basic bibliography in the field. Z2011.N45   016.82

The New York Times Book Review. N.Y.: The New York Times, 1896 to date, weekly. Current book reviews. Look here when you can't find a review in *Book Review Index* or *Book Review Digest.* Z1032.N45   028.1

Related Titles

> Other sources of current reviews: *Time, Newsweek,* and subject magazines like *Psychology Today,* which carry reviews of the books in specific fields.
>
> Remember, too: book reviews are indexed in a separate section of the *Readers' Guide to Periodical Literature*—often before they show up in the standard indexes. Similar sections are in the other Wilson indexes.

Oxford Companion to American Literature (James Hart), 4th ed. N.Y.: Oxford, 1965. Short articles, essays, and data on many aspects of literature in the U.S. and Canada. Includes biographies of authors with their major works, summaries and plots of novels, stories, poems, and essays; definitions of literary terms; outlines of different forms of literature; history; and notes on related items, from printers and periodicals to literary awards. PS21.H3   810.3

Related Title

> **The Reader's Encyclopedia of American Literature.** N.Y.: Crowell, 1962. Longer articles on authors and literary history than in Oxford. PS21.R4   810.3

Oxford Companion to English Literature (Paul Harvey), 4th ed. N.Y.:

Oxford, 1967. Short articles, essays, and data on many aspects of English literature. Follows same plan as *Companion to American Literature.* PR19.H3   820.3

Play Index.   N.Y.: Wilson, 1953–1973. 4 vols. Tells you where to find plays in collections and single plays. Covers all types of plays from one-act to television works. Z5781.W48   808.82

Related Titles

Chicorel Theater Index to Plays in Anthologies, Periodicals, Discs and Tapes.   N.Y.: Chicorel, 1970. 3 vols. Supplements the *Play Index,* but includes periodicals, discs, and tapes. Z5781.C485   802.82

Index to Full Length Plays   (Norma Ireland). Boston: Faxon, 1965. Index to 154 collections and 800 individual plays by author, title, and subject. Z5781.T52   808.82

Index to Plays in Collections   (John Ottemiller). Metuchen, N.J.: Scarecrow, various editions. Indexes over 3000 plays by author and by title. Z4781.08   808.82

Plot Summary Index   (Carol Koehmstedt). Metuchen, N.J.: Scarecrow Press, 1973. Tells you where to locate plots in standard reference books. You look up novel, play, or poem by author or by title. For literature after 1970, use annual *Masterplots.* Z6514.P66K63   809

Poetry Explication   (Joseph Kuntz). Denver: Swallow, 1962. Tells you where to find criticism about poetry in a select list of books and periodicals. Dated, but still useful. Z2014.P7K8   809.1

Related Title

An Index to Criticism of British and American Poetry.   Metuchen, N.J.: Scarecrow, 1973. Indexes critical remarks in books and periodicals. PR89.C5   821

Princeton Encyclopedia of Poetry and Poetics.   Princeton, N.J.: Princeton University Press, 1974. Covers many aspects of poetry, but *no biographies* of poets. Entries range from short notes to detailed essays. Covers all periods and most countries. PN1021.E5   809.103

Related Title

Poetry Handbook   (Babette Deutsch), 4th ed. N.Y.: Funk & Wagnalls, 1974. A dictionary approach to poetry and its terms and history. PN44.5D4   808.1

Reader's Encyclopedia   (William Rose Benet), 2nd ed. N.Y.. Crowell, 1965. Self-contained dictionary approach to literature, authors (dead only), and related topics from mythology and musical compositions to definitions of literary terms. One of the best in the field. PN41.B4   803

Related Titles

Dictionary of Literary Terms   (Harry Shaw). N.Y.: McGraw-Hill, 1972. Describes about 2000 terms, often with illustrations. PN44.5S46   803

Handbook of Literature   (Clarence Holman), 3rd ed. Indianapolis: Odyssey, 1972. Offers clear explanation of terms, schools, movements, and so on in literature. PN41.H6   803

Short Story Index.   N.Y.: Wilson, 1953. Supplements, 1956–1974; Annual, 1976 to date. Tells you where to locate over 100,000 short stories in books and periodicals. Z5917.S5C6   808.83

Related Titles

Science Fiction Story Index,   1950–1968. Chicago: American Library Assn., 1971. Z5917.S36S5   808.83

Index to Fairy Tales, Myths and Legends.   Boston: Faxon, 1926. Supplement, 1937, 1952. Z5983.F17E2   398.2

Speech Index   (Roberta Sutton). Metuchen, N.J.: Scarecrow, 1966. *Supplement*, 1972. Tells you where to find famous speeches in collections from all periods. AI3.S85   808.85

The Home Book of Quotations,   (Stevenson, Burton). rev. ed. N.Y.: Dodd, 1967. Arranged by subject. A basic source along with Bartlett. Index gives you entrance to quotes by key words, author, and subject. PN6081.S73   808.88

Related Titles

Dictionary of Quotations   (Evans, Bergen). N.Y.: Delacorte, 1968. PN6081.E9   808.88

Oxford Dictionary of English Proverbs.   N.Y.: Oxford, 1970. PN6421.09   398.9

Home Book of Proverbs   (Stevenson, Burton). N.Y.: Macmillan, 1948. PN6405.S8   398.9

Twentieth Century Short Story Explication   (Warren S. Walker). Hamden, Conn.: Shoe String, 1967. *Supplements,* 1970–1973. Tells you where to find critical articles, books, and essays on short stories and their writers. Emphasis is on English language stories and criticism in books and periodicals. Z5917.S5W33   808.83

Related Title

> ***Short Fiction Criticism: A Checklist of Interpretations since 1925 of Stories and Novelettes, 1800–1958.***   Denver: Swallow, 1960. Precedes the above, taking the same approach to earlier cricitism of the short story. PN3326.T48   016.8093

Writer's Market.   Cincinnati: Writer's Digest, 1930 to date, annual. Tells you over 4000 periodicals that might buy your short story, poem, article, or other work. There is a 100-page section on book publishers which is less detailed. PN161.S83   808

Related Titles

> ***Literary Market Place.***   N.Y.: Bowker, 1940 to date, annual. Lists under various classifications publishers, book clubs, review services, agents, and so on. PN161.L5   870.5
>
> ***Writer's Handbook.***   Boston: The Writer, 1936 to date, annual. First three quarters on how to write to sell, last quarter on markets, with section on radio and television. PN127.W73   808
>
> ***International Directory of Little Magazines and Small Presses.*** Paradise, Ca.: Dustbooks, 1954 to date, annual. An alphabetical listing of small presses, as well as a geographical index. Best source of information for a place to publish poetry or avant-garde fiction. Z6944.L5   051
>
> ***The Writer and Writer's Digest.***   Periodicals that include sections in each issue on markets for selling articles, poetry, fiction, photographs, and so on. Both incorporate this information into their annual guides, *Writer's Market* and *Writer's Handbook* (above).

Chapter **12**

Science

Medicine

Many sources of medical information are too technical for the untrained reader. This section will steer you to a variety of reference sources. Take time to read the descriptions of the sources, so you know the degree of difficulty of the source you choose.

BASIC GUIDES

There are two basic guides in medicine, at opposite extremes of difficulty:

1. *Medical Reference Works* (John Blake). Chicago: Medical Library Assn., 1967. Supplements, various dates. A classified arrangement of books useful in libraries, most annotated. Too technical for the lay person. Z6658.B63   016.6

2. *Medical Books for the Lay Person* (Marilyn McLean). Boston: Boston Public Library, 1976. Tells you where to find about 300 books on various aspects of medicine and health. All of the titles are chosen for the nonexpert and cover such areas as diet, health, and exercise. Z6658.P5   016.61

CLASSIFICATION NUMBERS

In the Dewey Decimal system, books on medicine are numbered 610. In the Library of Congress system, look for them simply under R.

SUBJECT HEADINGS

You might look up nontechnical medical materials under these subject headings:

"Allergy"
"Birth control"
"Children—Care and hygiene"
"Drugs"
"Exercise"
"First aid"
"Medical care"
"Medicine"
"Medicine, popular"
"Nutrition"
"Physical education"
"Pregnancy"

CHART 3: QUESTIONS AND SOURCES OF ANSWERS IN MEDICINE

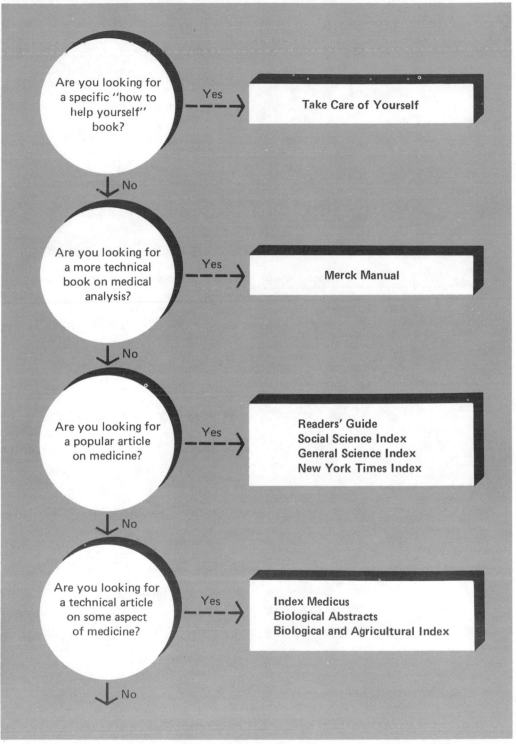

Are you looking for a specific "how to help yourself" book?

Yes → Take Care of Yourself

No

Are you looking for a more technical book on medical analysis?

Yes → Merck Manual

No

Are you looking for a popular article on medicine?

Yes → Readers' Guide
Social Science Index
General Science Index
New York Times Index

No

Are you looking for a technical article on some aspect of medicine?

Yes → Index Medicus
Biological Abstracts
Biological and Agricultural Index

No

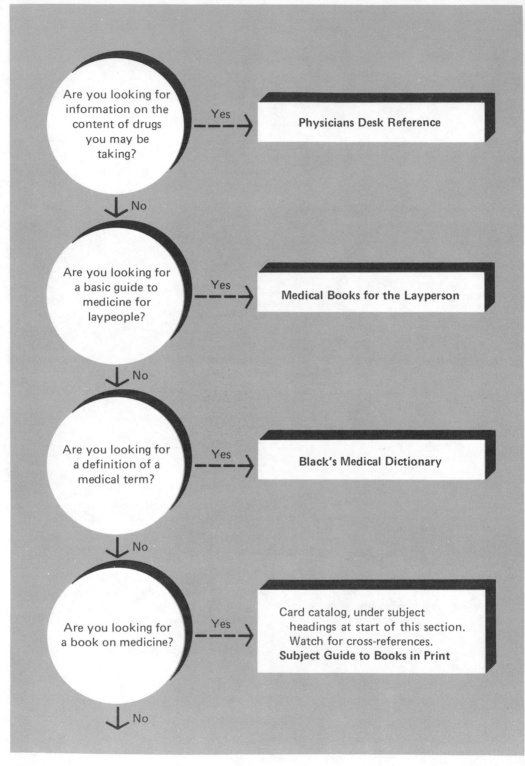

Are you looking for information on the content of drugs you may be taking?

Yes → **Physicians Desk Reference**

No ↓

Are you looking for a basic guide to medicine for laypeople?

Yes → **Medical Books for the Layperson**

No ↓

Are you looking for a definition of a medical term?

Yes → **Black's Medical Dictionary**

No ↓

Are you looking for a book on medicine?

Yes → Card catalog, under subject headings at start of this section. Watch for cross-references. **Subject Guide to Books in Print**

No ↓

144

See the librarian.

DESCRIPTIONS OF SOURCES

Black's Medical Dictionary. N.Y.: Barnes & Noble. A classic that has been used in libraries for over 75 years. Terms are clearly explained, and more technical information is avoided. R121.B598   610.3

Related Title

> ***Dorland's Illustrated Medical Dictionary.*** Philadelphia: Saunders, 1974. Frequently revised standard work, with particular emphasis on anatomy. Well illustrated. R121.D73   610.3

Index Medicus (National Library of Medicine). Washington, D.C.: U.S. Govt. Printing Office, 1960 to date, monthly. Tells you where to find material in over 3000 medical and related journals. Includes titles in English and other languages. Primarily for the expert, but you can use it to find basic materials. Try to choose articles that seem, by their titles and the periodicals in which they appear, to be of value to a lay person. Note: This famous service is available to you by computer. Ask your librarian for assistance. Z66660.I4   016.61

Merck Manual of Diagnosis and Therapy. Rahway, N.J.: Sharpe & Dohme, 1899 to date. A manual used by many physicians. While some of the language is technical, most of it is well within your reach. Gives basic symptoms and signs, diagnoses, analyses, and suggested treatments. Use it after you've exhausted the more popular titles, such as *Take Care of Yourself.* RC55.M4   616.075

Related Title

> ***Current Medical Diagnosis & Treatment*** (Marcus Krupp). Los Altos, Ca.: Lange, 1974. A frequently updated, standard guide for diagnosis and treatment. Primarily for the expert. RC55.C4   616.07

145

Physician's Desk Reference.   Oradell, N.J.: Medical Economics Co., 1947 to date, annual. Gives information on some 2500 drugs and products of drug manufacturers. You will find both the brand names and the generic names of drugs. A six-color section pictures and identifies over 1000 tablets and capsules. For physicians, but useful to you, although the first two related titles below may be more appropriate for everyday situations. QV772.P578   615

Related Titles

> ***Everyman's Guide to Drugs and Medicines.***   Washington, D.C.: Lucke, 1975. A lay guide to drugs, with numerous indexes. QV772.E56   615
>
> ***Good Housekeeping Guide to Medicine and Drugs.***   N.Y.: Hearst, 1977. Sound advice on various types of medicines and drugs. RC81.G7   616
>
> ***Merck Index: An Encyclopedia of Chemicals and Drugs.***   Rahway, N.J.: Sharpe & Dohme, various dates. A detailed description of substances, and 42,000 names of chemicals and drugs. Primarily for an expert. RS356.M524   615

Take Care of Yourself: A Consumer's Guide to Medical Care   (Donald M. Vickery). Reading, Mass.: Addison-Wesley, 1977. A self-contained, two-part work. The first section discusses medicine and health problems. The second part, an analysis of "common complaints," suggests steps you can take to treat yourself. RC81.V5   616

Related Titles

> ***Note:***   A group of reliable books on medicine for the lay person has been published since 1970. What follows are only two representative better titles.
>
> ***Our Bodies, Ourselves,***   2nd ed. N.Y.: Simon and Schuster, 1976. A classic title for women, which makes basic information easy to understand. HQ1426.B69   301.41
>
> ***Child Health Encyclopedia.***   N.Y.: Delacorte, 1975. An authoritative guide for parents, in nontechnical language. One of the best aids for parents. RJ26.C45   618.9

Science and Technology

Science and technology comprise a vast subject area. This section can help you find general information in many fields.

In any scientific or technological area, currency is of utmost importance. Usually it is best to begin with one of the many scientific indexes and abstracting services listed below. Many of these indexes and abstracts are now available by computer. Be sure to ask your librarian about computer searches, particularly when you are doing advanced work.

As currency is a major factor you should consider looking for material in such forms as reports, conference proceedings, and patents. Ask your librarian for assistance.

BASIC GUIDES

Most reference sources in this area are highly specialized. If you are doing more than superficial research, be sure to begin with one of these four guides:

1. *Scientific and Technical Information Sources* (Ching-chih Chen). Cambridge, Mass.: MIT Press, 1977. Close to 4000 current sources are annotated under 23 subjects. Good index. Most up-to-date of the literature guides. Z7401.C48   026

2. *Guide to Reference Books* (see p. 29), the "pure and applied sciences" section, pp. 691–830. Note that in each of the disciplines, from astronomy to zoology, you will find specific guides and bibliographies listed.

3. *Information Sources in Science and Technology* (C. C. Parker & R. V. Turley). London: Butterworth, 1975. For British readers, but an excellent general guide to research. A first choice, particularly for beginners. Q224.P37   507

4. *Science and Engineering Literature* (R. H. Malinowsky & Robert Gray), 2nd ed. Littleton, Colo.: Libraries Unlimited, 1976. A basic guide that stresses sources and practices in the U.S. Z7401.M28   016.5

Beyond these general guides are more specific guides, such as *The Use of Chemical Literature, Guide to the Literature of Mathematics,* and *The Use of Biological Literature.* You will find them listed and annotated in the four general guides.

CLASSIFICATION NUMBERS

Dewey Decimal System

If your library uses the Dewey Decimal classification system, you will find science and technology from 500 through 699. The basic divisions are:

510 Mathematics	610 Medical sciences
520 Astronomy and applied sciences	620 Engineering
530 Physics	630 Agriculture

540 Chemistry	640 Domestic arts and sciences
550 Earth sciences	650 Managerial services
560 Paleontology	660 Chemical
570 Life sciences	670 Manufacturers
580 Botanical Sciences	680 Miscellaneous manufacturers
590 Zoological sciences	690 Buildings

The surprise in this list is the 640s, which include home economics, cooking, clothing, and office and secretarial titles. The 620s include automobiles, boats and airplanes.

Library of Congress System

If your library uses the Library of Congress system, you will find science under Q, agriculture under S, and technology under T. TX is home economics (equivalent to 640).

SUBJECT HEADINGS

In science the chances of misunderstanding terminology are fewer than in the social sciences and humanities. Therefore, usually narrow down the subject. Instead of looking up "Mathematics," try "Algebra," "Calculus," "Geometry," or "Statistics."

For more general material, the most common headings are "Science," "Natural history," "Earth," "Ocean," "Evolution," "Life," and "Animals."

In technology, the most common headings you are likely to use may include "Manufacturing," "Automobiles," and "Buildings." You can also look under "Technology."

There are thousands of other subject headings. Again, look for the most precise term you associate with your subject. The odds are you will find that term as a subject heading.

OUTLINE OF SOURCES BY FORM

1. Atlases
   Atlas of the Universe
2. Biographical sources
   American Men and Women of Science
   A Biographical Dictionary of Scientists
3. Encyclopedias, yearbooks, handbooks, and dictionaries
   Dictionary of Biology

Dictionary of Technical Terms
McGraw-Hill Dictionary of Scientific and Technical Terms
McGraw-Hill Encyclopedia of Science and Technology
4. Indexes and abstracts
   Applied Science and Technology Index
   Biological and Agricultural Index
   General Science Index

CHART 4: QUESTIONS AND SOURCES OF ANSWERS IN SCIENCE AND TECHNOLOGY

General Information

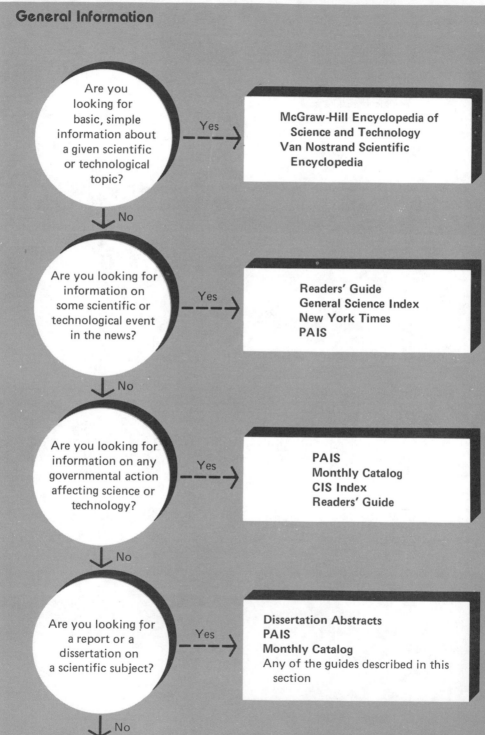

Are you looking for basic, simple information about a given scientific or technological topic?

Yes → McGraw-Hill Encyclopedia of Science and Technology
Van Nostrand Scientific Encyclopedia

No

Are you looking for information on some scientific or technological event in the news?

Yes → Readers' Guide
General Science Index
New York Times
PAIS

No

Are you looking for information on any governmental action affecting science or technology?

Yes → PAIS
Monthly Catalog
CIS Index
Readers' Guide

No

Are you looking for a report or a dissertation on a scientific subject?

Yes → Dissertation Abstracts
PAIS
Monthly Catalog
Any of the guides described in this section

No

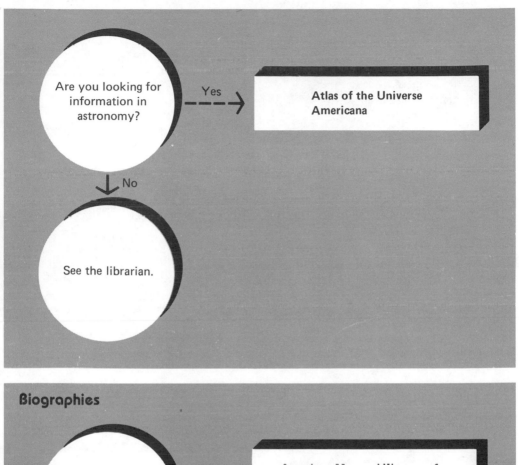

Are you looking for information in astronomy?

Yes → Atlas of the Universe
Americana

No ↓

See the librarian.

Biographies

Are you looking for brief data on a living scientist?

Yes → American Men and Women of
Science
Who's Who in America
Biographical Dictionaries Master
Index

No ↓

Are you looking for essay-length material on a living scientist?

Yes → Readers' Guide
General Science Index
Applied Science and Technology
Index
Current Biography
Biography Index
N.Y. Times Biographical Service

No ↓

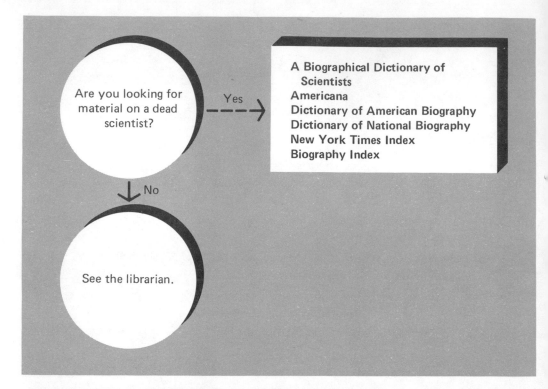

Are you looking for material on a dead scientist?

Yes →

A Biographical Dictionary of
   Scientists
Americana
Dictionary of American Biography
Dictionary of National Biography
New York Times Index
Biography Index

↓ No

See the librarian.

Current Literature[2]

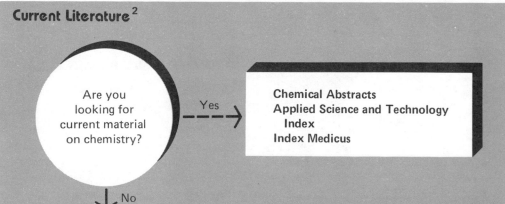

Are you looking for current material on chemistry?

Yes →

Chemical Abstracts
Applied Science and Technology
   Index
Index Medicus

↓ No

[2] Indexing and abstracting services are numerous in science and technology. This chart only represents a few of the questions and sources. Actually, almost any scientific or technological area has not only one, but several indexes and abstracts, which can be located in guides to the literature.

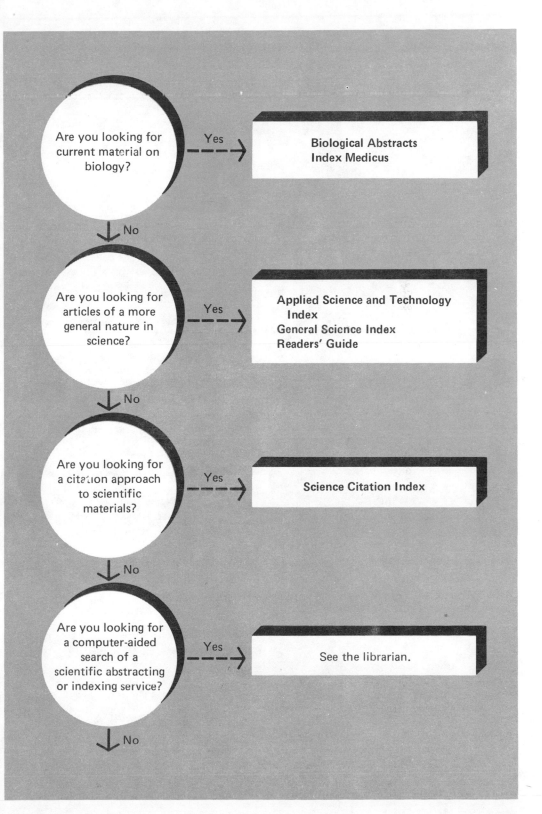

Are you looking for current material on biology?

Yes → Biological Abstracts / Index Medicus

No ↓

Are you looking for articles of a more general nature in science?

Yes → Applied Science and Technology Index / General Science Index / Readers' Guide

No ↓

Are you looking for a citation approach to scientific materials?

Yes → Science Citation Index

No ↓

Are you looking for a computer-aided search of a scientific abstracting or indexing service?

Yes → See the librarian.

No ↓

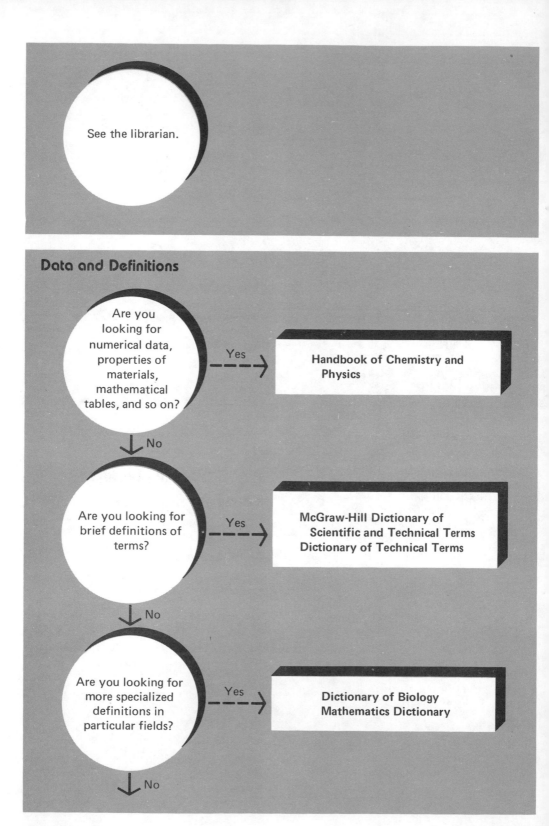

Data and Definitions

See the librarian.

Are you looking for numerical data, properties of materials, mathematical tables, and so on? — Yes → **Handbook of Chemistry and Physics**

↓ No

Are you looking for brief definitions of terms? — Yes → **McGraw-Hill Dictionary of Scientific and Technical Terms / Dictionary of Technical Terms**

↓ No

Are you looking for more specialized definitions in particular fields? — Yes → **Dictionary of Biology / Mathematics Dictionary**

↓ No

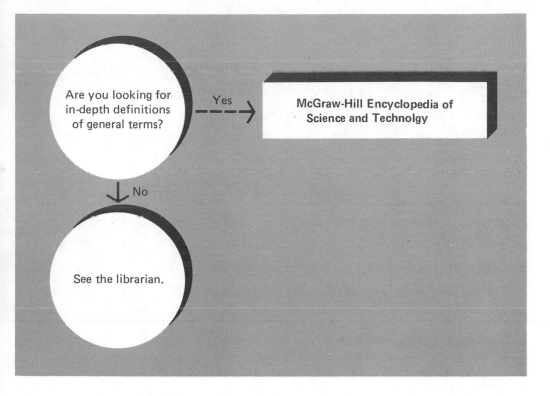

Are you looking for in-depth definitions of general terms?

Yes → McGraw-Hill Encyclopedia of Science and Technolgy

No → See the librarian.

DESCRIPTIONS OF SOURCES

American Men and Women of Science. N.Y.: Bowker, 1906 to date, various editions about every five years. Gives brief information about 110,000 individuals in the life sciences and physical sciences. Q141.A47   509

Applied Science and Technology Index. N.Y.: Wilson, 1913 to date, monthly. Tells you where to find articles on science and technology in about 300 periodicals. You will find aspects of science and technology including computers, energy, environment, food, oceanography, nuclear energy, transportation, and related subjects. Approach is by subject. *Note:* before 1958 this work was called the *Industrial Arts Index.* Z7913.I7   016.6

Related Titles

General Science Index.   (See p. 43).

Science Citation Index.   Philadelphia: ISI, 1961 to date, quarterly. Made up of a citation index, a source index, and a subject index. An approach to indexing that requires some experience to use; ask the librarian for help. Z7401.S365   016.5

Atlas of the Universe   (Patrick Moore). Skokie, Ill.: Rand McNally, 1970. A basic title that charts the universe, with photographs, diagrams, charts, and other illustrations. Articles at a popular level introduce or are part of the several sections. QB44.M54   523.2

Related Title

Encyclopedia of Astronomy.   N.Y.: St. Martin's, 1971. A dictionary approach, with long and short articles as well as numerous biographical sketches. QB14.S28   520.3

A *Biographical Dictionary of Scientists*   (Williams, Trevor), 2nd ed. N.Y.: Wiley, 1974. Gives brief entries (300 to 600 words) on about 1000 scientists around the world. All are dead. Q141.W62   509

Related Title

Dictionary of Scientific Biography.   N.Y.: Scribner's, 1971 to date. Essays on about 5000 international scientists. Q141.D5   509

Biological and Agricultural Index.   N.Y.: Wilson, 1964 to date, monthly. Tells you where to find material in about 185 periodicals on agriculture and biology. Among the numerous topics you will find covered here: botany, conservation, ecology, food science, forestry, genetics, nutrition, physiology, and veterinary medicine. *Note*: From 1948 to 1962 this work was called *Agricultural Index.* Z5073.A46   630.5

Related Titles

Bibliography of Agriculture   (U.S. National Agricultural library). N.Y.: Macmillan, 1942 to date, monthly. A service for experts that covers the literature of agriculture and allied sciences. Z5071.U58   016.63

Biological Abstracts.   Philadelphia: Biological Abstracts, 1926 to date, semimonthly. A service for experts that covers more than 5000 periodicals. Available by computer. Ask your librarian for assistance. QH301.B37   570.5

Chemical Abstracts.   Columbus, Ohio: American Chemical Society, 1907 to date, weekly. Tells you where to find material on chemistry and related disciplines in over 14,000 serials. Detailed indexing and abstracts. There are numerous parts to this service, and it requires a basic understanding of chemistry as well as of the service itself. You will need assistance, at least when you begin using the service. Also available by computer. QD1.A51   540

Dictionary of Biology   (Michael Abercrombie), 6th ed. Baltimore: Penguin, 1966. Supplement. Includes terms for botany, zoology, genetics, anatomy, and related subjects. Check the numerous abbreviations employed in the front of the dictionary. Generally easy. QH13.A25   574.03

Dictionary of Technical Terms   (F. S. Crispin), 11th ed. N.Y.: Bruce, 1970. A dictionary for the lay person. T9.C885   603

Handbook of Chemistry and Physics.   Cleveland: Chemical Rubber Co., 1913 to date, annual. Basic handbook used in many of the sciences. Updated about once a year, it includes several sections from mathematical tables to tables of properties. Presupposes some knowledge of science. QD65.H3   530

McGraw-Hill Encyclopedia of Science and Technology,   4th ed. N.Y.: McGraw-Hill, 1977, 15 vols. A basic set for lay persons. A beginning point for any in-depth study of science or technology. Updated by an annual yearbook. Q121.M3   503

Related Title

   Van Nostrand's Scientific Encyclopedia,   5th ed. N.Y.: Van Nostrand Reinhold, 1976. The standard one volume work with some 7,200 entries of various length. Q121.V3   503

McGraw-Hill Dictionary of Scientific and Technical Terms.   N.Y.: McGraw-Hill, 1974. Definitions of about 100,000 terms in lay language. Close to 3000 illustrations. Q123.M15   503

Mathematics Dictionary   (Glenn James and Robert C. James), 3rd ed. Princeton: Van Nostrand, 1968. Not only includes definitions, but features tables, formulas, mathematical symbols, and so on. Covers the whole of pure and applied mathematics. QA5.J32   510.3

Chapter **13**

Social Sciences

General Information

Many subjects fall under the social sciences. We shall take a broad, general look, and then devote separate parts of this chapter to nine of the subjects: Afro-Americans, business and economics, current events, education, history, political science, psychology, sociology, and women.

BASIC GUIDES

The basic guide to the social sciences is *Sources of Information in the Social Sciences* (see p. 162). In it you will find guides to each of the disciplines, such as history. See also *Guide to Reference Books* (p. 29), which devotes pp. 429–597 to the social sciences. When you are looking for annotated listings of indexes, bibliographies, encyclopedias, and so on, you should turn to either of these guides.

CLASSIFICATION NUMBERS AND SUBJECT HEADINGS

In the Dewey Decimal system, all the subjects in the social sciences fall into the 300s. General works belong between 300 and 310. In the Library of Congress system, general works on the social sciences are under H.

For the most general questions in the social sciences, you should look up the headings "Social sciences," "Social change," or "U.S.—Social conditions."

CHART 5: QUESTIONS AND SOURCES OF ANSWERS IN SOCIAL SCIENCES—GENERAL INFORMATION

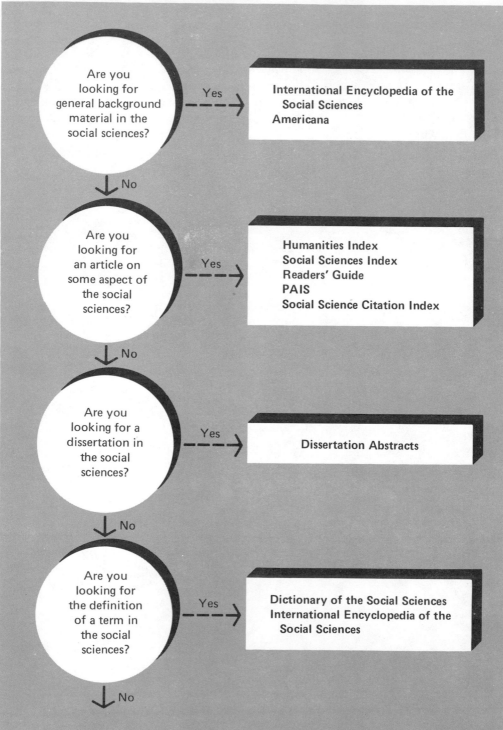

Are you looking for general background material in the social sciences?

Yes →

International Encyclopedia of the Social Sciences
Americana

↓ No

Are you looking for an article on some aspect of the social sciences?

Yes →

Humanities Index
Social Sciences Index
Readers' Guide
PAIS
Social Science Citation Index

↓ No

Are you looking for a dissertation in the social sciences?

Yes →

Dissertation Abstracts

↓ No

Are you looking for the definition of a term in the social sciences?

Yes →

Dictionary of the Social Sciences
International Encyclopedia of the Social Sciences

↓ No

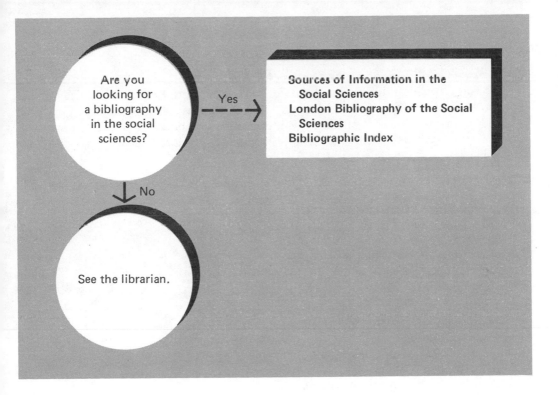

Are you looking for a bibliography in the social sciences?

Yes → Sources of Information in the Social Sciences
London Bibliography of the Social Sciences
Bibliographic Index

No → See the librarian.

DESCRIPTIONS OF SOURCES

A Dictionary of the Social Sciences (Julius Gould). N.Y.: Free Press, 1964. Full definitions of sometimes hard-to-find terms in sociology, political science, economics, social psychology, and social anthropology. H41.G6   303

London Bibliography of the Social Sciences. London: Mansell, 1931 to date, irregularly. A basic title for serious research, not for the casual reader. Covers the holdings of London libraries. Material is arranged by subject, with numerous cross-references. Z7161.L84   016.3

Social Sciences Citation Index. Philadelphia: ISI, 1973 to date, three/year. Tells you where to find articles, reviews, and so on in over 2000 journals. You may find the system of indexing difficult to use. Patterned after *Science Citation Index* (p. 155), it presupposes you have the name of one or more authorities in your field. Looking up that name in the citation index, you find others who cited your expert. Their articles can be run down in the source index. There is a subject index of significant words. Although this system takes time to get used to, it is a vast improvement over many indexes. If you are deeply involved with research in the social sciences, try to learn to use this index. Ask your librarian for assistance. Z7161.S65   016.3

Sources of Information in the Social Sciences   (Carl White), 2nd ed. Chicago: American Library Assn., 1973. Tells you where to find basic titles in the literature of the social sciences. Each of the titles usually is annotated. Furthermore, the nine sections begin with discursive introductions, and there are many notes in the subsections. The first place to turn for an overview of the subject area. Z7161.W49   016.3

Afro-Americans[1]

BASIC GUIDES

There are four basic guides to material about Afro-Americans:

1. *The Negro in America* (Mary L. Fisher), 2nd ed. Cambridge, Harvard University Press, 1970. Due for revision, this work is a subject listing of basic books and periodical articles. Z1361.N39M5   016.917

2. *Blacks in America.* Garden City, N.Y.: Doubleday, 1971. Combines essays and bibliographies under some 100 subject headings. Name and subject index. Z1361.N39B56   016.917

3. *An Annotated Guide to Basic Reference Books on the Black American Experience.* Wilmington, Del.: Scholarly Resources, 1974. An annotated listing of some 200 basic works for Afro-American studies. Z1039.N4W47

4. *The Negro in the United States* (Dorothy Porter). Washington, D.C.: Library of Congress, 1970. Close to 2000 titles listed by broad subject, with a detailed subject index. Z1361.N39P   016.9173

CLASSIFICATION NUMBERS AND SUBJECT HEADINGS

In the Dewey Decimal system, Afro-American studies are classified 301.45. In the Library of Congress system, they are E185 and Z1361.

Some representative subject headings begin with "Black": "Black artists," "Black bankers," "Black women," "Black youth," and so on. Other headings begin with "Negro": "Negroes—Civil rights," "Negroes—In literature," "Negroes—Social conditions," and so on. You might also look under "Slavery in the U.S.," "U.S.—Armed forces—Blacks," and "U.S.—Race relations."

---

[1] Some libraries may use the designations "Negroes" or "Blacks."

CHART 6: QUESTIONS AND SOURCES OF ANSWERS ABOUT AFRO-AMERCIANS

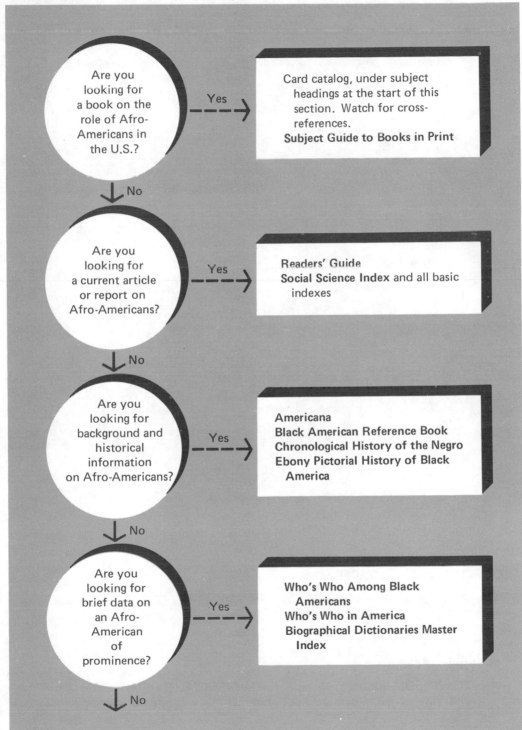

Are you looking for a book on the role of Afro-Americans in the U.S.?

Yes →

Card catalog, under subject headings at the start of this section. Watch for cross-references.
Subject Guide to Books in Print

No ↓

Are you looking for a current article or report on Afro-Americans?

Yes →

Readers' Guide
Social Science Index and all basic indexes

No ↓

Are you looking for background and historical information on Afro-Americans?

Yes →

Americana
Black American Reference Book
Chronological History of the Negro
Ebony Pictorial History of Black America

No ↓

Are you looking for brief data on an Afro-American of prominence?

Yes →

Who's Who Among Black Americans
Who's Who in America
Biographical Dictionaries Master Index

No ↓

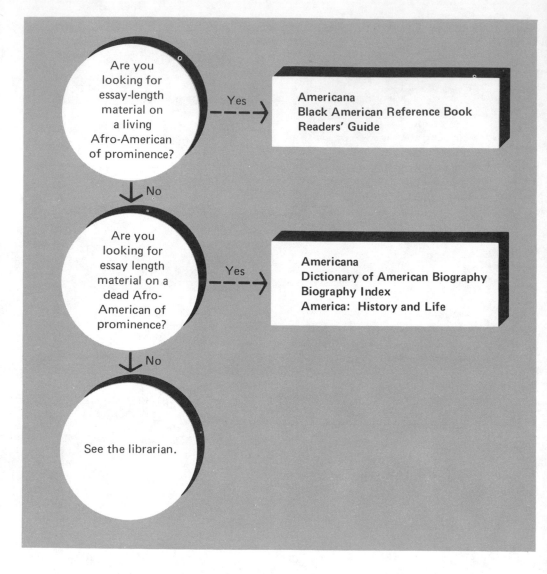

Are you looking for essay-length material on a living Afro-American of prominence?

Yes →

Americana
Black American Reference Book
Readers' Guide

No ↓

Are you looking for essay length material on a dead Afro-American of prominence?

Yes →

Americana
Dictionary of American Biography
Biography Index
America: History and Life

No ↓

See the librarian.

DESCRIPTIONS OF SOURCES

The Black American Reference Book.   Englewood Cliffs, N.J.: Prentice-Hall, 1976. Essays and short articles on numerous aspects of black history. One of the best of its type. E185.D25   301.451

Related Titles

The Negro Almanac.   N.Y.: Bellwether, 1967 to date, biennial. Covers both history and current events. Numerous biographical sketches. E185.P55   973

The Ebony Handbook. Chicago: Johnson, 1974. Divided into 20 sections covering both current and historical events and personalities. E185.D25   917.3

The Chronological History of the Negro in America. N.Y.: Harper, 1969. Badly arranged and not too accurate, but it does provide a running account of contributions of the blacks to the U.S. from 1492 through 1968. E185.B46   973

Related Title

Famous First Facts about Negroes (R. B. Garrett). N.Y.: Arno Press, 1972. A topical approach, with a detailed subject and name index. E185.G22   301.45

Ebony Pictorial History of Black America. Nashville, Tenn.: Southwestern, 1971–1973. 4 vols. Combines pictures and minimal text to trace the history of Afro-Americans from Africa up to 1973. Good illustrations and an easy text. E185.E23   973

Related Title

The Negro in American History. Chicago: Britannica, 1972. 3 vols. A collection of original documents from 1567 to 1971. Augments *Annals of America.* E185.N4   973

Who's Who Among Black Americans. Northbrook, Ill.: Who's Who, 1976 to date, biennial. Data on prominent black men and women. Includes an index of names by state and by profession. E185.96.W54   920

Business and Economics

BASIC GUIDES

You will find four basic guides to business and economics:

1. *Business Information Sources* (Lorna Daniels). Berkeley: University of California Press, 1976. Guide to basic reference sources in business with chapters on various forms and types of titles, which you would find useful in any extended study of business or economics. This work updates, but does not replace, Coman. Z7164.C81   016.33

2. *Sources of Business Information* (Coman, Edwin), rev. ed. Berkeley: University of California Press, 1964. Both a bibliography and a manual. A classic in the field and still useful. Z7164.C81C   016.65

3. *Guide to Reference Books* (see p. 29), section on economics and business, pp. 497–530.

4. *Sources of Information in the Social Sciences* (see p. 162), section on economics and business administration, pp. 181–242.

CLASSIFICATION NUMBERS AND SUBJECT HEADINGS

In the Dewey Decimal system, business and economics materials are divided under these numbers:

330 Economics
380 Commerce
650 Managerial services
670 Manufacturers
680 Miscellaneous manufacturers
690 Buildings

In the Library of Congress system, you must look under these letters:

HB Economic theory
HC Economic history
HG Finance
HJ Public finance
TS Manufacturers

You can look up the subject headings "Business" and "Economics," but try to think of a more precise heading. "Accounting," "Commerce," "Industry," "Investment," "Trade," and "U.S.—Economic conditions" are representative headings.

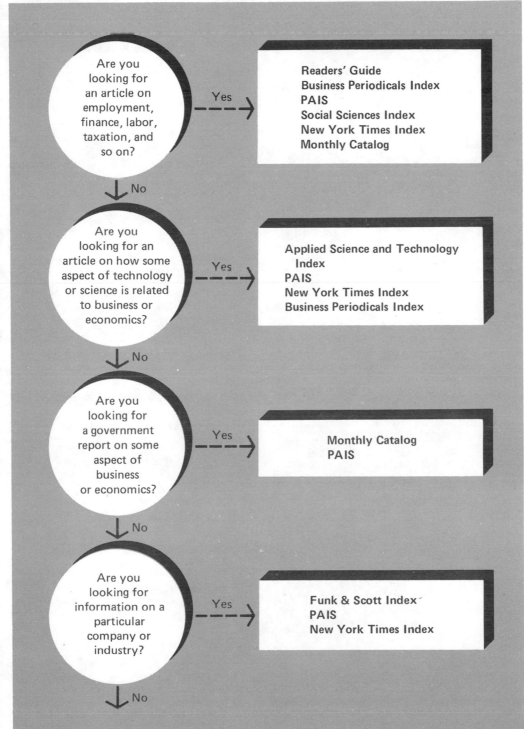

Are you looking for an article on employment, finance, labor, taxation, and so on?

Yes →

Readers' Guide
Business Periodicals Index
PAIS
Social Sciences Index
New York Times Index
Monthly Catalog

↓ No

Are you looking for an article on how some aspect of technology or science is related to business or economics?

Yes →

Applied Science and Technology Index
PAIS
New York Times Index
Business Periodicals Index

↓ No

Are you looking for a government report on some aspect of business or economics?

Yes →

Monthly Catalog
PAIS

↓ No

Are you looking for information on a particular company or industry?

Yes →

Funk & Scott Index
PAIS
New York Times Index

↓ No

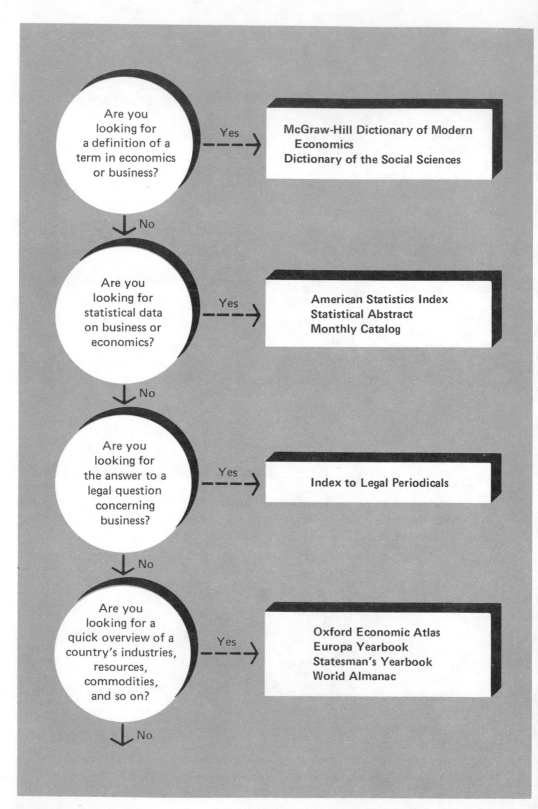

Are you looking for a definition of a term in economics or business? — Yes → McGraw-Hill Dictionary of Modern Economics
Dictionary of the Social Sciences

No ↓

Are you looking for statistical data on business or economics? — Yes → American Statistics Index
Statistical Abstract
Monthly Catalog

No ↓

Are you looking for the answer to a legal question concerning business? — Yes → Index to Legal Periodicals

No ↓

Are you looking for a quick overview of a country's industries, resources, commodities, and so on? — Yes → Oxford Economic Atlas
Europa Yearbook
Statesman's Yearbook
World Almanac

No ↓

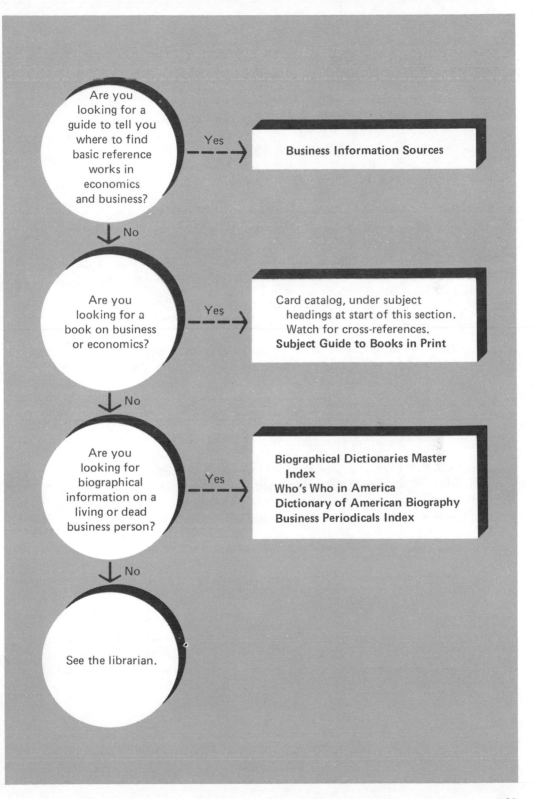

Are you looking for a guide to tell you where to find basic reference works in economics and business?

Yes → **Business Information Sources**

No ↓

Are you looking for a book on business or economics?

Yes → Card catalog, under subject headings at start of this section. Watch for cross-references. **Subject Guide to Books in Print**

No ↓

Are you looking for biographical information on a living or dead business person?

Yes → **Biographical Dictionaries Master Index**
Who's Who in America
Dictionary of American Biography
Business Periodicals Index

No ↓

See the librarian.

169

DESCRIPTIONS OF SOURCES

American Statistics Index. Washington, D.C.: Congressional Information Service, 1973 to date. Annual with monthly supplements. An index to statistics found in government publications only, not in other sources. Here you will find references to data on such matters as population, housing, employment, earnings, health, and education. The service is available for search by computer. Ask the librarian for assistance until you get used to the system. Z7554.U5A46   016.31

Business Periodicals Index. N.Y.: Wilson, 1958 to date, monthly. Covers not only business but also related subjects including economics, finance, investments, insurance, labor, marketing, and taxation. You can find most of what you need under a subject or under the name of the corporation or company. Z7164.C81   016.33

Related Titles

F & S Index of Corporations and Industries. Detroit: Funk & Scott, 1960 to date, weekly. Arranged by industry or subject. For detailed research. Z7164.C81F13   016.33

Wall Street Journal Index. N.Y.: Dow Jones, 1959 to date, monthly. Index in two parts: by company name and by general subjects. HG1.W26   332

McGraw-Hill Dictionary of Modern Economics, 2nd ed. N.Y.: McGraw-Hill, 1973. A dictionary for the lay person. The first part gives you direct, simple definitions to modern economic terms. The second, shorter section lists organizations in economics and marketing. HB61.M16   330

Related Title

Dictionary of Economics (Harold Sloan), 5th ed. N.Y.: Barnes & Noble, 1971. Wide coverage of economics and business. HB61.S54   330.3

Oxford Economic Atlas of the World, 4th ed. London: Oxford, 1972. In two parts. The first section divides the world into 13 subjects from crops to demography. The second is a statistical supplement arranged by country. While dated, still useful to locate quickly the primary industries, commodities, resources, and so on of a country or region. G1046.G1092   912

Current Events

This section will help you find information about major events, personalities, and other aspects of the news. The emphasis is on events in the U.S.

There are no guides to daily events, although once the day becomes history you can turn to the guides outlined in the history section, or in other sections whose subjects relate to the event.

By definition, there are no books (and therefore no subject headings in the card catalog) that are really current. With a few exceptions, a book will not be published on an event until months, or even years later.

You should rely primarily upon newspapers and magazines (as well as on some current government documents and reports) when you are looking for material on current happenings.

OUTLINE OF SOURCES BY FORM

1. Current surveys
   Facts on File
2. Encyclopedias
   International Encyclopedia of the Social Sciences
3. Indexes to government-published materials
   CIS Index
   Index to U.S. Government Periodicals
   Monthly Catalog of U.S. Government Publications
4. Indexes to newspapers
   New York Times Index
5. Indexes to periodicals
   Index to Legal Periodicals
   PAIS

CHART 8: QUESTIONS AND SOURCES OF ANSWERS IN CURRENT EVENTS

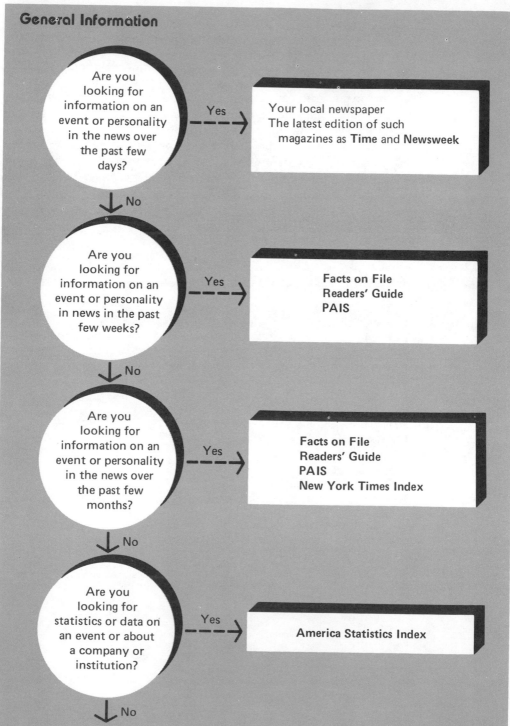

General Information

Are you looking for information on an event or personality in the news over the past few days? — Yes → Your local newspaper / The latest edition of such magazines as **Time** and **Newsweek**

No ↓

Are you looking for information on an event or personality in news in the past few weeks? — Yes → **Facts on File** / **Readers' Guide** / **PAIS**

No ↓

Are you looking for information on an event or personality in the news over the past few months? — Yes → **Facts on File** / **Readers' Guide** / **PAIS** / **New York Times Index**

No ↓

Are you looking for statistics or data on an event or about a company or institution? — Yes → **America Statistics Index**

No ↓

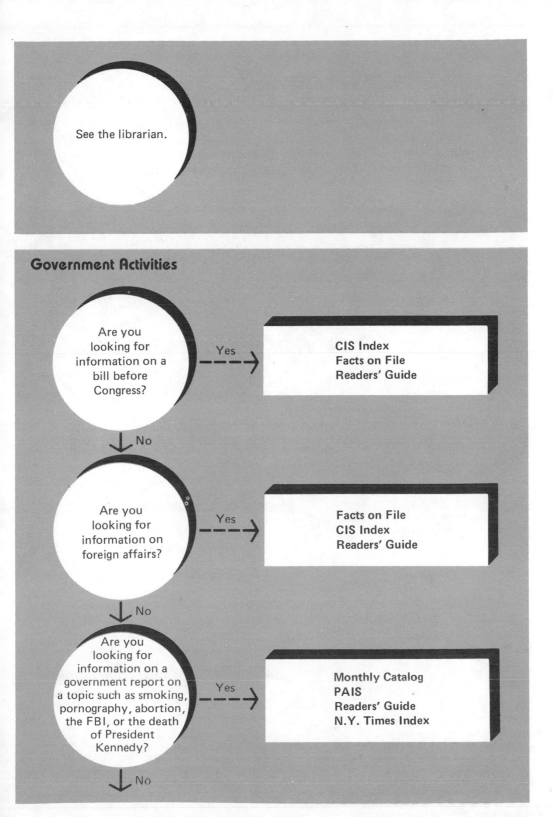

See the librarian.

Government Activities

Are you looking for information on a bill before Congress?

Yes → CIS Index
Facts on File
Readers' Guide

No ↓

Are you looking for information on foreign affairs?

Yes → Facts on File
CIS Index
Readers' Guide

No ↓

Are you looking for information on a government report on a topic such as smoking, pornography, abortion, the FBI, or the death of President Kennedy?

Yes → Monthly Catalog
PAIS
Readers' Guide
N.Y. Times Index

No ↓

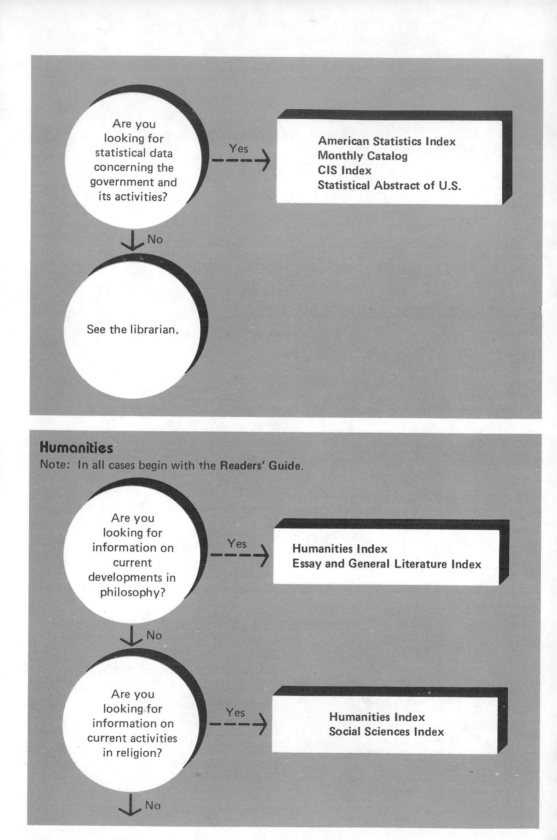

Are you looking for statistical data concerning the government and its activities?

Yes → American Statistics Index
Monthly Catalog
CIS Index
Statistical Abstract of U.S.

No

See the librarian.

Humanities

Note: In all cases begin with the **Readers' Guide.**

Are you looking for information on current developments in philosophy?

Yes → Humanities Index
Essay and General Literature Index

No

Are you looking for information on current activities in religion?

Yes → Humanities Index
Social Sciences Index

No

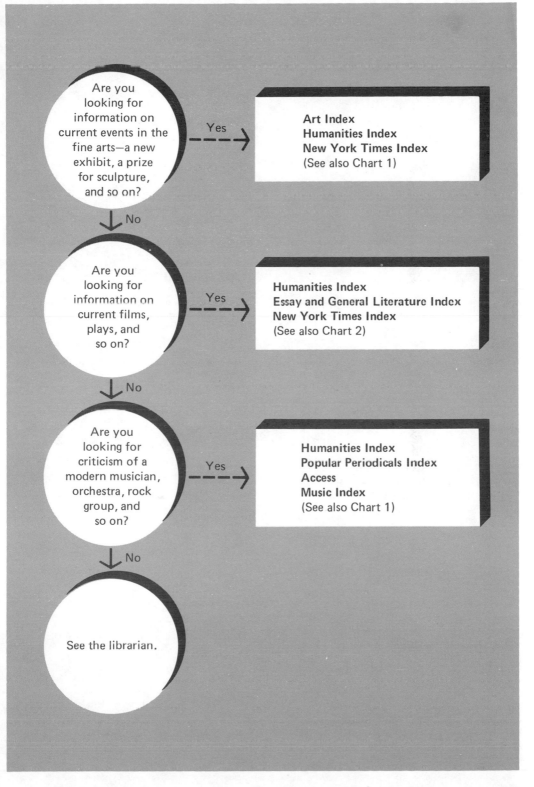

Are you looking for information on current events in the fine arts—a new exhibit, a prize for sculpture, and so on?

Yes →

Art Index
Humanities Index
New York Times Index
(See also Chart 1)

No ↓

Are you looking for information on current films, plays, and so on?

Yes →

Humanities Index
Essay and General Literature Index
New York Times Index
(See also Chart 2)

No ↓

Are you looking for criticism of a modern musician, orchestra, rock group, and so on?

Yes →

Humanities Index
Popular Periodicals Index
Access
Music Index
(See also Chart 1)

No ↓

See the librarian.

Science

Note: In all cases begin with the **Readers' Guide**. See also Chart 4.

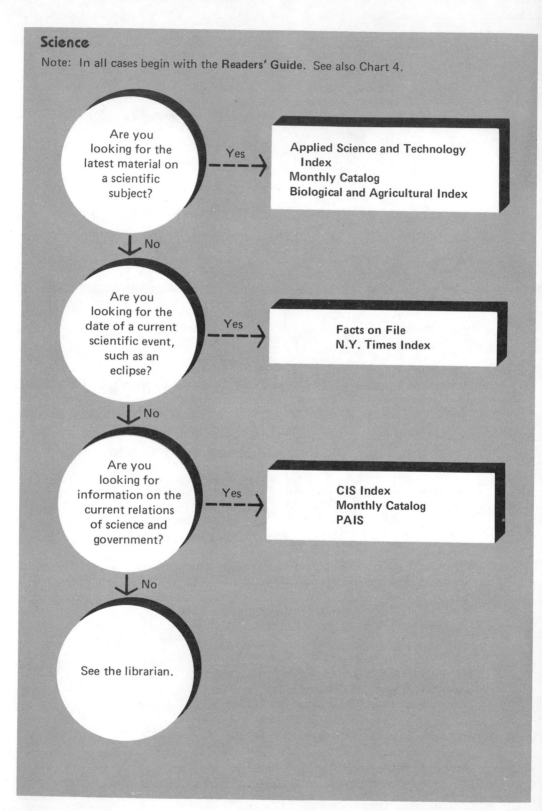

Are you looking for the latest material on a scientific subject?

Yes → **Applied Science and Technology Index**
Monthly Catalog
Biological and Agricultural Index

↓ No

Are you looking for the date of a current scientific event, such as an eclipse?

Yes → **Facts on File**
N.Y. Times Index

↓ No

Are you looking for information on the current relations of science and government?

Yes → **CIS Index**
Monthly Catalog
PAIS

↓ No

See the librarian.

Social Conditions and Issues

Note: In almost all cases begin with the **Readers' Guide**. See also Chart 13.

Are you looking for current articles on a social question in the U.S.—drugs, welfare, prisons, alcoholism?

Yes ----→

Readers' Guide
Social Science Index
PAIS
New York Times Index
Monthly Catalog

↓ No

Are you looking for the psychological aspects of a social problem?

Yes ----→

Psychological Abstracts
Education Index
(See also Chart 12)

↓ No

Are you looking for an overview of a U.S. social problem?

Yes ----→

International Encyclopedia of
Social Sciences
Americana
Social Sciences Index

↓ No

See the librarian.

Social Sciences

Note: In most cases begin with the **Readers' Guide**. See also Chart 5.

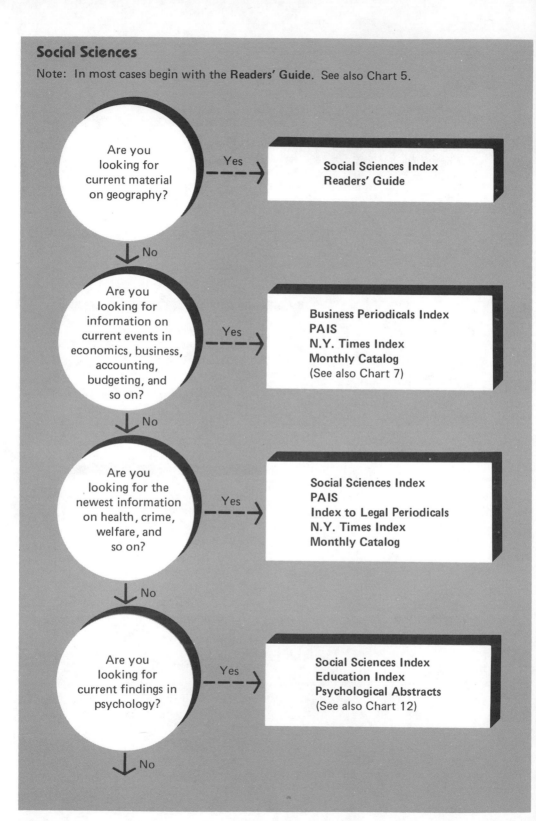

Are you looking for current material on geography?

Yes →

Social Sciences Index
Readers' Guide

↓ No

Are you looking for information on current events in economics, business, accounting, budgeting, and so on?

Yes →

Business Periodicals Index
PAIS
N.Y. Times Index
Monthly Catalog
(See also Chart 7)

↓ No

Are you looking for the newest information on health, crime, welfare, and so on?

Yes →

Social Sciences Index
PAIS
Index to Legal Periodicals
N.Y. Times Index
Monthly Catalog

↓ No

Are you looking for current findings in psychology?

Yes →

Social Sciences Index
Education Index
Psychological Abstracts
(See also Chart 12)

↓ No

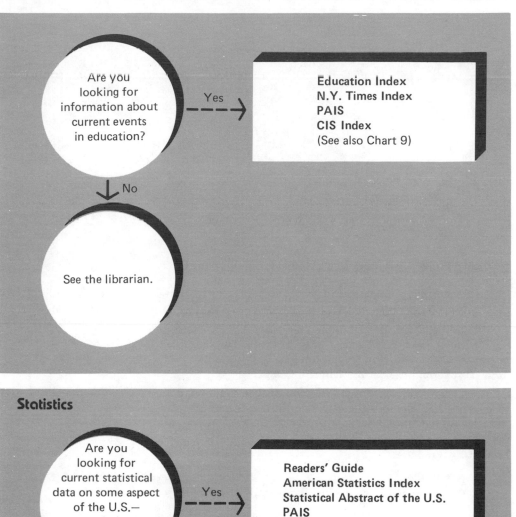

Are you looking for information about current events in education?

Yes →
Education Index
N.Y. Times Index
PAIS
CIS Index
(See also Chart 9)

No ↓

See the librarian.

Statistics

Are you looking for current statistical data on some aspect of the U.S.—population, politics, economics, and so on?

Yes →
Readers' Guide
American Statistics Index
Statistical Abstract of the U.S.
PAIS
Monthly Catalog
CIS Index

No ↓

Are you looking for general statistical data on population, religion, economics, and so on?

Yes →
World Almanac
Readers' Guide
PAIS

No ↓

See the librarian.

DESCRIPTIONS OF SOURCES

CIS/Index (Index to Publications of the United States Congress). Washington: Congressional Information Service, 1970 to date, monthly. Tells you where to find information on Congressional activities. Most of the material is abstracted. *Note*: Most large libraries have all of the indexed reports readily available on microform, and some even have the index itself available by computer search. You should ask for assistance, in any case.

The index is cumulated into *CIS/Annual* with abstracts in the first volume and an index by subject, titles, bill reports, names, and so on in the second volume. KF49.C62   348

Related Title

CQ Weekly Report. Washington: Congressional Quarterly, 1945 to date, weekly. A current summary of activities in government. JK1.C15   328.73

Facts on File. N.Y.: Facts on File, 1940 to date, weekly. Self-contained basic source for locating short descriptive notes on current events, particularly in the U.S. Valuable because it is almost on time; it is in the library usually the week after the events. Useful, too, to establish dates and names. (From there go to the *New York Times Index* or the *Readers' Guide* or other indexes for additional data.) In loose-leaf form. Every two issues there is a cumulative index. D410.F3   909.82

Related Titles

Keesing's Contemporary Archives. London: Keesing, 1931 to date, weekly. The English equivalent of *Facts on File*. D410.K4   909.8

News Dictionary. N.Y.: Facts on File, 1974 to date, annual. A condensation of *Facts on File* to cover the previous year. D410   909.82

Yearbooks for any of the basic encyclopedias from *Britannica* to *World Book.* Each is a compilation of the year's past events, like *News Dictionary,* but considerably more detailed.

Index to Legal Periodicals.   N.Y.: Wilson, 1908 to date, monthly. Tells you where to find material about law in close to 400 publications, including periodicals, yearbooks, annual institutes, and reviews. Z6453.I38   016.34

Index to U.S. Government Periodicals.   Chicago: Infordata, 1974 to date, quarterly. Tells you where to find information in 120 or so government periodicals. Useful as a supplement to *PAIS* and the *Social Science Index* when you are looking up any subject that has a bearing on government. Z1223.Z9I5   016.015

International Encyclopedia of the Social Sciences.   N.Y.: Macmillan, 1968. 17 vols. Best source for information on any of the social sciences from anthropology and geography to law and sociology. Articles are by experts and are excellent overviews. Biographical articles and a good index. Based upon the earlier **Encyclopedia of the Social Sciences**, which you will still find useful for additional historical material. A40.A2I5   303

Monthly Catalog of U.S. Government Publications.   Washington, D.C.: U.S. Govt. Printing Office, 1895 to date, monthly. Tells you where to find government-published documents on a wide variety of subjects. Each issue has a subject, author, and title index and an index of series and reports. You can find a government report or study here on almost any topic. Once you find what you need, it is a good idea to ask for assistance—at least until you are used to the catalog and the documents collection. Z1223.A18   015.73

Related Titles

Cumulative Subject Index to the Monthly Catalog of the United States Government Publications, 1900–1971.   Washington: Carrollton, 1973. 15 vols. Z1223.A182   015.73

Monthly Checklist of State Publications.   Washington, D.C.: U.S. Govt. Printing Office, 1910 to date, monthly. Z1223.5A1U5   015.73

A Popular Guide to Government Publications   (W. Phillip Leidy), 4th ed. N.Y.: Columbia University Press, 1976. Arranges about 3000 titles under broad subject headings. Useful for standard queries about such matters as social security, the census, and Medicare. Z1223.L7   015.73

The New York Times Index.   N.Y.: The New York Times, 1951 to date, twice a month. Tells you where to find material in the newspaper. Also a self-contained source; most of the items indexed have short descriptive annotations.

As the closest to a national newspaper, the *Times* has extensive coverage, which makes it a paper of record. You will find almost anything you need here relating to current events. Most libraries have the newspaper on microfilm. Search is available via computer. The drawback, and a great one: the index is several months late, and the annual cumulation may not come out for six or seven months into the new year. Therefore, it can't be used for events a week or two old. AI26.N45   016.076

Related Title

Newspaper Index.   Wooster, Ohio: Bell & Howell, 1972 to date, monthly. An umbrella name for indexes to six newspapers from San Francisco to Washington, D.C. AI21.L65N49   016.071

PAIS   (Public Affairs Information Service Bulletin). N.Y.: PAIS, 1915 to date, twice a month. Tells you where to find material in periodicals, reports, books, government documents, and so on that have any relation to public affairs. The most useful of the indexes when you are doing in-depth papers or talks on almost any current subject in areas like political science, government, legislation, economics, business, education, and sociology. The service is available by computer; ask your librarian. Z7163.P9   016.3

Related Title

Cumulative Subject Index to the PAIS, 1915–1974.   N.Y.: Carrollton, 1976. Z7163.P8   016.3

Education

This section will help you find general information on the theory and history of education, specific data on schools at any level, and works related to teaching. The emphasis is on education in the U.S.

BASIC GUIDES

For a basic guide to information in education, use these five sources in about the order listed:

   1. *Guide to Reference Books* (see p. 29), the education section, pp. 437–454.

   2. *A Guide to Sources of Educational Information* (Marda Woodbury). Washington: Information Resources Press, 1976. Most comprehensive and best guide with emphasis on current sources. Well annotated. Z5811.W65   016.37

3. *Sources of Information in the Social Sciences* (see p. 162).
Z7161.W49   016.3

4. *Documentation in Education* (Arvid Burke & Mary Burke). N.Y.: Teachers College, 1967. A basic guide to the literature for both beginners and experts.
Z711.B93   029.7

5. *Essentials of Educational Research* (Carter Good), 2nd ed. N.Y.: Appleton, 1972. Details on research methodology, sources, and interdisciplinary topics. LB1023.G58   370.78

CLASSIFICATION NUMBERS

Dewey Decimal System

If your library uses the Dewey Decimal system, you will find education in the 370s. The basic breakdown is:

371 Teaching and administration
372 Elementary education
373 Secondary schools
374 Adult and continuing education
375 Curriculum
378 Colleges and universities
379 Education and the state

Library of Congress System

If your library uses the Library of Congress system, you will find education in the L section. The history of education is LA; theory and practice is LB.

SUBJECT HEADINGS

Look up material on education under the name of a specific form of education, such as "Adult education" or "Private schools." A specific country's educational system is listed under "Education"; for example, "Education—United States." Primary and secondary education are listed under "School."

These representative headings may help you:

Your term	*Subject heading*
Administration	"Schools—Administrators"
	"School management and
	organization"
Audiovisual aids	"Teaching—Aids and devices"
	"Instructional materials"
Biography	"Educators"
Colleges and universities	"Education, higher"
Equal opportunity	"Equalization, educational"
	"Discrimination in education"
Finance	"Education—Finance"
	"Scholarships, fellowships, etc."
	"Student loan funds"
Politics	"Politics and education"
	"Education and state"
Test scores	"Educational attainment"
	"Accountability (education)"

OUTLINE OF SOURCES BY FORM

1. Bibliographies
   Guides to Educational Media
2. Biographical sources
   Leaders in Education
3. Directories
   Comparative Guide to American Colleges
   Education Directory
4. Encyclopedias, yearbooks, handbooks, and dictionaries
   Digest of Educational Statistics
   Encyclopedia of Education
   Requirements for Certification
   Scholarships, Fellowships and Loan News Service
5. Indexes and abstracts
   Current Index to Journals in Education (see *Education Index*)
   Education Index
   NICEM Media Indexes
   Resources in Education (see *Education Index*)

CHART 9: QUESTIONS AND SOURCES OF ANSWERS IN EDUCATION

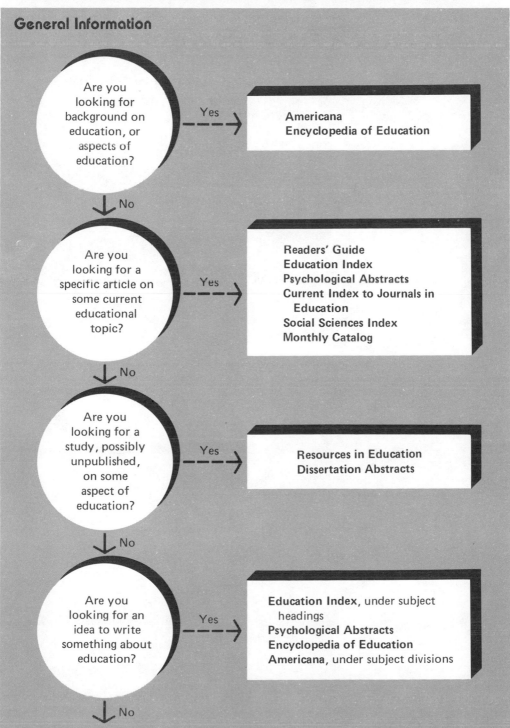

General Information

Are you looking for background on education, or aspects of education?

Yes → Americana
Encyclopedia of Education

No ↓

Are you looking for a specific article on some current educational topic?

Yes → Readers' Guide
Education Index
Psychological Abstracts
Current Index to Journals in Education
Social Sciences Index
Monthly Catalog

No ↓

Are you looking for a study, possibly unpublished, on some aspect of education?

Yes → Resources in Education
Dissertation Abstracts

No ↓

Are you looking for an idea to write something about education?

Yes → Education Index, under subject headings
Psychological Abstracts
Encyclopedia of Education
Americana, under subject divisions

No ↓

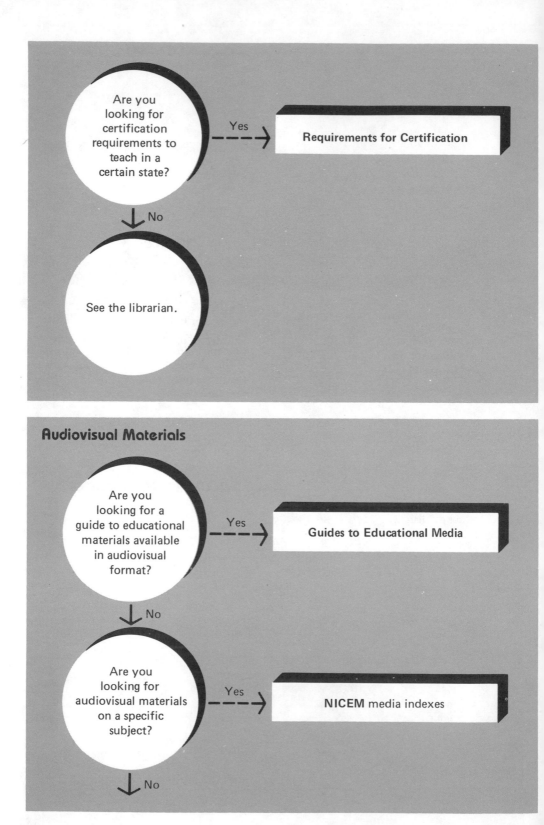

Are you looking for certification requirements to teach in a certain state?

Yes → **Requirements for Certification**

No ↓

See the librarian.

Audiovisual Materials

Are you looking for a guide to educational materials available in audiovisual format?

Yes → **Guides to Educational Media**

No ↓

Are you looking for audiovisual materials on a specific subject?

Yes → **NICEM** media indexes

No ↓

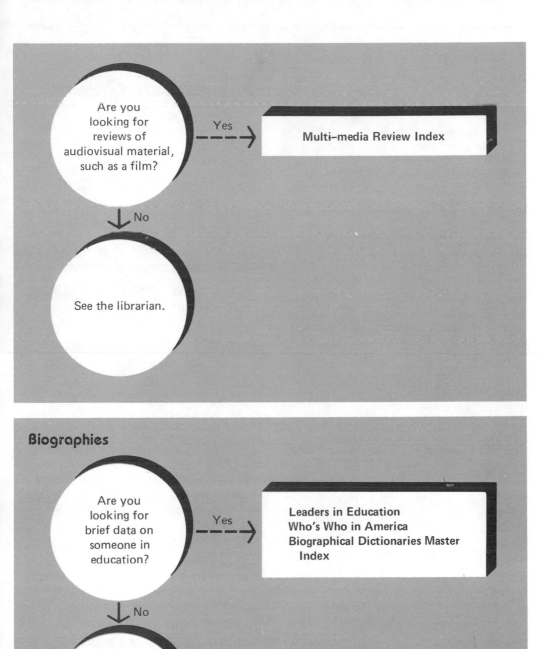

Are you
looking for
reviews of
audiovisual material,
such as a film?

Yes → **Multi–media Review Index**

No ↓

See the librarian.

Biographies

Are you
looking for
brief data on
someone in
education?

Yes →
**Leaders in Education
Who's Who in America
Biographical Dictionaries Master
Index**

No ↓

Are you
looking for an
essay-length
treatment of a
dead figure
in U.S.
education?

Yes →
**Dictionary of American Biography
Americana
Encyclopedia of Education
Biography Index**

No ↓

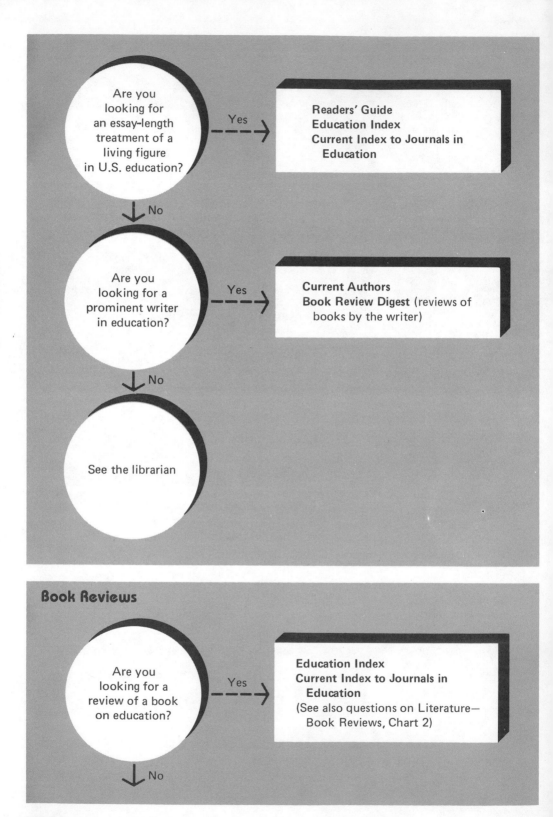

Are you looking for an essay-length treatment of a living figure in U.S. education?

Yes → Readers' Guide
Education Index
Current Index to Journals in Education

No ↓

Are you looking for a prominent writer in education?

Yes → Current Authors
Book Review Digest (reviews of books by the writer)

No ↓

See the librarian

Book Reviews

Are you looking for a review of a book on education?

Yes → Education Index
Current Index to Journals in Education
(See also questions on Literature—Book Reviews, Chart 2)

No ↓

See the librarian.

Financial Help

Are you looking for a scholarship to a U.S. university or college?

Yes →

Scholarships, Fellowships and Loan News Service
Comparative Guide to American Colleges

↓ No

Are you looking for information on an educational loan?

Yes →

Scholarships, Fellowships and Loan News Service

↓ No

Are you looking for information about other types of assistance?

Yes →

Guide to Federal Assistance for Education

↓ No

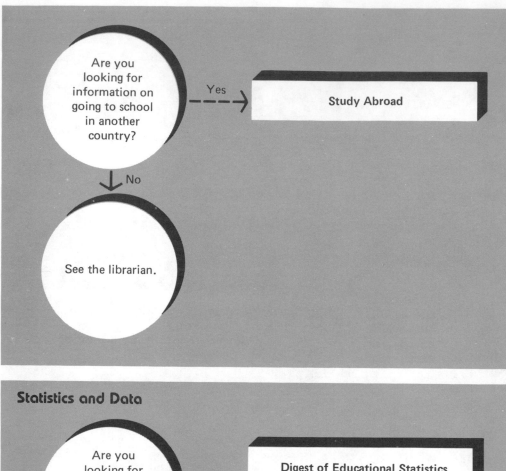

Are you looking for information on going to school in another country?

Yes → Study Abroad

No ↓

See the librarian.

Statistics and Data

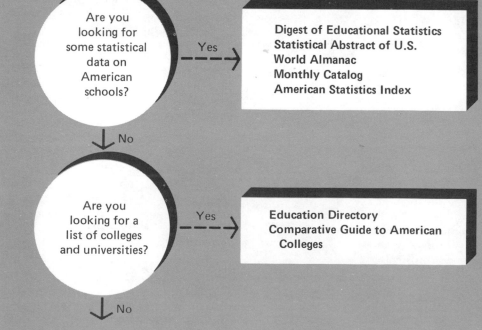

Are you looking for some statistical data on American schools?

Yes →
Digest of Educational Statistics
Statistical Abstract of U.S.
World Almanac
Monthly Catalog
American Statistics Index

No ↓

Are you looking for a list of colleges and universities?

Yes →
Education Directory
Comparative Guide to American Colleges

No ↓

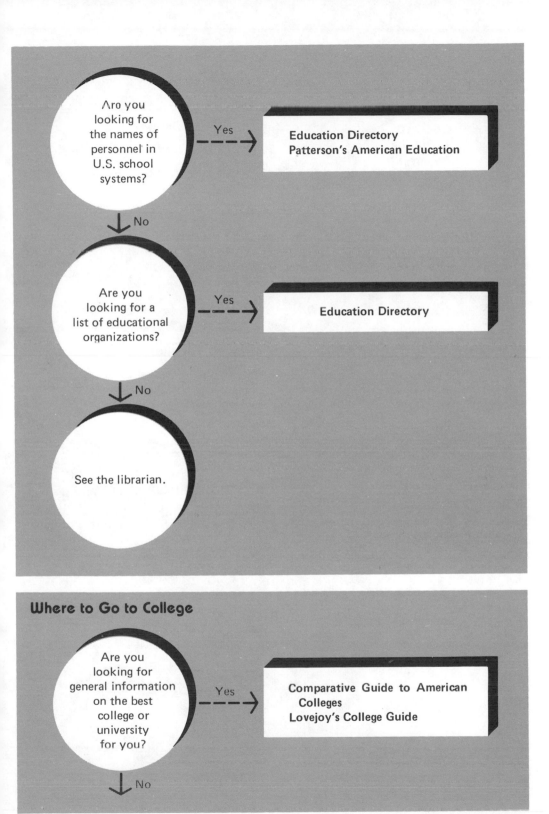

Are you
looking for
the names of
personnel in
U.S. school
systems?

Yes → **Education Directory
Patterson's American Education**

No ↓

Are you
looking for a
list of educational
organizations?

Yes → **Education Directory**

No ↓

See the librarian.

Where to Go to College

Are you
looking for
general information
on the best
college or
university
for you?

Yes → **Comparative Guide to American
Colleges
Lovejoy's College Guide**

No ↓

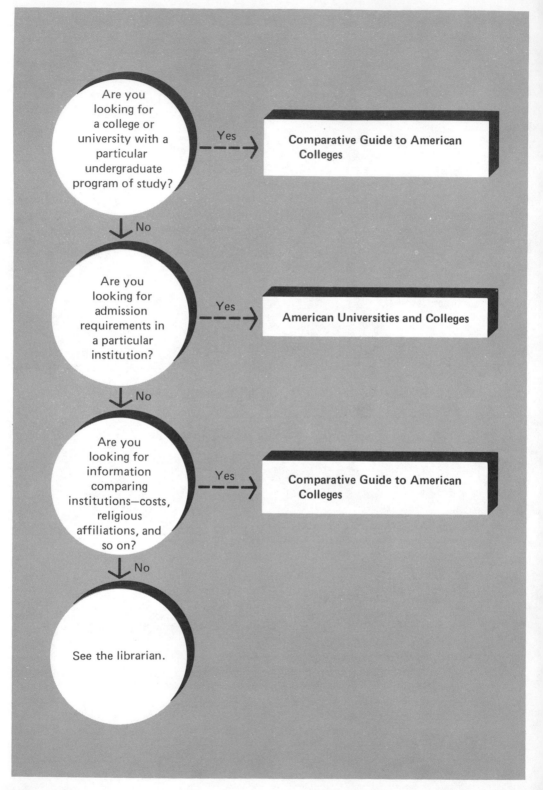

Are you looking for a college or university with a particular undergraduate program of study?

Yes → Comparative Guide to American Colleges

No ↓

Are you looking for admission requirements in a particular institution?

Yes → American Universities and Colleges

No ↓

Are you looking for information comparing institutions—costs, religious affiliations, and so on?

Yes → Comparative Guide to American Colleges

No ↓

See the librarian.

DESCRIPTIONS OF SOURCES

Comparative Guide to American Colleges (James Cass & Max Birnbaum), 8th ed. N.Y.: Harper & Row, 1977. Data on all accredited four-year institutions. Gives opinion on level of campus life. L901.C33   378.73

Related Titles

Lovejoy's College Guide (Clarence Lovejoy). N.Y.: Simon & Schuster, 1940 to date, biennial. More emphasis on concise information, less opinion. Includes unaccredited four- and two-year schools as well. LA226.L6   378.73

Barron's Profiles of American Colleges. N.Y.: Barron's, 1972 to date, frequency varies. Includes more information on campus sports. L901.F5   378.73

American Universities and Colleges (American Council on Education), 11th ed. Washington, D.C.: The Council, 1973. The most complete and objective, but not as up-to-date as other guides. A companion volume is *American Junior Colleges.* LA226.A65 (Jr. colleges: L901.A53)   378.73

Digest of Educational Statistics. (U.S. Office of Education). Washington, D.C.: U.S. Govt. Printing Office, 1962 to date, annual. Self-contained annual data on U.S. education from elementary through graduate programs. The first place to look for up-to-date statistical data. L112.A35   370.78

Education Directory (U.S. Office of Education). Washington, D.C.: U.S. Govt. Printing Office, 1912 to date, annual. Four-volume guide to various types of schools. The first and second volumes include detailed, state-by-state information on elementary and secondary schools. The third volume is a directory of colleges and universities, and the last volume gives you a listing of educational associations. A fifth volume is sometimes issued, which lists federal personnel in education. L901.A3   378.73

Related Title

Patterson's American Education. Mt. Prospect, Ill.: Educational Directories, 1904 to date, annual. Another comprehensive directory to school systems, their personnel, and so on. Includes primary schools, secondary schools, and colleges and universities. L901.P3   370.25

Education Index. New York: Wilson, 1929 to date, monthly. Tells you where to find articles on education and related areas in about 230 periodicals. Some other sources are included, but most emphasis is on journals. Z5813.E23   016.37

Related Titles

Current Index to Journals in Education. N.Y.: Macmillan, 1969 to date, monthly. Indexes 750 periodicals, many covered in *Education Index.* Most of the material is abstracted. Begin with the subject index near the back of each issue. Z5813.C8   016.37

Resources in Education. Washington, D.C.: U.S. Govt. Printing Office, 1966 to date, monthly. Abstracts of reports and related materials. Begin with subject and author index. Along with *Current Index to Journals in Education* (see p. 00) it is part of the ERIC system (Educational Resources Information Center), a common reference aid in medium to large libraries. Most libraries have ERIC reports on microform. Larger libraries offer this service by computer. Z5813.R4   016.37

The Encyclopedia of Education. N.Y.: Macmillan, 1971. 10 vols. Survey of education, with more than 1000 articles on virtually all aspects of the subject. Emphasis is on history and theory. LB15.B56   370.3

Related Titles

Encyclopedia of Educational Research, 4th ed. N.Y.: Macmillan, 1969.LB15.E48   370.3

Dictionary of Education (Carter Good), 3rd ed. N.Y.: McGraw-Hill, 1973. Close to 40,000 terms defined, some at considerable length. LB15.G6   370.3

Guides to Educational Media, 4th ed. Chicago: American Library Association, 1978. Tells you where to find information, dealers, and so on for films, instructional materials, slides, videotapes, and other audiovisual material. Also lists periodicals that review or otherwise take note of audiovisual materials. Z5814.V8R8   016.37

Related Titles

A Reference Guide to Audiovisual Information. N.Y.: Bowker, 1972. Primarily a listing of books and periodicals. Z5814.V8L55   016.37

Audiovisual Marketplace: A Multimedia Guide. N.Y.: Bowker, 1969 to date, annual. A directory of some 5000 firms and individuals involved with audiovisual aids, including manufacturers and dealers in equipment. LB1043.A817   371.33

Leaders in Education, 5th ed. N.Y.: Bowker, 1974. Self-contained data on about 17,000 educators in the U.S. and Canada. LA2311.L4   920.03

Related Titles

Who's Who in American Education. Nashville, Tenn.: 1928 to date, biennial. LA2311.W45   920.03

The National Faculty Directory. Detroit: Gale, 1971 to date. 2 vols. Names and institutional addresses of close to 450,000 members of academic teaching faculties throughout the U.S. L901.N34   378.1

NICEM Media Indexes (National Information Center for Educational Media). Los Angeles: Nicem, 1967 to date. A set of indexes found in the catalog under separate titles such as *Index to 16mm Educational Films* and *Index to 8mm Motion Cartridges.* Tells you where to find a wide range of audiovisual materials. Although not current enough, it is the best subject index available. The set, which is periodically revised, includes such features as multimedia approaches to psychology, an index to filmstrips, and an index to safety. Ask your librarian for help if you want any of the materials listed.

Related Titles

Educator's Grade Guide to Free Teaching Aids. Randolph, Wisc.: Educators Progress Service, 1955 to date, annual. A listing of free materials, including maps, pamphlets, charts, books, and periodicals. The same publisher issues a number of similar titles such as *Educator's Guide to Free Films.* AG600.E3   016.37

Multi-Media Reviews Index. Ann Arbor, Mich.: Pierian Press, 1970 to date. Tells you where to find reviews of all kinds of audiovisual materials. Z5784.M9M85   016.37

Requirements for Certification for Elementary Schools, Secondary Schools, Junior Colleges. Chicago: University of Chicago Press, 1935 to date, annual. Tells you requirements you must fulfill to be certified as a teacher, administrator, or librarian in the U.S. Also includes certification requirements for such jobs as school counselor and speech therapist. LB1771.W6   371.1

Scholarships, Fellowships and Loan News Service. Cambridge, Mass.: Bellman, 1955 to date, quarterly. Loose-leaf service that tells you where to find money for education. LB2338.F41   378.3

Related Titles

How to Obtain Money for College (William Lever). N.Y.: Arco, 1976. LB2337.4.L48   378.3

The Grants Register.   Chicago: St. James, 1969 to date, biennial. Lists scholarships and fellowships in education and teaching for advanced study. LB2338.G7   378.3

Study Abroad.   N.Y.: Unipub, 1948 to date, biennial. Tells you where to find money for study abroad. LB2376.U63   378.3

History

This section will help you find information about many aspects of history. The emphasis is on U.S. and English history.

BASIC GUIDES

The following sources are the basic guides in history. Use them in the order listed:

1. *Guide to Reference Books* (see p. 29). The history section is extensive, pp. 598–690.

2. *Sources of Information in the Social Sciences* (see p. 162). Includes a discursive information to history and guides to the literature, pp. 83–137.

3. *The Modern Researcher* (Jacques Barzun), 3rd ed. N.Y.: Harcourt, 1977. This basic manual on how to write acceptable research papers has a special emphasis on history. D13.B334   808

4. *A Guide to Historical Method* (Robert Shafer). Homewood, Ill.: Dorsey, 1974. A classic in the field. Primarily for students of history at the college level. D16.S47   907.2

5. See also *Guide to Historical Literature* (see p. 216) and *Harvard Guide to American History* (see p. 216).

CLASSIFICATION NUMBERS

Dewey Decimal System

If your library uses the Dewey Decimal system, you will find history from 930 to 990. The basic divisions are:

930   Ancient world
940   Europe
     942   Great Britain
950   Asia

960   Africa
970   North America
   970.1 Indians of North America
   971 Canada
   973 United States
980   South America
990   Other areas

Within 973, titles progress in time through U.S. history as the numbers progress after the decimal point:

973.1 Discovery
973.9 20th century

Library of Congress System

If your library uses the Library of Congress system, you will find history under D, E, and F. You will be involved primarily with DA (Great Britain) and E (United States). F includes U.S. local history.

SUBJECT HEADINGS

Basic subject headings you should look for first when you are searching for material in history in the card catalog or periodical index.

  Generally begin looking up history under the name of the country: for example, "United States—History," "Great Britain—History," or "Canada—History." Also look under larger headings, such as "Europe—History." Watch next for chronological development in the subdivisions: for example, "United States—History—Colonial period," or "United States—History—Civil War, 1861–1865."

  The following headings may help you look up U.S. history:

Your term	*Subject headings*
Biography	"U.S.—Biography" and under name of person
Discovery and exploration	"America—Discovery and explorations" "Explorers"
Modern history	"U.S.—History—20th century"
Politics	"U.S.—Politics and government"
Revolutionary War	"U.S.—History—Revolution"
Social history	"U.S.—Social conditions"
World War I	"European War, 1914–1918"
World War II	"World War, 1939–1945"

OUTLINE OF SOURCES BY FORM

World History	U.S. History

1. Bibliographies

Guide to Historical Literature	*Guide to the Study of the U.S.A.*
	Harvard Guide to American History
	National Union Catalog of Manuscript Collections
	Writings on American History

2. Biographies

Who Was When	*Facts about the Presidents*
	Who Was Who in America

3. Encyclopedias, yearbooks, handbooks, and dictionaries

Cambridge Ancient History	*Album of American History* (see Dictionary)
Cambridge Medieval History	*Atlas of American History* (see Dictionary)
(New) *Cambridge Modern History*	
Encyclopedia of World History	
Sheperd's Historical Atlas	*Dictionary of American History*
	Documents of American History
	Encyclopedia of American History
	Encyclopedia of the American Revolution
	Historical Statistics of the U.S.
	Oxford Companion to American History

4. Indexes and abstracts

Historical Abstracts	*America: History and Life*
Nineteenth Century Readers' Guide to Periodical Literature	*Index to Book Reviews in Historical Periodicals*

CHART 10: QUESTIONS AND SOURCES OF ANSWERS IN HISTORY

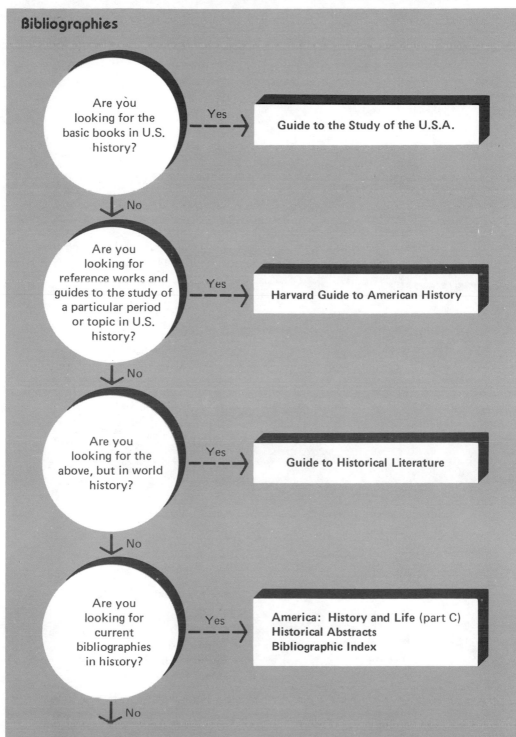

Bibliographies

Are you looking for the basic books in U.S. history?

Yes → **Guide to the Study of the U.S.A.**

No ↓

Are you looking for reference works and guides to the study of a particular period or topic in U.S. history?

Yes → **Harvard Guide to American History**

No ↓

Are you looking for the above, but in world history?

Yes → **Guide to Historical Literature**

No ↓

Are you looking for current bibliographies in history?

Yes → **America: History and Life** (part C)
Historical Abstracts
Bibliographic Index

No ↓

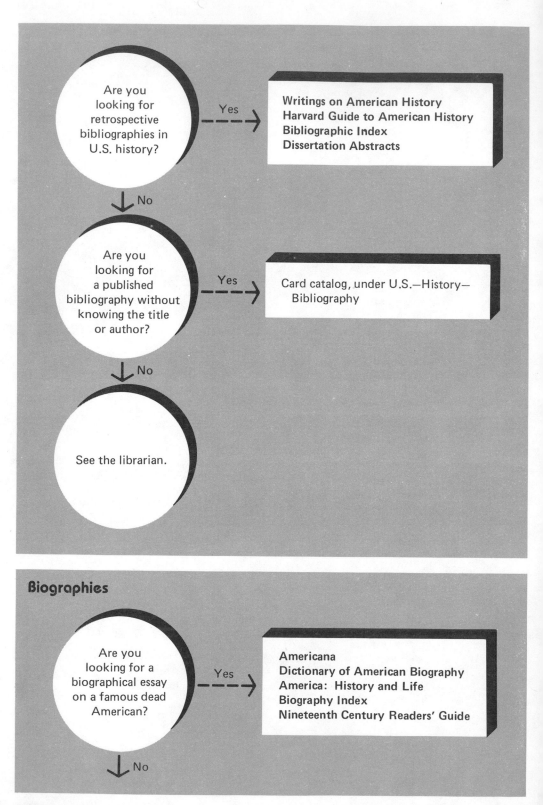

Are you looking for retrospective bibliographies in U.S. history?

Yes → Writings on American History
Harvard Guide to American History
Bibliographic Index
Dissertation Abstracts

No ↓

Are you looking for a published bibliography without knowing the title or author?

Yes → Card catalog, under U.S.—History—Bibliography

No ↓

See the librarian.

Biographies

Are you looking for a biographical essay on a famous dead American?

Yes → Americana
Dictionary of American Biography
America: History and Life
Biography Index
Nineteenth Century Readers' Guide

No ↓

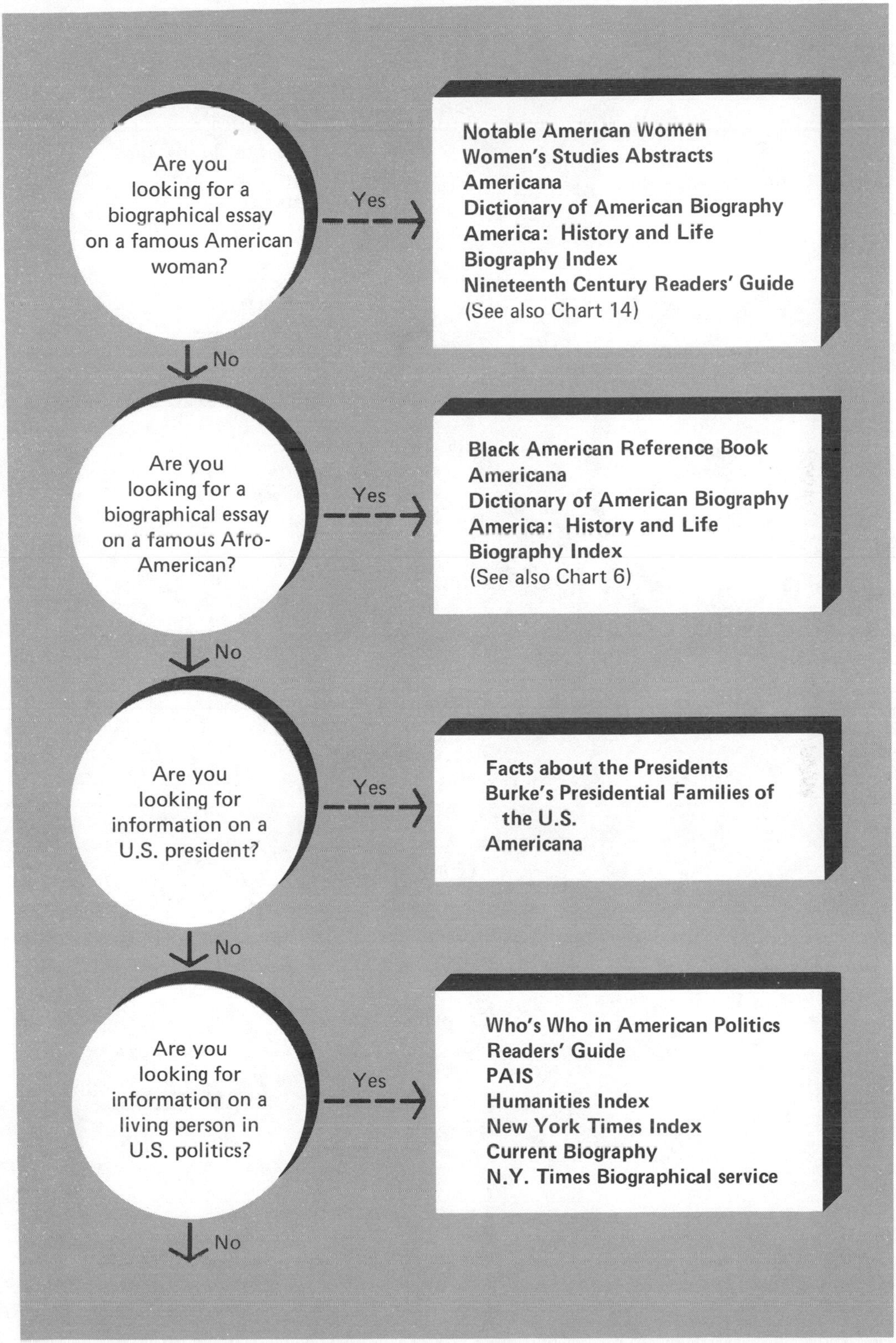

Are you looking for a biographical essay on a famous American woman?

Yes →

Notable American Women
Women's Studies Abstracts
Americana
Dictionary of American Biography
America: History and Life
Biography Index
Nineteenth Century Readers' Guide
(See also Chart 14)

↓ No

Are you looking for a biographical essay on a famous Afro-American?

Yes →

Black American Reference Book
Americana
Dictionary of American Biography
America: History and Life
Biography Index
(See also Chart 6)

↓ No

Are you looking for information on a U.S. president?

Yes →

Facts about the Presidents
Burke's Presidential Families of the U.S.
Americana

↓ No

Are you looking for information on a living person in U.S. politics?

Yes →

Who's Who in American Politics
Readers' Guide
PAIS
Humanities Index
New York Times Index
Current Biography
N.Y. Times Biographical service

↓ No

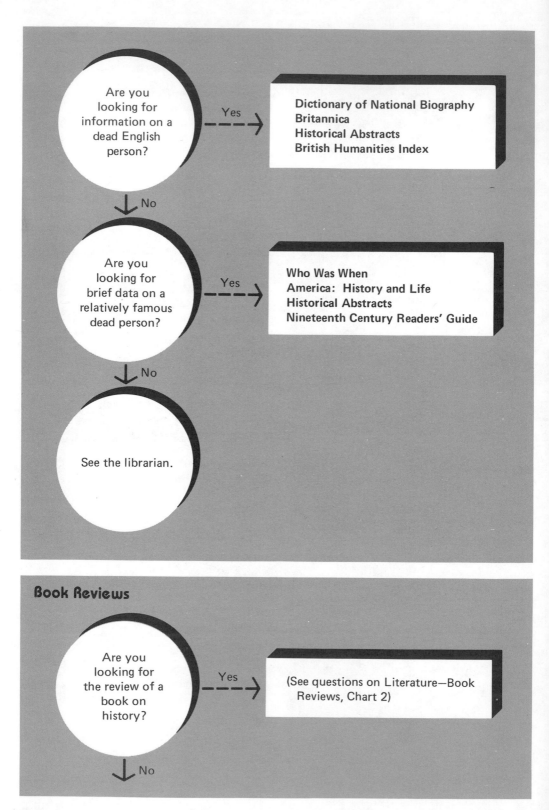

Are you looking for information on a dead English person?

Yes → Dictionary of National Biography
Britannica
Historical Abstracts
British Humanities Index

No

Are you looking for brief data on a relatively famous dead person?

Yes → Who Was When
America: History and Life
Historical Abstracts
Nineteenth Century Readers' Guide

No

See the librarian.

Book Reviews

Are you looking for the review of a book on history?

Yes → (See questions on Literature—Book Reviews, Chart 2)

No

202

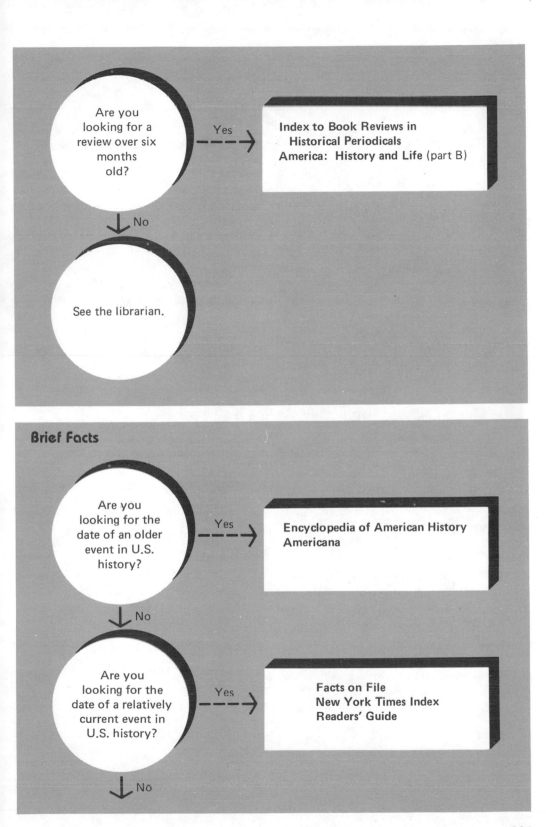

Are you looking for a review over six months old?

Yes → **Index to Book Reviews in Historical Periodicals**
America: History and Life (part B)

No ↓

See the librarian.

Brief Facts

Are you looking for the date of an older event in U.S. history?

Yes → **Encyclopedia of American History**
Americana

No ↓

Are you looking for the date of a relatively current event in U.S. history?

Yes → **Facts on File**
New York Times Index
Readers' Guide

No ↓

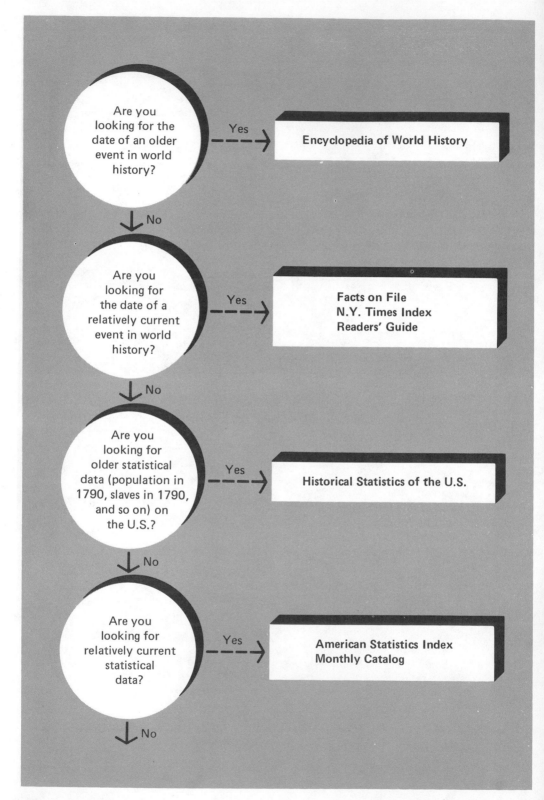

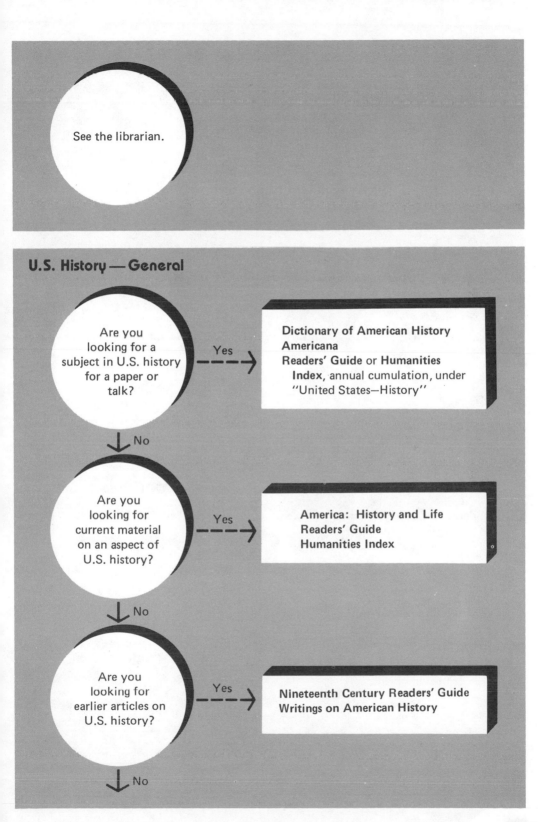

See the librarian.

U.S. History — General

Are you looking for a subject in U.S. history for a paper or talk?

Yes → Dictionary of American History
Americana
Readers' Guide or **Humanities Index**, annual cumulation, under "United States—History"

No ↓

Are you looking for current material on an aspect of U.S. history?

Yes → **America: History and Life**
Readers' Guide
Humanities Index

No ↓

Are you looking for earlier articles on U.S. history?

Yes → **Nineteenth Century Readers' Guide**
Writings on American History

No ↓

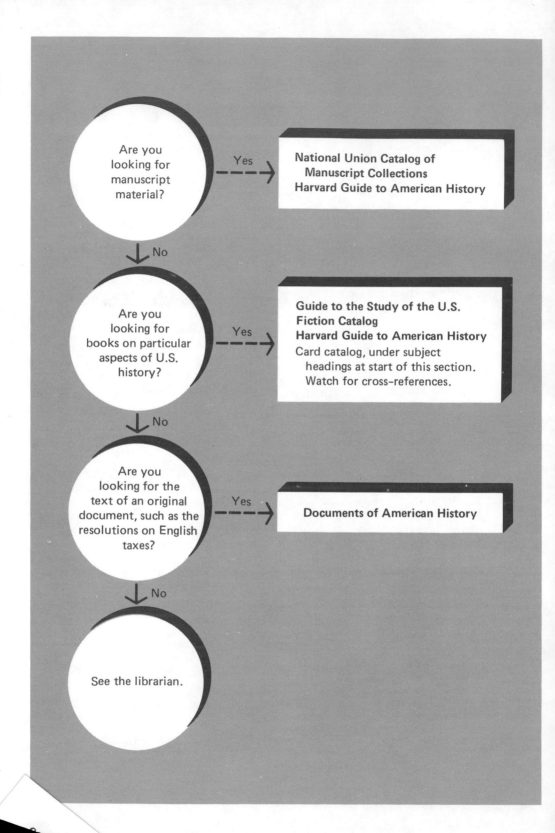

Are you looking for manuscript material?

Yes → National Union Catalog of Manuscript Collections
Harvard Guide to American History

No ↓

Are you looking for books on particular aspects of U.S. history?

Yes → Guide to the Study of the U.S.
Fiction Catalog
Harvard Guide to American History
Card catalog, under subject headings at start of this section. Watch for cross-references.

No ↓

Are you looking for the text of an original document, such as the resolutions on English taxes?

Yes → Documents of American History

No ↓

See the librarian.

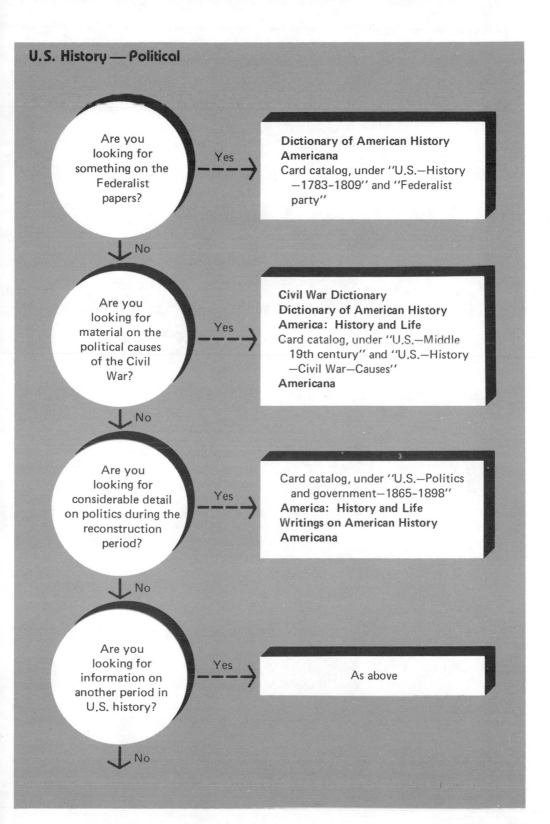

Are you looking for something on the Federalist papers?

Yes →

Dictionary of American History
Americana
Card catalog, under "U.S.—History
—1783-1809" and "Federalist
party"

No ↓

Are you looking for material on the political causes of the Civil War?

Yes →

Civil War Dictionary
Dictionary of American History
America: History and Life
Card catalog, under "U.S.—Middle
19th century" and "U.S.—History
—Civil War—Causes"
Americana

No ↓

Are you looking for considerable detail on politics during the reconstruction period?

Yes →

Card catalog, under "U.S.—Politics
and government—1865-1898"
America: History and Life
Writings on American History
Americana

No ↓

Are you looking for information on another period in U.S. history?

Yes →

As above

No ↓

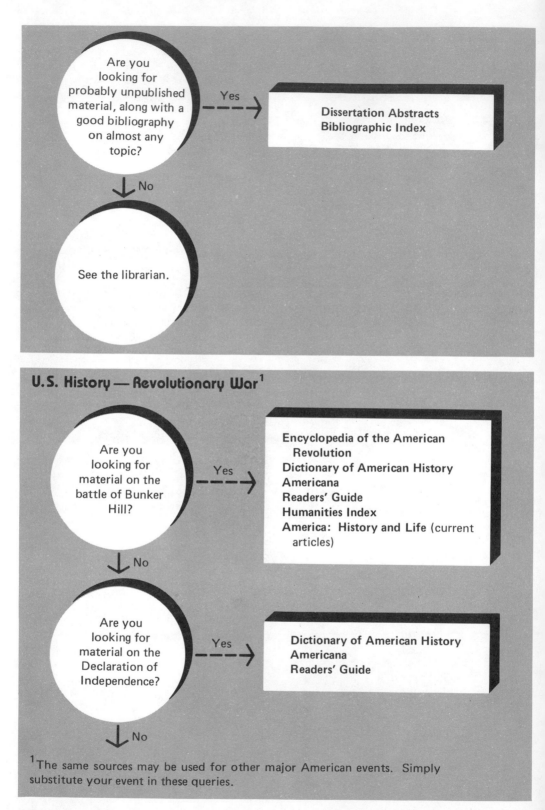

U.S. History — Revolutionary War[1]

[1]The same sources may be used for other major American events. Simply substitute your event in these queries.

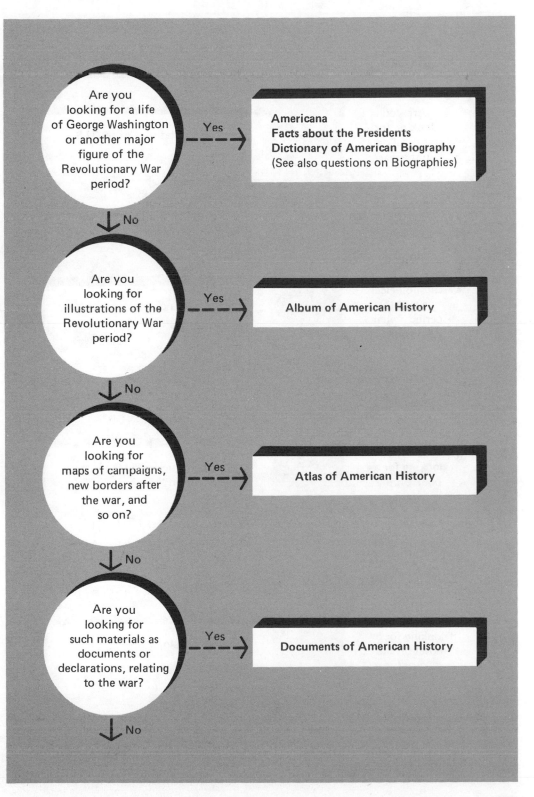

Are you looking for a life of George Washington or another major figure of the Revolutionary War period?

Yes → **Americana**
Facts about the Presidents
Dictionary of American Biography
(See also questions on Biographies)

No ↓

Are you looking for illustrations of the Revolutionary War period?

Yes → **Album of American History**

No ↓

Are you looking for maps of campaigns, new borders after the war, and so on?

Yes → **Atlas of American History**

No ↓

Are you looking for such materials as documents or declarations, relating to the war?

Yes → **Documents of American History**

No ↓

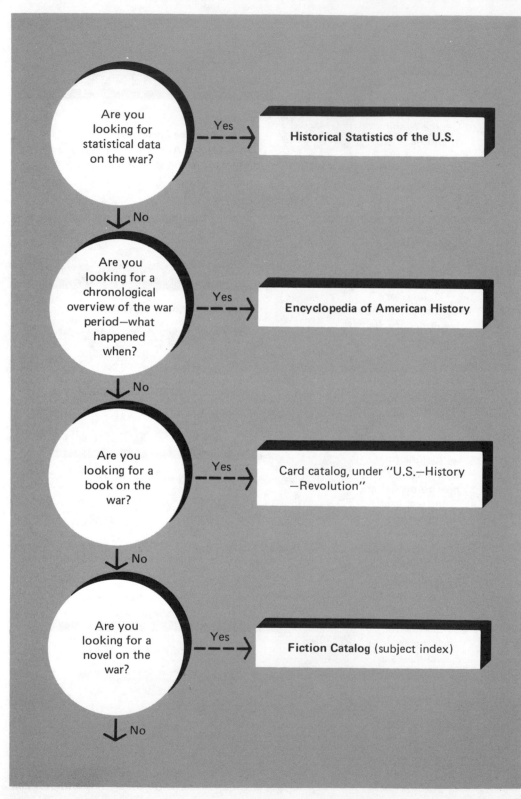

Are you looking for statistical data on the war? — Yes → **Historical Statistics of the U.S.**

No ↓

Are you looking for a chronological overview of the war period—what happened when? — Yes → **Encyclopedia of American History**

No ↓

Are you looking for a book on the war? — Yes → Card catalog, under "U.S.—History —Revolution"

No ↓

Are you looking for a novel on the war? — Yes → **Fiction Catalog** (subject index)

No ↓

See the librarian.

World History

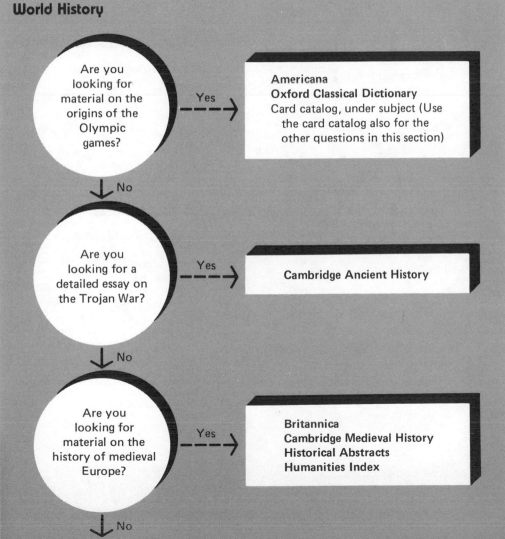

Are you looking for material on the origins of the Olympic games?

Yes →

Americana
Oxford Classical Dictionary
Card catalog, under subject (Use the card catalog also for the other questions in this section)

↓ No

Are you looking for a detailed essay on the Trojan War?

Yes →

Cambridge Ancient History

↓ No

Are you looking for material on the history of medieval Europe?

Yes →

Britannica
Cambridge Medieval History
Historical Abstracts
Humanities Index

↓ No

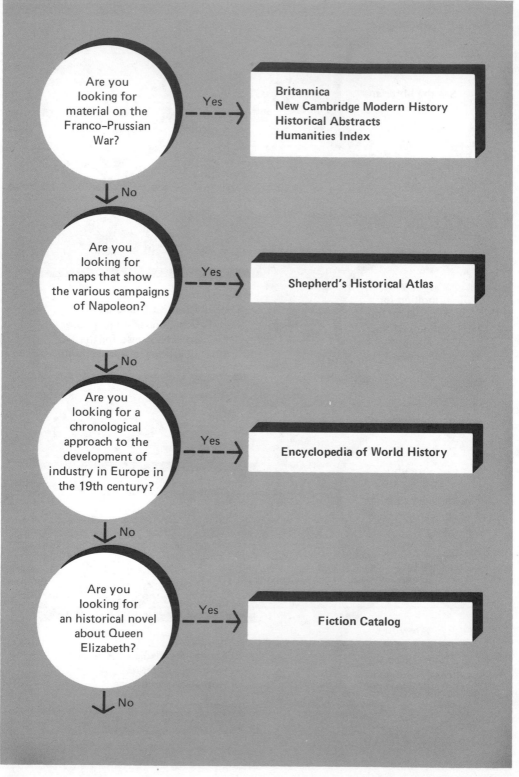

Are you looking for material on the Franco–Prussian War?

Yes →

Britannica
New Cambridge Modern History
Historical Abstracts
Humanities Index

No

Are you looking for maps that show the various campaigns of Napoleon?

Yes →

Shepherd's Historical Atlas

No

Are you looking for a chronological approach to the development of industry in Europe in the 19th century?

Yes →

Encyclopedia of World History

No

Are you looking for an historical novel about Queen Elizabeth?

Yes →

Fiction Catalog

No

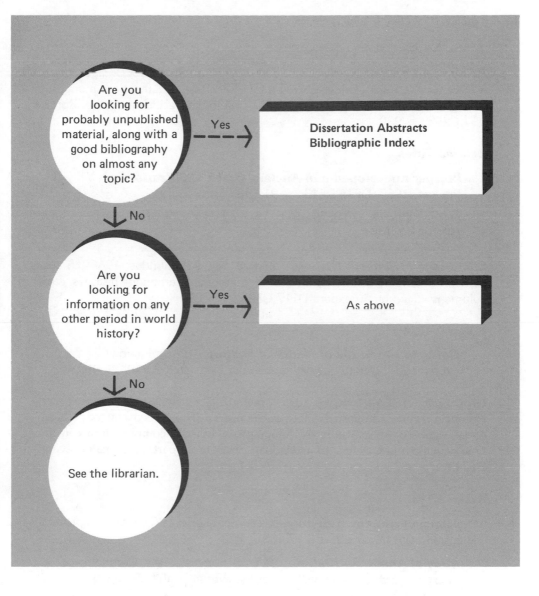

Are you looking for probably unpublished material, along with a good bibliography on almost any topic?

Yes → Dissertation Abstracts Bibliographic Index

No ↓

Are you looking for information on any other period in world history?

Yes → As above

No ↓

See the librarian.

DESCRIPTIONS OF SOURCES

America: History and Life.   Santa Barbara, Calif.: American Bibliographical Center, Clio Press, 1964 to date, seven/year. Tells you where to find material about the U.S. and Canada in periodicals, book reviews, dissertations, and books in the field. An excellent subject index describes the various articles in depth. It is called the subject profile index. Begin with the annual index, and then work back to the individual issues. The index not only will give you sources for specific subjects, but will indicate sections to scan in the individual issues. Z1236.A48   016.973

Cambridge Ancient History,   3rd ed. N.Y.: Cambridge, 1970– in progress. A basic history. Each chapter is written by a specialist, and there are numerous bibliographies. It deals with history from Egypt to the decline and fall of Rome. D57.C252   930

Related Titles

Praeger Encyclopedia of Ancient Greek Civilization.   N.Y.: Praeger, 1967. DF16.D513   913.38

Oxford Classical Dictionary,   2nd ed. N.Y.: Oxford, 1970. DE5.09   913.38

Cambridge Mediaeval History,   2nd ed. N.Y.: Cambridge, 1966– in progress. The standard history for the period. Like other Cambridge histories, each volume is edited by an expert. D117.C32   940.1

Related Title

Guide to the Study of Medieval History   (Louis Paetow). N.Y.: Crofts, 1931. Dated, but still basic in the field. Z6203.P19   016.94

Dictionary of American History,   rev. ed. N.Y.: Scribner's, 1976. 8 vols. Material on almost any aspect of American history. The set is useful for political, social, and economic history. No biographies, but the complete index in the final volume often refers to individuals who took part in a major event. E174.A4   973.03

Related Titles

Album of American History.   NY.: Scribner's, 1969. 6 vols. A pictorial history with minimal text. E178.5   973

Atlas of American History.   N.Y.: Scribner's, 1943. Chronological maps with index. Useful with either the *Album* or the *Dictionary.* G1201.S1A2   911

Documents of American History (Henry Steele Commanger), 9th ed. Englewood Cliffs, N.J.: Prentice-Hall, 1973. 2 vols. Reprints the text of significant American historical documents from 1492 through the mid-1970s. E173.C66   973

Related Title

Documentary History of American Life.   N.Y.: McGraw-Hill, 1966. 8 vols..Emphasis on original documents of political history, but covers social, cultural, and other aspects. E173.D58   973

Encyclopedia of the American Revolution (Mark Boatner). N.Y.: McKay, 1974. In dictionary form, with emphasis on biography and the war. E203.B68   973.703

Related Title

The Civil War Dictionary (Mark Boatner). N.Y.: McKay, 1959. Same author, style, and emphasis on biography. E468.B7   973.703

Encyclopedia of American History (Richard Morris). N.Y.: Harper, 1976. Chronological approach to American history, from 50,000 B.C. to the 1970s. E174.5M847   973.03

Related Titles

Webster's Guide to American History. Springfield, Mass.: Merriam, 1971. The same approach as above. Includes some quotes from contemporary documents. E174.5W4   973.03

The Encyclopedia of American Facts and Dates (Gorton Carruth), 6th ed. N.Y.: Crowell, 1972. From beginning through 1968, chronology in parallel columns. E174.5.C3   973.03

Encyclopedia of World History (William Langer), 5th ed. Boston: Houghton-Miffln, 1972. A chronological approach to world history from the beginning to about 1970. Maps concentrate on political, military, and diplomatic developments. D21.L27   902

Related Titles

Timetables of History (Berard Grun). N.Y.: Simon & Schuster, 1975. From 5000 B.C. to 1974, with seven columns for each year (some years are missing). Covers areas like politics, literature, and the visual arts. D11.G78   902.02

Harper Encyclopedia of the Modern World (Richard Morris). N.Y.: Harper, 1970. Same approach as *Encyclopedia of American History.* D025.H35   903

Facts about the Presidents (Joseph N. Kane), 3rd ed. N.Y.: Wilson, 1974. Data on the presidents from Washington to the beginning of Nixon's second term. Also lists presidential and vice-presidential candidates, State of the Union messages, and other information. A good index brings facts and people together. E176.K3   973

Related Titles

Burke's Presidential Families of the United States of America.
N.Y.: Arco, 1974. Vast amount of material. Good illustrations and
chronology. C569.B82   973

Guide to Historical Literature   (American Historical Association). N.Y.:
Macmillan, 1961. Tells you where to find material in reference sources. Check
the index first, which will refer you to an event, personality, country, or topic
in the main text. The annotated text is arranged by broad subject and country.
Now dated, but useful. Z601.A55   016.9

Related Title

Historical Bibliographies   (Edith Coulter). Berkeley: University of
California, 1936. An annotated list of major bibliographies arranged by
country. Dated, but still useful. Z6201.A1C8   016.9

A Guide to the Study of the United States of America   (U.S. Library of
Congress). Washington, D.C.: U.S. Govt. Printing Office, 1960. Supplement,
1956–1965, 1976. Tells you where to find books on aspects of U.S. history
from the beginning years to the mid-1950s. Some 6500 titles are listed under
broad subject headings. There is a descriptive annotation for each of the titles.
The supplement lists 3000 titles published from 1956 to 1965.
Z1215.U53   016.917

Harvard Guide to American History   (Frank Freidel, ed.), rev. ed. Cambridge, Mass.: Belknap, 1974. 2 vols. The basic bibliographic guide to U.S.
history, the first source to consult for detailed study. The first volume includes
material on research methods, and references are arranged by broad topics.
The second volume is arranged chronologically and ends with the late 1960s.
When you use the set, turn first to the extensive index, which includes both
authors and subjects. Also useful is the detailed table of contents in each of the
volumes. Z1236.H27   016.9

Related Title

Bibliographies in American History   (Henry Beers). N.Y.: Wilson,
1942. A classified listing of over 11,000 bibliographies. Dated, yet useful.
Z1236.A1B4   016.9

Historical Abstracts.   Santa Barbara, Calif.: American Bibliographical Center, Clio Press, 1955 to date, quarterly. Tells you where to find historical material
in periodicals. In two parts: one section covers the period from 1450 to 1914;

the other from 1914 to the present. Scope is worldwide. Material from over 2000 periodicals is arranged in a way that requires some knowledge of the field. Consult the annual subject index to find out the classifications for your subject. D299.H5   909.808

Historical Statistics of the United States, Colonial Times to 1970. Washington, D.C.: U.S. Govt. Printing Office, 1975. 2 vols. Self-contained data on more than 12,500 different subjects and time series. The information is in tabular form. See also *Statistical Abstract of the United States* (p. 71) which this work supplements. HA202.A38.   317.3

Index to Book Reviews in Historical Periodicals   (John W. Brewster). Metuchen, N.J.: Scarecrow, 1972 to date, annual. Tells you where to find reviews of history books in about 110 periodicals. Z6205.B75   016.9

Related Title

> ***Reviews in American History.***   Westport, Conn.: Redgrave, 1973 to date, quarterly. A periodical, not a book. Z1236.R47   973

The National Union Catalog of Manuscript Collections   (U.S. Library of Congress). Washington, D.C.: U.S. Govt. Printing Office, 1962 to date, Hamden, Conn.: Shoe String, 1962 to date, annual. Tells you where to find manuscript material such as letters, memoirs, and diaries in your field of interest. Z6620.U5N3   016.091

Related Title

> ***A Guide to Archives and Manuscripts in the United States***   (Philip M. Hamer). New Haven: Yale, 1961. Gives detailed descriptions of major holdings in 1300 depositories.
> CD3022.A45   025.171

New Cambridge Modern History,   2nd ed. N.Y.: Cambridge, 1957–1970. 14 vols. Linked to the other two sets in the Cambridge series on ancient history and medieval history. Moves from the Renaissance through World War II. It emphasizes Europe but does consider the remainder of the world, particularly economics, politics, and culture. D208.N4   909

Nineteenth Century Readers' Guide to Periodical Literature.   N.Y.: Wilson, 1944. 2 vols. Tells you where to find articles in 51 periodicals published between 1890 and 1899. Has author, subject, and illustrator index. AI3.R496   015

Related Title

> ***Poole's Index to Periodical Literature, 1802–1881.***   Boston: Houghton, 1891. Supplement, Jan. 1882–Jan. 1907. The basic index to articles in 500 periodicals and fiction published during the 19th century in the U.S. and England. Entries only by subject. (An author index issued in 1971 by C. Edward Wall is usually found with the set.) Confusing abbreviations of titles, and neither paging nor date of article is given. A13.P7   015

Oxford Companion to American History   (Thomas Johnson). N.Y.: Oxford, 1966. A source of data and short articles on the "lives, events, and places significant in the founding and growth of the nation." E174.J6   973.03

Related Title

> ***Oxford Companion to Canadian History and Literature.***   N.Y.: Oxford, 1967. Supplement, 1973. PR9106.S7   810.3

Sheperd's Historical Atlas,   9th ed., rev. N.Y.: Barnes & Noble, 1973. Maps of historical events from 1450 B.C. to the mid-1960s. G1030.S4   911

Related Titles

> ***Atlas of American History.***   N.Y.: Scribner's, 1943. Chronological maps with index. G1201.S1A2   911

> ***Atlas of World History.***   Chicago: Rand McNally, 1965. Detailed North American maps. Also maps of Latin America, Asia, and Africa. G1030.R3   911

Who Was When? A Dictionary of Contemporaries   (Miriam DeFord). N.Y.: Wilson, 1976. A ready reference source chronologically listing some 10,000 major historical figures from 500 B.C. through the early 1970s. CT103.D4   920.03

Who Was Who in America, Historical Volume, 1607–1896.   Chicago: Marquis, 1967. Brief biographical data on 13,000 people. See also *Who Was Who in America, 1942 to date,* which picks up dead entries from the regular *Who's Who in America.* E176.W64   920.03

Related Titles

> ***Appleton's Cyclopaedia of American Biography.***   N.Y.: Appleton: 1894–1900. 7 vols. Useful for out-of-the-way names. Be sure to use the index. E176.A659   920.03

National Cyclopaedia of American Biography. N.Y.: White, 1892 in progress. Ongoing "vanity" sketches. You must use the index.
E176.N27   920.03

Writings on American History (American Historical Association) N.Y.: Kraus-Thomson, 1974 to date. (Under different publishers, began publication in 1906.) Tells you where to find books and articles on periods of U.S. history. Use it only after the other basic indexes and bibliographies. It is best to begin with the index, which covers 1902–1940, move to the 1948 volume (nothing has been issued for 1941–1947), and then go to the current volumes.
Z1236.L331   016.973

Political Science

BASIC GUIDES

For information on political science, make these three basic guides your main-stays:
    1. *The Information Sources of Political Science* (Frederick Holler), rev. ed. Santa Barbara, Calif.: ABC-Clio, 1975. 5 vols. A comprehensive guide to the basic works in political science. Most of the entries have descriptive annotations.
Z7161.H64   016.32
    2. *Guide to Reference Books* (see p. 29), the section on political science, pp. 531–553.
    3. *Sources of Information in the Social Sciences* (see p. 162), the section on political science, pp. 493–564.

CLASSIFICATION NUMBERS

Materials on political science are classified in the 320s under the Dewey Decimal system. In the Library of Congress system, look under J; for political science in the United States, look under JK. Socialism, communism, and anarchism are under HX.

SUBJECT HEADINGS

When you are looking up applications of political science to a particular country, you should look under the name of the country. For example, you would look

up "France—Politics and government" or "Spain—Foreign relations."
These subject headings are representative:

"Citizenship"
"Civil rights"
"Communism"
"Conservatism"
"Democracy"
"International relations"
"Nationalism"
"Political parties"
"Political science"
"Politics"
"The state"
"U.S.—Congress"
"U.S.—Foreign relations"
"U.S.—Politics and government"
"World politics"

CHART II: QUESTIONS AND SOURCES OF ANSWERS IN POLITICAL SCIENCE

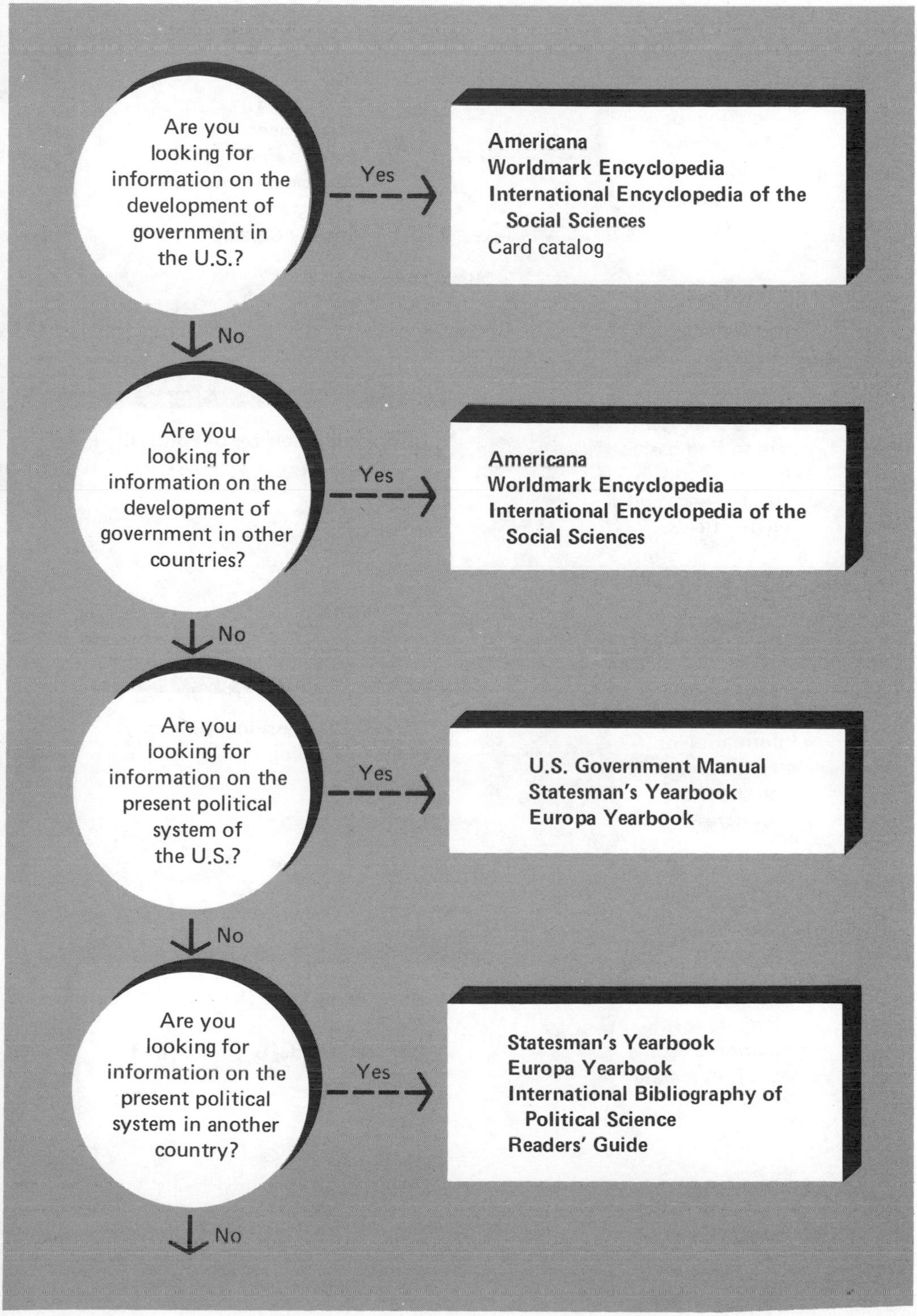

Are you looking for information on the development of government in the U.S.?

Yes →

Americana
Worldmark Encyclopedia
International Encyclopedia of the
    Social Sciences
Card catalog

↓ No

Are you looking for information on the development of government in other countries?

Yes →

Americana
Worldmark Encyclopedia
International Encyclopedia of the
    Social Sciences

↓ No

Are you looking for information on the present political system of the U.S.?

Yes →

U.S. Government Manual
Statesman's Yearbook
Europa Yearbook

↓ No

Are you looking for information on the present political system in another country?

Yes →

Statesman's Yearbook
Europa Yearbook
International Bibliography of
    Political Science
Readers' Guide

↓ No

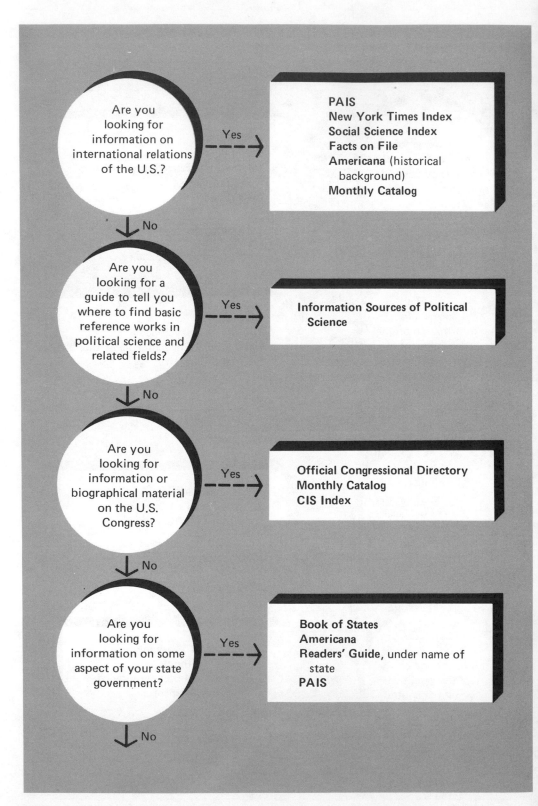

Are you looking for information on international relations of the U.S.?

Yes →

PAIS
New York Times Index
Social Science Index
Facts on File
Americana (historical background)
Monthly Catalog

No ↓

Are you looking for a guide to tell you where to find basic reference works in political science and related fields?

Yes →

Information Sources of Political Science

No ↓

Are you looking for information or biographical material on the U.S. Congress?

Yes →

Official Congressional Directory
Monthly Catalog
CIS Index

No ↓

Are you looking for information on some aspect of your state government?

Yes →

Book of States
Americana
Readers' Guide, under name of state
PAIS

No ↓

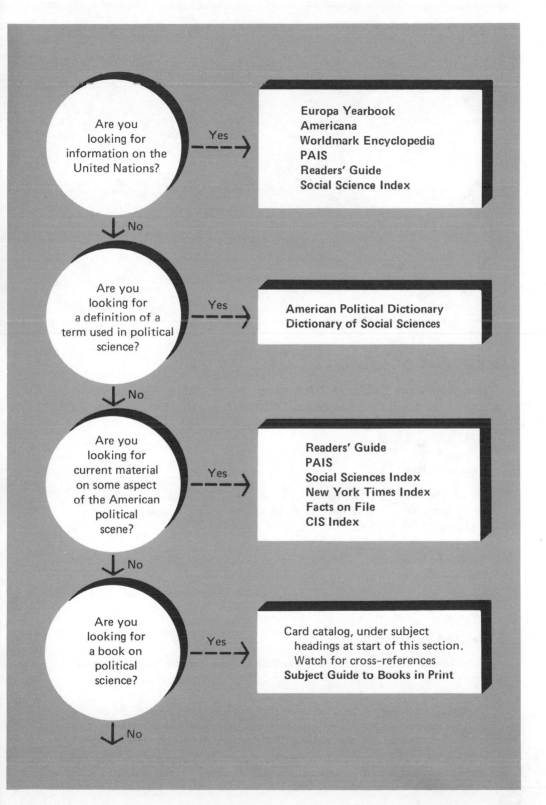

Are you looking for information on the United Nations?

Yes →
Europa Yearbook
Americana
Worldmark Encyclopedia
PAIS
Readers' Guide
Social Science Index

No ↓

Are you looking for a definition of a term used in political science?

Yes →
American Political Dictionary
Dictionary of Social Sciences

No ↓

Are you looking for current material on some aspect of the American political scene?

Yes →
Readers' Guide
PAIS
Social Sciences Index
New York Times Index
Facts on File
CIS Index

No ↓

Are you looking for a book on political science?

Yes →
Card catalog, under subject headings at start of this section. Watch for cross-references
Subject Guide to Books in Print

No ↓

See the librarian.

DESCRIPTIONS OF SOURCES

The American Political Dictionary (Jack Plano), 4th ed. N.Y.: Holt, 1976. A standard reference encyclopedia in dictionary form. Provides you with detailed articles and brief entries on political life in the United States. JK9.P55   320.9

Related Title

> ***A Dictionary of Politics*** (Al Laqueur). London: Weidenfeld, 1971. Information on international politics, with some biographical material. D419.L36   320

Book of the States.   Chicago: Council of State Governments, 1935 to date, biennial. Gives comparative data on state governments, including their constitutions, legislatures, and services. Concludes with state-by-state lists of state officers and statistics, etc. JK2403.B6   352

Related Titles

> Most states have their own manuals and yearbooks, published both privately and by the government. Ask your librarian for them.

Europa Yearbook.   London: Europa, 1959 to date, annual. 2 vols. The first volume covers international organizations, including the United Nations, and Europe; the second covers the rest of the world. Countries are arranged alphabetically in each volume. Extensive data on political parties, religion, transportation, tourism and other aspects of life. JN1.E85   341.184

Related Titles

Political Handbook and Atlas of the World.   N.Y.: Harper & Row, 1927 to date, annual. Covers much the same material as *Europa.* JF37.P6   342

International Yearbook and Statesman's Who's Who.   London: Burke's Peerage, 1953 to date. Includes data on countries and a special section on world leaders. JA51.I57   305.8

International Bibliography of Political Science.   Chicago: Aldine, 1953 to date, annual. Tells you where to find materials of all kinds related to political science. Includes titles in other languages. Although annual, the material is dated and can be used only for background. Z7163.I64   016.32

Related Title

ABC Pol Sci.   Santa Barbara, Calif.: ABC-Clio, 1969, 9/yr. Reprints the content pages of about 300 journals. There is a subject index. Z7161.A214   016.32

Official Congressional Directory.   Washington, D.C.: U.S. Government Printing Office, 1965 to date, annual. Information on various current aspects of Congress, such as biographical sketches, committee assignments, and staff members. Also includes information on Congress from 1789 to the present, a list of reporters and media agencies recognized by Congress, and a section on the executive and judiciary branches. JK1011   328.73

Related Title

Who's Who in American Politics.   N.Y.: Bowker, 1967 to date, biennial. Brief data on about 19,000 federal, state, and local officials. E176.W6424   320

Worldmark Encyclopedia of Nations,   5th ed. N.Y.: Wiley, 1976. 5 vols. Concise information for over 160 countries. Easy to follow. G103.W65   909.82

Psychology

BASIC GUIDES

There are three basic guides to information in psychology:
1. *Guide to Library Research in Psychology* (James Bell). Dubuque, Iowa: Brown, 1971. Basic approach to how to use the library, followed by a detailed

bibliography of reference works in the field. BF76.8B43   016.16

2. *Guide to Reference Books* (see p. 29), the section on psychology and psychiatry, pp. 768–774.

3. *Sources of Information in the Social Sciences* (see p. 162) the section on psychology, pp. 374–424.

CLASSIFICATION NUMBERS AND SUBJECT HEADINGS

In the Dewey Decimal system, look for material in the 150s and under 618.8. In the Library of Congress system, look for psychology under BF and psychiatry under RC.

Representative subject headings include "Dreams," "Emotions," names of specific emotions such as "Love" or "Anger," and "Mental tests." You can look also under "Psychology" and "Psychiatry."

CHART 12: QUESTIONS AND SOURCES OF ANSWERS IN PSYCHOLOGY

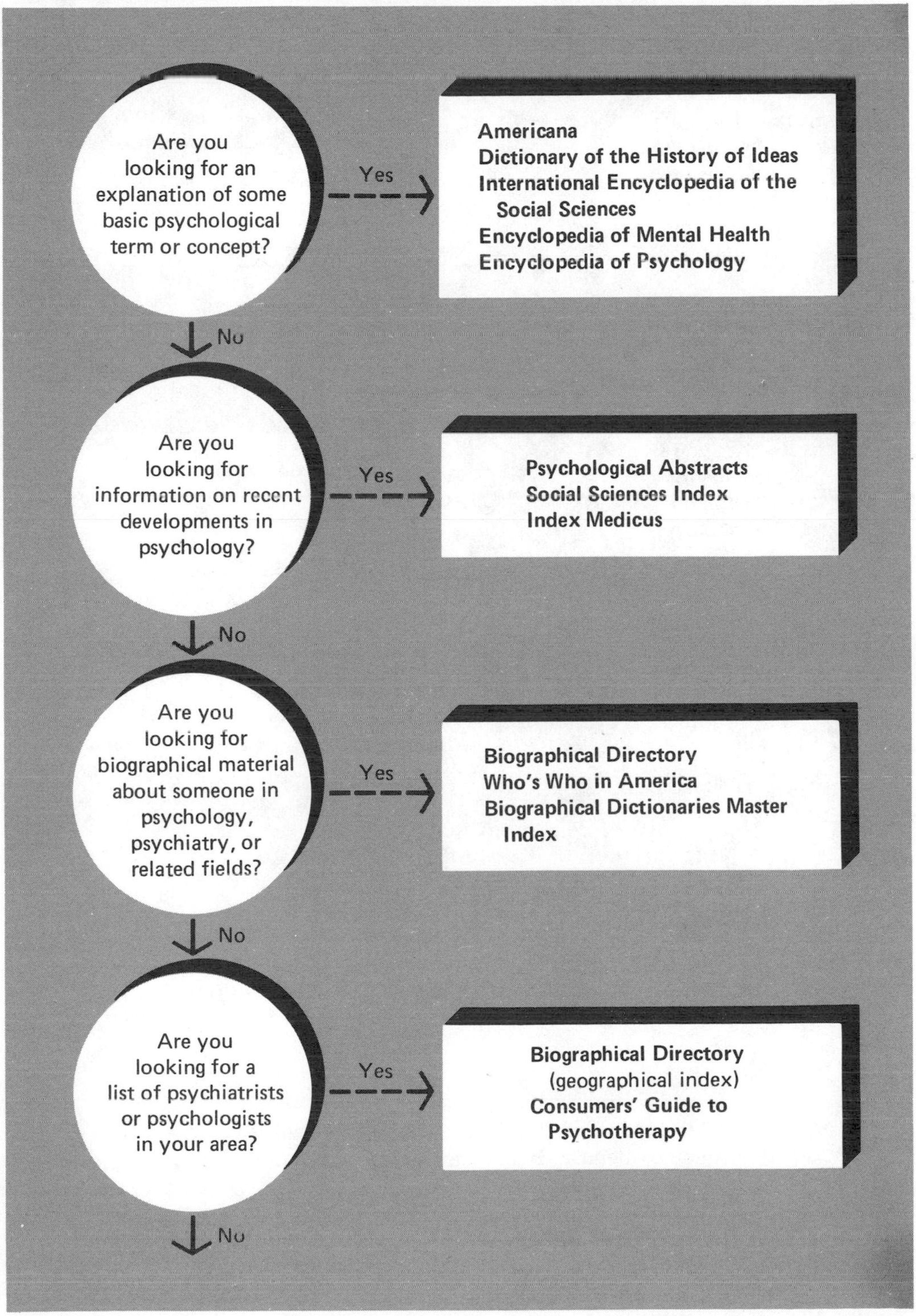

Are you looking for an explanation of some basic psychological term or concept?

Yes →

Americana
Dictionary of the History of Ideas
International Encyclopedia of the
  Social Sciences
Encyclopedia of Mental Health
Encyclopedia of Psychology

↓ No

Are you looking for information on recent developments in psychology?

Yes →

Psychological Abstracts
Social Sciences Index
Index Medicus

↓ No

Are you looking for biographical material about someone in psychology, psychiatry, or related fields?

Yes →

Biographical Directory
Who's Who in America
Biographical Dictionaries Master
  Index

↓ No

Are you looking for a list of psychiatrists or psychologists in your area?

Yes →

Biographical Directory
  (geographical index)
Consumers' Guide to
  Psychotherapy

↓ No

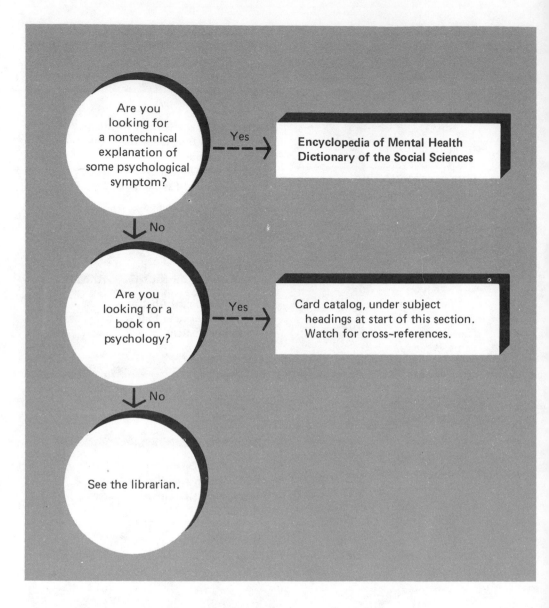

DESCRIPTIONS OF SOURCES

Biographical Directory. Washington, D.C.: American Psychological Association, 1970 to date, triennial. Brief data on 28,000 members of the American Psychological Association. BF11.A67   150

Encyclopedia of Mental Health. N.Y.: Watts, 1963. 6 vols. A set for the lay person on many aspects of mental health. About 170 topics are considered by a question and answer method. You should begin with the subject index in the last volume. Some of the material is dated. RA790.E56   614.58

Related Titles

A Guide to Mental Health Services.   Pittsburgh: University of Pittsburgh, 1973. Overview of subject, with a chapter on sources of information. RA790.H42   362.2

A Consumer's Guide to Psychotherapy   (Daniel Wiener), rev. ed. N.Y.: Hawthorn, 1975. A lay person's guide to various aspects of the field, including how to know whether you need help and what to do about it. RC480.W53   616.8

Encyclopedia of Psychology.   N.Y.: Herder, 1972, 3 vols. Includes both short definitions and long articles. Some biographies. BF31.E52   150

Related Title

Encyclopedia of Human Behavior.   N.Y.: Doubleday, 1970. 2 vols. Dictionary arrangement of definitions, case histories, and long overview articles. BF31.G6   150

Psychological Abstracts.   Lancaster, Pa.: American Psychological Association, 1927 to date, monthly. Tells you where to find material in books, journals, reports, and other sources on various aspects of psychology and allied fields. Material is abstracted and arranged under broad subject headings. Unless you are familiar with the field, check the brief subject index—preferably in the cumulative volumes. Available for search by computer. BF1.P65   016.15

Sociology

BASIC GUIDES

The two basic guides in sociology are:
1. *Socioloy of America: A Guide to Information Sources* (Charles Mark). Detroit, Gale, 1976. Tells you where to find some 2000 sources for the study of society, culture, and life in the United States. Most of the sources are annotated. Z7164.S66M37   016.3091
2. *Sources of Information in the Social Sciences* (see p. 162).

CLASSIFICATION NUMBERS AND SUBJECT HEADINGS

In the Dewey Decimal system, look for sociology under 301. In the Library of Congress system, look under HM; the family, marriage, and women are under HQ.

Here are a few representative subject headings:

"Child study"
"Cities and towns"
"Divorce"
"Family"
"Human ecology"
"Human relations"
"Population"
"Social change"
"Social psychology"
"Sociology"
"U.S.—Foreign population"
"U.S.—Social conditions"
"Violence"

CHART 13: QUESTIONS AND SOURCES OF ANSWERS IN SOCIOLOGY

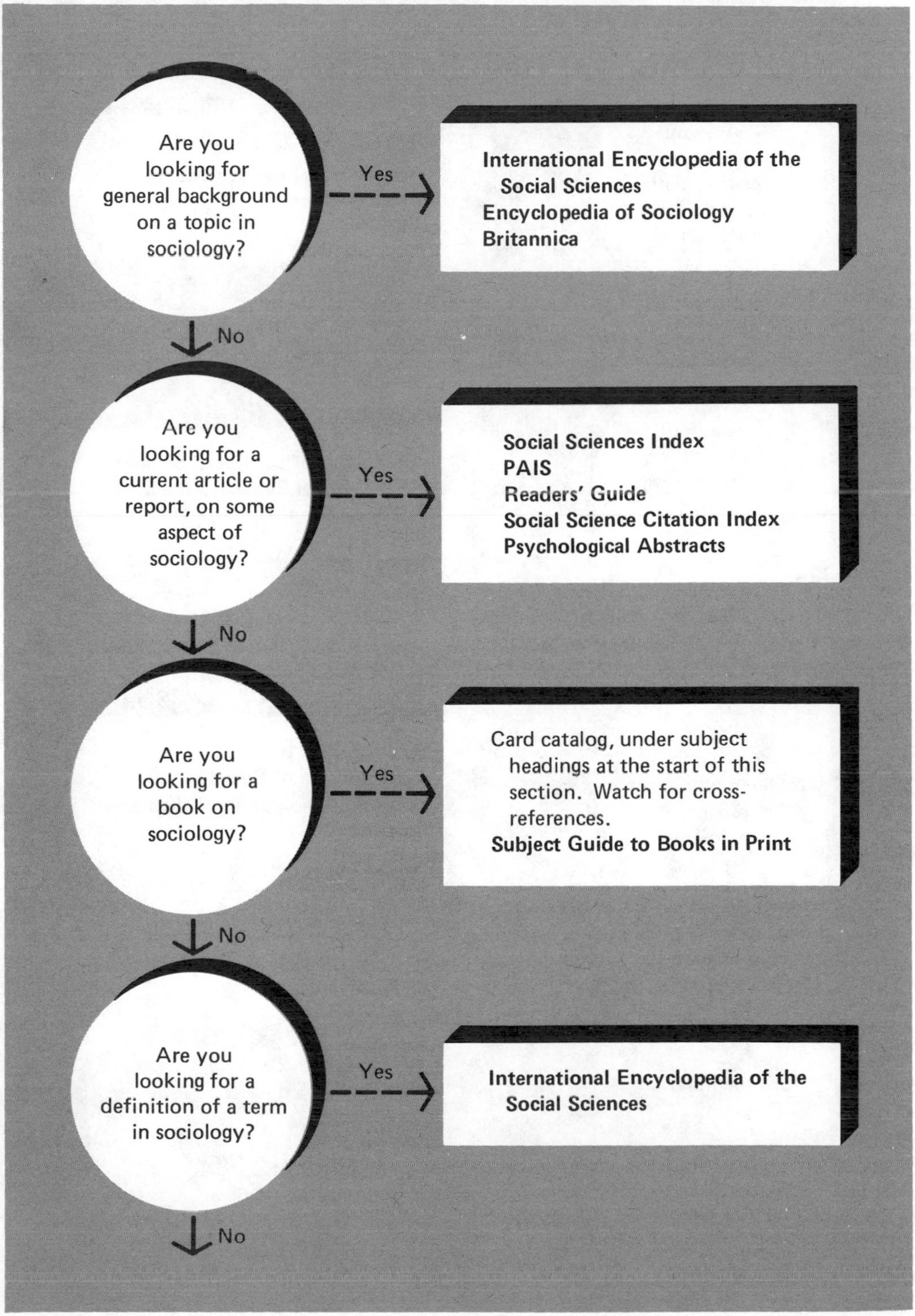

Are you looking for general background on a topic in sociology?

Yes ⇢

International Encyclopedia of the Social Sciences
Encyclopedia of Sociology
Britannica

No ↓

Are you looking for a current article or report, on some aspect of sociology?

Yes ⇢

Social Sciences Index
PAIS
Readers' Guide
Social Science Citation Index
Psychological Abstracts

No ↓

Are you looking for a book on sociology?

Yes ⇢

Card catalog, under subject headings at the start of this section. Watch for cross-references.
Subject Guide to Books in Print

No ↓

Are you looking for a definition of a term in sociology?

Yes ⇢

International Encyclopedia of the Social Sciences

No ↓

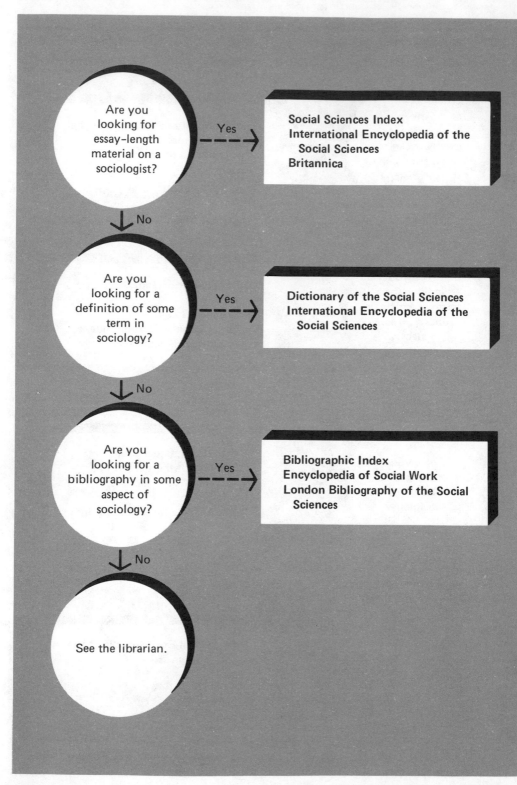

Are you looking for essay-length material on a sociologist?

Yes → Social Sciences Index
International Encyclopedia of the Social Sciences
Britannica

No

Are you looking for a definition of some term in sociology?

Yes → Dictionary of the Social Sciences
International Encyclopedia of the Social Sciences

No

Are you looking for a bibliography in some aspect of sociology?

Yes → Bibliographic Index
Encyclopedia of Social Work
London Bibliography of the Social Sciences

No

See the librarian.

DESCRIPTIONS OF SOURCES

Encyclopedia of Social Work.   N.Y.: National Association of Social Workers, 1965 to date, irregular. A summary of the year's activities in social work. Includes articles, bibliographies, and numerous statistical tables.
HV35.S6   360

Encyclopedia of Sociology.   Guilford, Conn.: Dushkin, 1974. Articles on most aspects of sociology. Material by experts touches on related fields such as political science. Numerous illustrations, bibliographies, and cross-references.
HM17.E5   301

Women

BASIC GUIDES

You should turn to three basic guides for material about women:
    1. *Women and Society: A Critical Review of the Literature* (Marie Rosenberg and Len Bergstrom). Beverley Hills, Calif.: Sage, 1975. Covers women in history, politics, and work. Carefully annotated entries for books and articles. Has a section on general reference works on women. Z7961.W8   016.301
    2. *Women's Studies Sourcebook,* 2nd ed. Allendale, Mich.: Grand Valley State College, 1976. Lists, but does not annotate, 1000 books and pamphlets. Z7961.K55   016.301
    3. *Women's Guide to Books.* N.Y.: MSS information, 1974 to date, annual. A distributor's list of carefully chosen current titles. Z7961.W66   016.301

CLASSIFICATION NUMBERS AND SUBJECT HEADINGS

Materials devoted specifically to women are classified 301.41 in the Dewey Decimal system. In the Library of Congress system, they are under HQ.
    Most subject headings begin wtih "Woman" or "Women"; for example:

"Woman—Employment"
"Woman—Social conditions"
"Women artists"
"Women athletes"
"Women bankers"
"Women—Equal rights"
"Women in the U.S."
"Women's liberation movement"

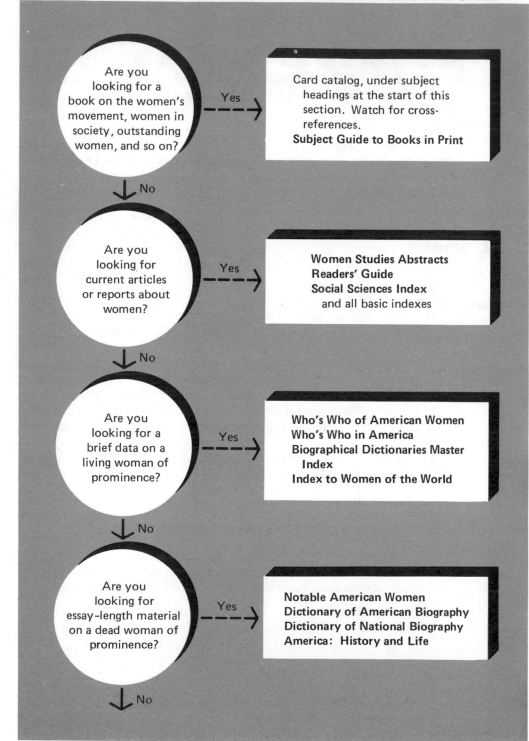

Are you looking for a book on the women's movement, women in society, outstanding women, and so on?

Yes →

Card catalog, under subject headings at the start of this section. Watch for cross-references.
Subject Guide to Books in Print

No

Are you looking for current articles or reports about women?

Yes →

Women Studies Abstracts
Readers' Guide
Social Sciences Index
and all basic indexes

No

Are you looking for a brief data on a living woman of prominence?

Yes →

Who's Who of American Women
Who's Who in America
Biographical Dictionaries Master Index
Index to Women of the World

No

Are you looking for essay-length material on a dead woman of prominence?

Yes →

Notable American Women
Dictionary of American Biography
Dictionary of National Biography
America: History and Life

No

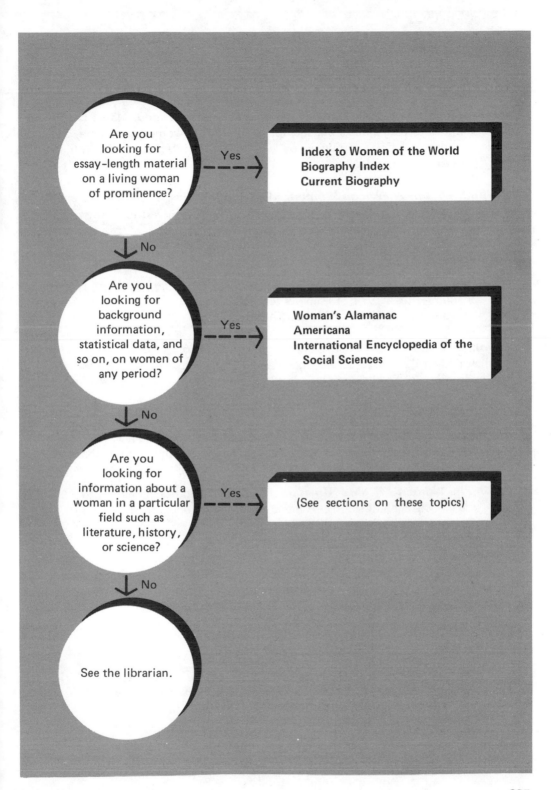

Are you looking for essay-length material on a living woman of prominence?

Yes → Index to Women of the World
Biography Index
Current Biography

No ↓

Are you looking for background information, statistical data, and so on, on women of any period?

Yes → Woman's Alamanac
Americana
International Encyclopedia of the Social Sciences

No ↓

Are you looking for information about a woman in a particular field such as literature, history, or science?

Yes → (See sections on these topics)

No ↓

See the librarian.

DESCRIPTIONS OF SOURCES

Index to Women of the World (Norma Ireland). Westood, Mass.: Faxon, 1970. Index to biographical material for about 13,000 women of all times and places. Also includes information on where to find pictures of the women. Z7963.B6I73   016.92

Who's Who of American Women. Chicago: Marquis, 1958 to date, biennial. Supplements the same publisher's *Who's Who in America.* Some duplication between them. E176.W647   920.72

Related Title

> *Who's Who and Where in Women's Studies.* Old Westbury, N.Y.: Feminist Press, 1974. A listing of teachers and of women's studies programs as of 1973. HQ1181.U5W48   375

Woman's Almanac. Philadelphia: Lippincott, 1976. A collection of short articles rather than a regular almanac. Useful for directory of agencies that aid women and a good bibliography. HQ1115.I37   301

Related Titles

> *The Book of Women's Achievements.* N.Y.: Stein & Day, 1976. A catchall of data about women. Coverage is international and emphasis is on women who achieved a first. HQ1123.M31976   301.41

> *The Women's Rights Almanac.* Bethesda, Md.: E. Stanton, 1974 to date. Collection of statistical data at both the national and international levels. HQ1406.S65   301.41

Women Studies Abstracts. Rush, N.Y.: Women Studies, 1972 to date, quarterly. Tells you where to find articles by and about women in a wide range of periodicals. Includes some books and pamphlets. The annotatons are written by volunteers, and the abstracts appear under numerous broad headings. Z7961.W64   016.301

Related Title

> *Women's Work and Women's Studies.* N.Y.: Barnard College, 1972 to date, annual. Lists books, pamphlets, periodical articles, dissertations, and other sources for works published or being researched. Z7961.W64   016.301

Women's Movement Media. N.Y.: Bowker, 1975. A listing of over 550 organizations and services of interest to women in the liberation movement and in women's studies. Includes feminist publishers, women's research centers, and women's library research collections. Z7964.U49H37   016.301

Related Title

Womanhood Media.   Metuchen, N.J.: Scarecrow, 1972. Supplement, 1975. Primarily a listing of books, periodicals, audiovisual material, and other sources. Z7961.W8   016.301

Title Index

Titles described in this manual are listed here in letter-for-letter alphabetical order, with page numbers. In addition you will find their Library of Congress and Dewey Decimal classification numbers.

In your library, the numbers might be slightly different, so if you do not find the book, check in your card catalog. *Since most of the books are in the reference section of the library, you may find an "R" before Dewey numbers or a "Ref" before Library of Congress numbers.*

Subject Index